Discovering Polish

Liliana Madelska

with Geoffrey Schwartz

A LEARNER'S GRAMMAR

Contents

1 Introduction: *wstęp*

Fans of detective stories enjoy figuring out the mystery on their own. Likewise, every language contains clues to how the grammatical system works: some are quite simple and easy to spot, some are less obvious and may be quite intricate in nature. This book presents Polish grammar as if it were a mystery, giving clues so the reader can discover the rules on his/her own. Maybe this way grammar can be a little more fun.

This book encourages independent work on the part of readers, even those who may not be familiar with linguistic terminology. This method allows for the deployment of self-organizing processes of language acquisition.[1] We hope that the graphic symbols, *grammicons*, that accompany the linguistic terms will be of help to learners in this endeavour.

We have taken great care in formulating grammatical explanations that are as clear as possible, and illustrating grammatical problems with carefully chosen examples. We strive to present the interrelationships among the various subsystems of Polish grammar.[2] Throughout the book readers will find information on how sentences are constructed – there is thus no need for a separate chapter on syntax.

Discovering Polish is designed for:

- those who have had some contact with Polish but wish to deepen their knowledge, e.g. young people of Polish origin living abroad;
- foreigners learning Polish;
- teachers of Polish who run courses with English-speaking groups or groups with a multilingual background (especially for those using the grammar books *Odkrywamy język polski* in the Polish or in the German version, see Madelska 2007, 2008a and 2008b).

This course book is intended for learners at both the beginner and intermediate levels, introducing all grammatical topics relevant to level B2 of the Common European Framework of Reference and beyond. In order to pass an examination at that level, the learner is advised not only to master the grammar, but also to acquire reading, writing and speaking competence; it is essential to develop one's vocabulary and repertoire of idiomatic phrases.

I would like to thank Anna Maria Adaktylos, Katarzyna Dziubalska-Kołaczyk, Kamil Kaźmierski, Hans Christian Luschützky, Stefan Michael Newerkla and Joanna Śmiecińska for their valuable support. Special thanks to Geoffrey Schwartz for preparing this English language edition based on my grammar books in Polish and in German.

Without the co-operation and help of my students, I would have had neither the idea nor the motivation to write this book. It is always a pleasure to discover the secrets of language together with young people, and for the many happy hours of doing so I wish to thank my students most warmly.

Liliana Madelska

---

[1] On *self-organizing processes* of language acquisition see Gass & Selinker (2002) and Flynn & O'Neil (1988).

[2] On *pedagogical grammar* see De Knop & De Rycker (2008); on *contrastive English-Polish grammar* see Fisiak at al. (1978).

2 On the art of language learning: *o sztuce uczenia się*

Learning a foreign language requires a lot of work; one must learn many things by heart – however, grammar is not one of them. The purpose of grammar is to show how the linguistic system functions, and it is much more important to understand the system as a whole than it is to memorise any one particular rule.

Our goal is to enable the reader to learn the fundamentals of Polish grammar in his or her own way. Almost every chapter of this grammar book begins with an introduction to the subject, followed by questions about Polish grammar, and then tables with carefully chosen examples. These examples allow the curious reader to find the answers to questions on their own, and in this way proceed step by step through the structure of the Polish language. Whenever it has been possible, the most commonly encountered Polish words[1] are chosen as examples; internationally known words (e.g. *hotel, komputer*) that are easy to remember are also used frequently. We invite you to play: we provide the data so you can discover the secrets of Polish grammar for yourself. There are two possibilities:

 1. When you want to play along you will need a piece of paper with which to cover a section of the text. When you find a question in the text, read the examples (words, texts, dialogues, etc.) in the following tables and try to find clues. Then you can compare your answer with our explanation; it is even possible that your answers and explanations might be even more accurate and detailed than ours, a better fit to your own interests, linguistic knowledge, and grammatical terminology.[2] Also, when you occasionally miss the clues in the examples, it is worth working independently: the comments in the book are meant to serve your memory and intellect, and are not intended to be memorised without real understanding. In this way you can discover the rules and tendencies that make Polish easier to learn. This is true as well for the translations: based on your own linguistic knowledge you can try to translate the examples into English, and then afterwards compare them with ours (This is of course only possible when you cover up what you want to translate!). If necessary, both British and American English expressions are given, e.g. *tramwaj* 'tram / streetcar'. Since there are many ways to translate a given text, it is expected that there will be some differences in the translations; in this area as well your translations may be more successful than ours.

2. You can also use this book to study in a 'classic' manner, seeking information on given topics that you can find in the index or table of contents.

One cannot learn a foreign language using only a grammar textbook, so we recommend that learners take part in spoken activities as often as possible. Such activities include the following:

---

[1] The following sources were consulted concerning frequency of use: Zgółkowa 1983, Kurzowa & Zgółkowa 1993, Mizerski 2000, Madelska 2004.

[2] This book does not avoid grammatical terminology, which many readers may find useful. However, it should be possible to understand the relationships between the various forms based on the examples, even without knowing the grammatical terminology. Therefore we recommend that you try to answer the questions in the text on your own.

- **Language courses:** particularly effective are intensive language courses in the target language country; all courses, including those that take place outside of Poland, bring more to a learner than simple independent language study;

- **Computer games:** many courses can easily be found on the Internet, for example *Lost in*, both in its English and German versions (www.lost-in.info), or *Grampol – computer programme facilitating the learning of Polish* (which is more suitable for advanced students): www.sjikp.us.edu.pl.

- **Reading newspapers:** you will see that as a European language, Polish has a large number of words in common with the European languages you may already know, so even beginners may be able to understand some of what they read in the press;

- **Watching films:** by watching films one can pick up entire phrases that are appropriate for given situations; contact with the spoken language, including intonation and phonetic variation, is invaluable; DVDs or films are thus highly recommended, since the learner can stop the film and repeat useful words and phrases; beginners may use versions with English subtitles, and then repeat various excerpts;

- **Communication:** it is worth communicating with native speakers; even if you do not know any you can find one in an internet chatroom;

- **Studying vocabulary:** since both Polish and English (as well as most languages spoken in Europe) are Indo-European languages, one can occasionally find common patterns. Also, English speakers will find that Polish has borrowed a large number of English words. From the beginning of the learning process, it is worth becoming 'a linguistic detective', looking for those common roots that may be reconstructed if one learns a few language-specific processes.

- **Textbooks:** in addition to a grammar of Polish written in Polish, English and German, the series "Hurra!" contains textbooks designed in the vein of a communicative approach to language learning (cf. www.hurra.edu.pl). We also recommend Miodunka's audiovisual course *Uczmy się polskiego*, both on videotape (2006) and on DVD (2007). The linguistic material is presented systematically in thirty half-hour episodes, during which the viewer gets to know the Grzegorzewskis, a very interesting family, and is able to combine acoustic and visual perception, which is not only entertaining, but above all makes learning much easier.

- **Assessment and documentation of proficiency:** even those who do not wish to take examinations and learn just for themselves will want to assess their proficiency from time to time. This not only helps to find weak spots in the learning process, but may also be good motivation for systematic work[3].

---

[3] In the relevant literature, many valuable approaches can be found, cf. Pasieka 2001 Seretny et al. 2004, Dąbrowska et al. 2005. Suggestions for testing procedures and information on certificate exams of Polish as a foreign language can be found on the following website: www.buwiwm.edu.pl/certyfikacja.

So-called grammicons (a combination of grammar and icon) have already been introduced in the grammar book *Polnisch entdecken* (Madelska 2007) in order to make the grammatical concepts appearing in the tables more conspicuous. This system has been developed mainly for those who are not familiar with grammatical terminology, and for visual learners, who remember graphic items more easily than text. The grammicons are not intended to replace the grammatical terms, but to accompany them. It is easy to remember that a small picture of a woman indicates feminine gender, and that a small head indicates neuter.[4] The vast majority of grammatical terms, however, refer to abstract concepts, and it is difficult to find a straightforward pictographic equivalent for them. In the Polish grammar books of the present series, the following solutions are carried through:

- **cases**

- the basket symbolizes the nominative, where almost everything can be "thrown in";

- an angry face symbolizes the genitive, expressing its close relationship with negation;

- the hand symbolizes the dative, which is related to expressions of giving, receiving and thanking;

- verbs expressing positive emotions, like *lubić*, *kochać* or *uwielbiać*, govern the accusative, therefore this case is symbolized with a heart;

- constructions of the type *interesuje się…* take the instrumental; that is why this case is expressed with the information sign;

- many verbs expressing speech acts (*mówić o, opowiadać o, plotkować o*) are connected to the locative, which is therefore symbolized with a mouth;

- the vocative is the case used for calling over, appealing to and addressing others; it is symbolized by a person shouting;

- **selected examples from the sphere of grammatical gender**

- a dog symbolizes animacy;

- a skull expresses inanimacy;

- woman, child and man is the symbol for groups containing a male person;

- scissors are used for groups without a male person (here the men are "cut out").

The remaining symbols are easier to interpret; we count on the reader's imagination. In order to have all the grammicons at hand while working through the book, the reader can just unfold the back flap of the cover.

---

[4] The illustration of grammatical categories like gender with symbols can also be found in other works on grammar (cf. Serafin & Achtelik 2005); in the present book we propose a more elaborate system of icons and they accompany the grammatical terms consistently.

3 Pronunciation and spelling: *wymowa i ortografia*

3.1. The Polish alphabet

Many "international" words (so-called *internationalisms*: words with similar meaning and spelling in various languages) often appear in Polish, especially in the contemporary Polish press. English speakers may be able to use these words to grasp the general idea of articles that they look through.

Polish has been written with the Latin alphabet since the early Middle Ages. Since Polish has many more sounds than the Latin alphabet has letters, many diacritic marks and letter combinations are used.

 Table 3.1.a. shows some Polish words whose meaning should be familiar. Ask a native speaker to read these words aloud, and notice the spelling. Cover up the English examples and try to guess the meaning. In Polish it is generally the second-to-last syllable of a word that is stressed, e.g. *atletyczny* (more about it in § 3.4.).

Table 3.1.a. Spelling of "international" words

ADJECTIVES		NOUNS		VERBS	
atletyczny	athletic	alfabet	alphabet	dyskutować	to discuss
elitarny	elite	bokser	boxer	informować	to inform
czeski	Czech	ortografia	orthography	faksować	to fax
arogancki	arrogant	precyzja	precision	eksplodować	to explode
centralny	central	szal	shawl	instalować	to install
elegancki	elegant	czekolada	chocolate	fantazjować	to fantasize
fizyczny	physical	fragment	fragment	szokować	to shock
interesujący	interesting	frekwencja	frequency	cytować	to cite
fantastyczny	fantastic	komunikacja	communication	tolerować	to tolerate
polityczny	political	garaż	garage	komplikować	to complicate
aktywny	active	wirus	virus	ilustrować	to illustrate
instynktowny	instinctive	komputer	computer	interesować się	to be interested

In the spelling of these "international" words, we see that Polish has a tendency to adjust the spelling of such words to their pronunciation. For example, while in English we see spellings with *ph* in words such as 'telephone', in Polish the word has been spelled *telefon* (with an *f*).

Since it causes softening of consonants in Polish, the letter *i* is often avoided in international words: *y* or *j* often appear where English uses *i* (e.g. *fantastyczny*).

The letter *j* after *s*, *c*, and *z* signals a softened version of those sounds, while *i* changes these sounds to palatals. Compare *Twoja misja to pilnować misia* 'Your mission is to guard the bear'; *Po pierwszym akcie kup akcje* 'Buy shares (of stock) after the first act'.

In Polish the letter *k* is used in international words, even when other languages use the letter *c*, for the sound *k* (e.g. *komputer*).

Please also remember that double letters in Polish reflect a double pronunciation, e.g. *Anna* [an:a].

The letters *x*, *v*, and *q* generally do not appear in Polish, and are replaced by *ks*, *w*, and *k(u)*. Only in a few foreign words may we find these letters. For example, both spellings, *video* and *wideo*, are acceptable.

The above examples show that as far as the spelling of international words is concerned, Polish is more consistent than English, and therefore should not be too difficult to master; for those studying Polish orthography we recommend Lipińska's (1999) textbook.

In the Middle Ages, when the first writings appeared in Polish, it was necessary to adjust the Latin alphabet to the rich inventory of Polish sounds: about 45 phonemes needed to be represented using only 24–26 letters. At that time digraphs like *cz* and *dz* were introduced, as well as diacritic marks.

Although at first glance the Polish spelling system looks quite daunting, it is in fact quite regular, unlike the English system. Once you have learnt the relatively small number of patterns presented in this chapter, you will know how to pronounce every word you come across.

Table 3.1.b. presents the modern Polish alphabet. Comments are made in the case of letters that may cause problems in interpretation. Phonetic script is for specialists; for non-linguists the only help is orthography (see also http://www.polish-translators.com/wymowa.html). Examples are given that provide an approximation of the Polish pronunciation (it is difficult to find the equivalents in English of Polish vowels). Many international words have been used, and thanks to repetition the number of examples has been limited.

For English speakers studying the Polish spelling system, a few items must be mentioned immediately:
– the Polish letter *w* is pronounced like *v* in English (see *wiza* 'visa');
– the Polish letter *j* is pronounced like *y* in English 'yes', not like English *j* in 'jazz';
– the Polish letter *c* is pronounced like *ts* in English, as in 'Betsy', and not like *k* in 'kiss';
– the Polish letter combinations *sz*, *rz*[1] and *cz*, are quite regular in their pronunciation: they are pronounced harder than English *sh*, *z*, and *ch*, as in: 'shop', 'azure', and 'chop', respectively;
– the Polish letters or letter combinations *ś (si)*, *ź (zi)* and *ć (ci)*, although they look somewhat exotic, are quite regular in their pronunciation: they are pronounced softer (more palatal) than English *sh*, *si*, and *ch* as in: 'sheep', 'Asia', and 'cheap', respectively.
– in Polish it is generally the second-to-last syllable of a word that is stressed; see § 3.4.

---

[1] The letters *rz* and *ż* are pronounced the same. There are a couple of cases where *rz* is not pronounced as the letter combination but as separate *r* and *z* sounds, e.g. *marznąć* 'to freeze'.

Table 3.1.b. The Polish alphabet

Printed letter	Hand-written letter	IPA[2]	Examples		Comment
A a	*A a*	a	start	start, strut	the Polish **a** is articulated between the vowels in the two (British) English examples
Ą ą	*Ą ą*	ɔ̃	oni idą 'they are going'	—	sounds like the vowel in the French word 'bon', as in 'bon voyage'
B b	*B b*	b	bar	bar	
C c	*C c*	ts	centrum 'centre'	Betsy	this is a single sound in Polish, written with a single letter
Ć ć	*Ć ć*	t͡ɕ	pić 'to drink'	cheap	close to **ch** in 'cheap', but softer
D d	*D d*	d	data	date	
E e	*E e*	ɛ	element	element	closest to the first vowel in the English example
Ę ę	*Ę ę*	ɛ̃	męski 'manly; masculine'	—	sounds like the vowel in the French word *vin*[3]
F f	*F f*	f	faks	fax	
G g	*G g*	g	grupa	group	
H h	*H h*	x	hotel 'hotel'	loch	sounds close to 'Loch Ness' in English, Scottish; Polish **h** and **ch** are pronounced the same
I i	*I i*	i	idealista 'idealist'	ski	this vowel has a pure quality to it in Polish, while in English it is often pronounced as a diphthong
J j	*J j*	j	jacht	yacht, yes	not like English **j** in 'jazz'
K k	*K k*	k	kawa	coffee	without aspiration
L l	*L l*	l	lekcja	lesson	"clear" in all phonetic contexts
Ł ł	*Ł ł*	w	łazienka 'bathroom'	wine	the Polish **ł** is articulated like English **w**
M m	*M m*	m	moment	moment	
N n	*N n*	n	numer	number	
Ń ń	*Ń ń*	ɲ	tańczyć 'to dance'	cognac	like English **n** in 'new' or 'cognac'
O o	*O o*	ɔ	organizacja	organisation	

---

[2] This chapter will utilize the phonetic symbols from the International Phonetic Alphabet (IPA).

[3] At the end of the word, this letter is often pronounced like a regular (oral) -e.

Printed letter	Hand-written letter	IPA	Examples		Comment
Ó ó	*Ó ó*	u	mówić 'to speak'	pool, pull	the Polish **ó** is articulated between the vowels in the two English examples (see also Polish **u**)
P p	*P p*	p	**p**ark	**p**ark	without aspiration
R r	*R r*	r	**r**eferat 'paper, article'	—	a trill like in Scottish, Spanish or Italian
S s	*S s*	s	**s**ystem	**s**ystem	
Ś ś	*Ś ś*	ɕ	**ś**roda 'Wednesday'	**sh**eep	close to **sh** in 'sheep', but softer
T t	*T t*	t	**t**est	**t**est	without aspiration
U u	*U u*	u	p**u**ls 'pulse'	p**oo**l, p**u**ll	the same sound as **ó**
W w	*W w*	v	**w**iza 'visa'	**v**isa	the Polish **w** is articulated like English **v**
Y y	*Y y*	ɨ	m**y** 'we'	b**i**ll, poli**ti**cs	darker than Polish **i**
Z z	*Z z*	z	**z**upa 'soup'	**z**oo	
Ź ź	*Ź ź*	ʑ	**ź**le (ADV) 'badly'	A**si**a	close to **s** in 'Asia', but softer
Ż ż	*Ż ż*	ʒ	**ż**ona 'wife'	a**z**ure	close to **z** in 'azure' or to **s** in 'measure', but harder
Letter combinations					
ch	*ch*	x	**ch**arakter 'character'	Lo**ch** Ness	Polish **h** and **ch** are pronounced the same
ci	*ci*	tɕ	**ci**ocia 'aunt'	**ch**eap	the same sound as **ć**
cz	*cz*	tʃ	**Cz**ech	**ch**op	close to **ch** in 'chop' but harder
dz	*dz*	dz	ro**dz**aj 'type, gender'	a**dz**e, he a**dds** it	this is a single sound in Polish
dzi	*dzi*	dʑ	**dzi**ecko 'child'	**j**ingle	close to **j** in 'jingle', but softer
dź	*dź*	dʑ	**dź**więk 'sound'	**j**ingle	the same sound as **dzi**
dż	*dż*	dʒ	**dż**entelmen	**g**entleman	close to **g** in 'gentleman', but harder
ni	*ni*	ɲ	**ni**e 'no'	co**gn**ac	the same sound as **ń**
rz	*rz*	ʒ	**rz**ecz 'thing'	a**z**ure	the same sound as **ż**
si	*si*	ɕ	**si**edem 'seven'	**sh**eep	the same sound as **ś**
sz	*sz*	ʃ	**sz**al 'shawl'	**sh**op	close to **sh** in 'shop', but harder
zi	*zi*	ʑ	**zi**ma 'winter'	A**si**a	the same sound as **ż**

3.2. The sounds of Polish

Polish pronunciation has a reputation for being difficult. In fact, the difficulty of the Polish consonantal system is comparable to that of English or German, and the Polish vowel system is much simpler. The Polish literary language is very homogeneous in comparison with some European languages like English or German. Differences between regional dialects are not terribly dramatic, though a speaker's intonation will give a clue as to what part of Poland he or she comes from.

The following outlines a schematic view of the speech articulators and where the Polish obstruent consonants[4] are articulated. The figure and the following tables present a rough sketch (intended for non-linguists) of Polish consonants and vowels.

Table 3.2.a. Place of articulation of Polish obstuent consonants

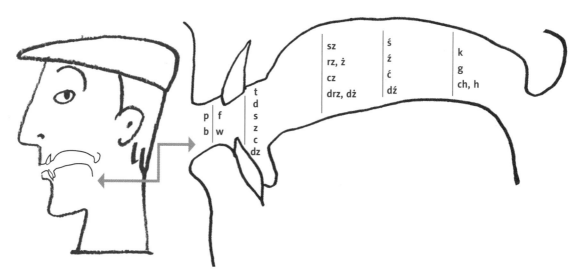

Table 3.2.b. The Polish consonants (in IPA phonetic transcription)

Manner of articulation		Place of articulation	bilabial	labio-dental	dental	alveolar	palatal (soft)[5]	labial / velar	velar
Conso-nants	Obstru-ents	Plosives	p b		t d				k g
		Fricatives		f v	s z	ʃ ʒ	ɕ ʑ		x
		Affricates			ts dz	tʃ dʒ	tɕ dʑ		
	Sono-rants	Nasals	m		n		ɲ		(ŋ)[6]
		Liquids				l r			
		Approximants					j	w	

---

[4] An obstruent consonant is one that is produced with the greatest blockage of the airstream during speech, as opposed to sonorant consonants and vowels, which allow relatively free passage of air through the vocal tract.

[5] In soft consonants, also called palatals, the body of the tongue (not the tip) is raised toward the palate.

[6] This sound is pronounced in words like *bank* 'bank', where the nasal /ŋ/ is followed by a velar consonant.

Table 3.2.c. Polish vowels[7]

Vowels		front	central	back
	high	i [i]	y [ɨ]	u [u]
	mid	e [ɛ]		o [ɔ]
	nasal	ę [ɛ̃]		ą [ɔ̃]
	low		a [a]	

You will notice that the Polish vowel system is much simpler than the English one. There are six oral vowels and two nasal vowels. One challenge to minimising an English accent in Polish is to avoid the tendency of English speakers to diphthongise vowels. The vowels in Polish are very pure in quality.

3.3. Learning Polish pronunciation

 Foreign language pronunciation can be easily acquired if one heeds the following pieces of advice:

- It is never too early to begin pronunciation exercises; the later a learner starts working on his or her pronunciation, the more ingrained the early pronunciation mistakes become, and the longer it takes to get rid of them.

- Only linguistic geniuses or children can master the pronunciation of a foreign language independently. A normal adult needs a good teacher in order to acquire pronunciation in a foreign language.

- One should practice as often as one can; better daily or at least 2–3 times a week for a couple of minutes then one hour once per week. Practising too many categories at once (e.g. voicing, place of articulation) should be avoided.

- One should always first work on listening comprehension, and only when one is comfortable with that, go on to work on pronunciation. Since difficulties typically have much more to do with perception than pronunciation, exercises should be designed accordingly.

Table 3.3.a. is designed to help learners exercise their listening and pronunciation skills. Minimal pairs[8] are presented for various categories of Polish speech sounds. Also included are comments as to the expected difficulty of various contrasts for English speakers.

---

[7] Orthographic representation on the left, phonetic transcription on the right.

[8] Pairs of words differing by only one sound. More exercises: see Styczek (1982), Madelska (in print).

It's best to begin listening exercises with the help of minimal pairs: the teacher shows the learner two pictures representing the words of the minimal pair and says one of the words aloud. When the learner reliably points to the correct picture, he or she has managed to perceive the difference. Then, the teacher and the learner can change roles: the learner says the word and the teacher points to the picture representing the word perceived. In this way the learner can see whether listeners perceive his or her pronunciation as accurate.

One begins with the minimal pairs which most learners find relatively easy, while more difficult units are practiced later. The following tendencies should be considered for Polish consonants (the arrows represent an increasing level of difficulty):

- Manner of articulation:
  plosives > fricatives > affricates
- Position:
  stressed syllable > unstressed syllable;
  onset (initial syllable margin) > coda (final syllable margin)
- Complexity:
  sequences Consonant + Vowel are easier than consonant clusters.

As far as obstruent consonants are concerned, one does not only need to master those differences connected with place or manner of articulation, but also differences in voicing. Minimal pairs allow one to concentrate on one feature and master the relevant contrast. This brings success to adult learners much more quickly than simply looking for difficult words to repeat. As one can see in **Table 3.2.b.** the twelve sounds: *s, z, c, dz* and *ś, ź, ć, dź* as well as *sz, ż, cz, dż* form a subsystem in which the three categories of voicing, place of articulation, and manner of articulation play a role. This type of targeted practice also allows learners to see which categories (both for listening and pronunciation) are the most problematic for them. Sometimes it can be helpful to isolate phonological categories from the learner's first language. For example, the difference between fricative and affricate can be seen in the English pair *ship* : *chip*.

The systematic difference between *sz* and *ś* is not found in English. It can be approximated, however, with the English words *show* and *sheep*. If you listen carefully, the **sh** sound is slightly different in the two words – the **sh** in *show* is close to the Polish *sz*, while the **sh** in *sheep* sounds a little like Polish *ś*. While this difference is difficult, in most cases Polish listeners will be able to reconstruct which sound was intended even if they were not pronounced perfectly. What is less relevant for communication can thus be given less attention.

A strong English accent sounds foreign to the Polish ear and many basic words may be incomprehensible. The main problem is diphthongization of vowels: compare such pairs as *puka* : *półka* '(he) is knocking : shelf', which many speakers of English pronounce identically[9]. Poles perceive diphthongs as two separate sounds, that is with an extra sound added to an original vowel. Extra elements in speech often cause greater comprehension problems than those that are elided (see Madelska 2004).

---

[9] In Scottish English, this diphthongization is generally minimal. English speakers might use the Scottish accent as something of a model to produce authentic sounding Polish vowels.

Table 3.3.a. Models for listening and pronunciation exercises[10]

Phonological category	Examples			Comments
	A. Medial position	**B. Initial position**	**C. Final position**	
vowels and ł	puka : półka kuka : kółka koki : kołki doki : dołki stoki : stołki	łóżko : uszko łożyć : ożyć łono : ono łowi : owi łania : Ania	da nam : dał nam my : mył mu : muł biega : biegał czyta : czytał	
l : ł : r	palę : pałę : parę kula : kuła : kura	lasy : łasy : rasy lata : łata : rata	pal : pał : par mól : muł : mur	
manner of articulation	masa : maca w lesie : w lecie razi : radzi uszy : uczy grozi : grodzi	sali : cali siebie : ciebie sen : cen szyja : czyja siało : ciało	pies : piec nos : noc grasz : gracz działasz : działacz	fricative : affricate

my : mył

koki : kołki

łóżko : uszko

lata : łata : rata

mól : muł : mur

---

[10] Unfortunately, many of the examples for minimal pair exercises are not frequently heard.
'**A.** (he/she) knocks : shelf; (it) cuckoos : wheels; buns : stakes; docks : holes; slopes : stools; (I) smoke : club ACC : couple ACC; sphere : (she) hammered : hen; mass : matzah; in a wood LOC : in summer LOC; (it) dazzles : (he/she) advises; ears : (he/she) teaches; (he/she) threatens : (it) fences; **B.** bed : ear (DIM); provide for : revive; womb : it; (he/she) hunts : those (men); doe : Ann; forests : greedy : races; years : patch : instalment; room GEN : inches GEN; oneself : yourself; dream : prices GEN; neck : whose FEM; (it) sowed : body; **C.** will give us : gave us; we washed; him : mule; (he/she) runs : was running; (he/she) reads : was reading; stilt : clubs GEN : couples GEN; moth : mule : wall; dog : furnace; nose : night; (you) play : player; (you) are active : activist'

Phonological category	Examples			
	A. Medial position	**B. Initial position**	**C. Final position**[12]	**Comments**
voiceless : voiced [11]	ko**d**y : ko**t**y (o) ro**g**u : (o) ro**k**u	**b**ułka : **p**ółka **g**óra : **k**ura **d**om : **t**om	ko**t** : ko**d**	Plosives
	ko**z**a : ko**s**a wie**ż**a : wie**sz**a	**ż**uka : **sz**uka **ż**yj! : **sz**yj	je**ż** : je**sz**	Fricatives
	(na) no**dz**e : no**c**e bu**dz**iki : bu**c**iki sie**dz**i : sie**c**i	**dż**emu : **cz**emu **dz**iało : **ci**ało **dz**ień : **ci**eń	cho**dź**! : cho**ć**	Affricates

kody : koty

dom : **t**om

koza : kosa

dżemu : **cz**emu

bu**dz**iki : bu**c**iki

---

[11] 'A. (bar) codes : cats; horn LOC : year LOC; goat : scythe; tower : (he/she) hangs; on a leg : nights; alarm clocks: shoes; (he/she) sits : networks; B. roll : shelf; mountain : chicken; house : volume; beetle GEN : (he/she) looks for; live! : sew!; jam GEN : why?; (it) took place : body; day : shadow; C. cat : (bar) code; hedgehog : (you) eat; come! : though'

[12] In Polish, consonants at the end of words are pronounced voicelessly; in other words, pairs like **kot** : **kod** are pronounced the same.

	A. Medial position	B. Initial position	C. Final position	Comments
Place of articulation (important)[13]	ka**s**a : ka**sz**a : Ka**si**a pro**sz**ę : pro**si**ę (w) bar**z**e : ba**zi**e	**sz**yny : **si**ny (w) **Rz**ymie : (w) **zi**mie	ko**s** : ko**sz** : ko**ś**!	Fricatives
	u**cz**eszę : u**ci**eszę le**cz**y : le**ci**	**cz**apki : **ci**apki **cz**yha : **ci**cha **cz**y : **ci**	le**cz** : le**ć**!	Affricates
Manner of articulation[14]	u**sz**y : u**cz**y gro**z**i : gro**dz**i	**sz**yja : **cz**yja **si**ało : **ci**ało	gra**sz** : gra**cz** działa**sz** : działa**cz**	Fricative : Affricate
Manner of articulation[15]	o**cz**yma : o**trz**yma	**dż**emy : **drz**emy **cz**y ma : **trz**yma **cz**y : **trz**y	wypa**cz**! : wypa**trz**!	Affricate : Plosive + Fricative

kasa : kasza : Kasia

proszę : prosię

szyny : siny

lecz : leć!

czapki : ciapki

uszy : uczy

oczyma : otrzyma

dżemy : drzemy

---

[13] 'A. cash register : buckwheat / grits / groats : Kasia (name); please : piglet; in a bar : in a base; (I'll) comb : (I'll) be glad; (he/she) treats : (he/she) flies; B. tracks : bluish; (in) Rome : (in) winter; caps : spots; (he/she) lurks : quiet FEM; whether : you DAT; C. blackbird : basket : mow!; but : fly!'

[14] 'A. ears : (he/she) teaches; (he/she) threatens : (he/she) encloses; B. neck : whose FEM; (it) sowed : body; C. (you) play : player; (you) are active : activist'

[15] This type of stop fricative combinations are in many Polish dialects pronounced as affricates. 'A. eyes INST : (he will) obtain; B. jam PL : (we) tear; does he have? : he holds; whether : three; C. distort! : look out for!'

	A. Medial position	B. Initial position	C. Final position	Comments
Gemination – quite difficult[16]	po**d**any : po**dd**any pa**n**a : pa**nn**a	—	—	one versus "two" speech sounds
Sonority – not difficult[17]	pi**ł**em : pi**w**em la**ł**y : la**w**y umy**ł**am : umy**w**am	**ł**ata : **w**ata **ł**ódź : **w**ódź! **ł**ożę : **w**ożę	—	
Vowel contrasts[18]	m**i**ła : m**y**ła : m**e**łła w**i**je : w**y**je : w**ie**je b**i**ł : b**y**ł	—	grub**i** : grub**y** : grub**e** now**i** : now**y** : now**e** m**i** : m**y** : m**e**	

podany : po**dd**any   pana : pa**nn**a

żyły : żywy   łata : wata

wije : wyje : wieje   nowi : nowy : nowe

---

[16] '**A.** given : surrendered; you : maiden'

[17] '**A.** (I) drank : beer INST; (they) were pouring water : lava GEN; (I) washed : (I) am washing; **B.** patch : cotton wool; boat : lead!; (I) provide for : (I) transport'

[18] '**A.** nice FEM : (he/she) washed : (he/she) ground (old form); (he/she) winds : (he/she) howls : (the wind) blows; (he/she) beat : (he/she) was; **C.** fat PL : fat MASC SG : fat FEM PL; new PL : new MASC SG : new FEM PL; me : we : my PL (short form of *moje*)'

	A. Medial position	B. Initial position	C. Final position	Comments
Presence vs. absence of r – difficult for British speakers[19]	karta : kata warta : wata	—	zator : za to dar : da	
Nasality – not so difficult[20]	kosa : kąsa proszki : prążki też : tęż	—	drogo : drogą pisze : piszę	see Table 3.5.c.

karta : kata

dar : da

kosa : kąsa

drogo : drogą

3.4. Stress

Stress in Polish generally falls on the second to last syllable of a word, e.g. *Macie słownik? Nie, nie mamy słownika* 'Have you got a dictionary? No, we haven't got a dictionary'. Exceptions to this pattern are relatively uncommon and not very difficult to learn. They include, as can be seen in **Table 3.4.a.** compound numerals (often stressed on the first syllable), acronyms (often stressed on the last syllable), and words of foreign origin (mostly Latin or Greek, especially with the suffixes *-ika* or *-yka*, often stressed on the third to last syllable). Sometimes Poles themselves will extend the standard stress pattern to these words.

Table 3.4.a. Exceptions to the stress rule

siedemset	700	gra**ma**tyka	grammar	US**A**	USA
osiemset	800	uni**wer**sytet	university	UE (Unia Europejska)	EU
dziewięćset	900	**fi**zyka	physics	PK**P** (Polskie Koleje Państwowe)	Polish National Railways

---

[19] When *r* is written, it must be pronounced. In most dialects of British English *r* is not pronounced at the end of a syllable. 'A. card : executioner GEN; C. gridlock : for that; gift : he will give'

[20] The letter *-ę* at the end of a word is often pronounced as *-e*. The letter *-ą* at the end of a word retains its nasality. 'A. scythe : (he/she) bites; powder PL : stripes; also : flex (muscles)!; C. expensive ADV : way INST; he writes : I write'

Enclitic words (small words that are not used by themselves, like *n't* in English *don't*), have no influence on the stress, so words like **chciałabym** ⌂ 'I would like', **chcielibyśmy** 🐕 'we would like', should be in fact stressed on the first syllable. When one-syllable verbs are negated, the stress falls on the *nie*, e.g. **nie pij, nie jedź** 'don't drink, don't go'. Also, prepositions are generally pronounced together with the words they join with, and as such are often stressed, e.g. **dla** mnie 'for me', but *dla ciebie* 'for you'. In Polish, the difference between stressed and unstressed syllables is much less noticeable than it is in English.

3.5. Reading rules

Unlike English, Polish orthography is, to a large extent, phonetic. This means that once a few rules of correspondence between spelling and pronunciation are learned, one knows how to pronounce every word one comes across. Nevertheless, before the learner tries to read aloud independently, it is recommended that he or she listens to a text on DVD (or a video recording) while following along with the written text. Then the learner may try to read along with the DVD (in this way the learner can also practice intonation), and then finally he or she should go on to read completely independently. It would be a mistake to try first to memorize all the rules and then try to read Polish out loud, since in this way one delays the self-organization of the learning process. We favour DVDs over CDs; it is much better to practice communication if one can not only hear but also see the speakers.

 One of the most difficult and important aspects of the Polish spelling system is the variety of roles that the letter *i* can play. **Table 3.5.a.** shows each of these roles (illustrated using Polish orthography and the phonetic transcription). Try to describe them on your own.

Table 3.5.a. The letter *i* in the Polish spelling system[21]

A. vowel		B. softening		A. + B.		C. (vowel) + (j) + i	
spelling	pron.	spelling	pron.	spelling	pron.	spelling	pron.
ile	ilɛ	siostra	ɕɔstra	zima	ʑima	moi	mɔji
inny	innɨ	ciocia	tɕɔtɕa	nosić	nɔɕitɕ	stoi	stɔji

- In column **A.** *i* represents a single vowel at the beginning of a word, e.g. *ile* 'how many?' *inny* 'other'.
- **B.** When *i* follows a consonant and precedes a vowel, the *i* is not pronounced as a separate vowel. Rather, the letter *i* indicates that the preceding sound is soft (as if it were spelled *ś, ź, ć, dź, ń*, etc.). Thus, a word like *siostra* 'sister' is pronounced as if it were spelled *śostra*. The letter combination **sio** in fact represents two sounds, a soft fricative (*ś*) followed by a vowel.
- **A. + B.** When the letter *i* stands by itself between two consonants, it plays both of the roles outlined in columns **A.** and **B.** It represents the vowel *i*, and also indicates that the preceding consonant is soft, e.g. *zima* 'winter', *nosić* 'to wear'.
- **C.** In grammatical alternations the letter *j* is never written before the vowel *i*, so the letter combination *ji* is not permitted in Polish. However, a letter combination like *oi* in *moi* generally implies the presence of the sound [j] even if it is not spelled. Thus, we can observe many alternations of the type **mój** brat : *moi bracia* 'my brother : my brothers', **stój :** *stoi* 'stop (or stand still) : he is standing'.

21 'A. how many; other; B. sister; aunt; A.+B. winter; wear; C. my (PL); he stands'

Knowing the rules associated with the letter *i* is crucial to understanding the sense behind many of the alternations and orthographic phenomena involved in the Polish inflectional system.

To read what you see is easy; to write what you hear is more complicated: one needs a lot of practice.[22]

The following tables serve to illustrate that in Polish the relation between spelling and pronunciation (the reading rules) is clear.

Read the examples in **Table 3.5.b.** Try to explain the effect sounds may have on the pronunciation of neighbouring sounds.

Table 3.5.b. Groups of consonants

spelling	pronunciation	ENG	spelling	pronunciation	ENG
w domu	v dɔmu	at home	podgrzać	pɔdgʒatɕ	to warm up
w sali	f sali	in the (class)room	podpisać	pɔtpisatɕ	to sign
od brata	ɔd brata	from (my) brother	odwaga	ɔdvaga	courage
od syna	ɔt sɨna	from (my) son	odpowiedź	ɔtpɔvjetɕ	answer
w Rzymie	v ʒɨmjɛ	in Rome	trzy grzyby	tʃɨ gʒɨbɨ	three mushrooms

In Polish a group of consonants can either be voiced or voiceless, but it generally cannot contain both a voiced and voiceless consonant. Generally the last consonant of a group will determine this. For example in the phrase *w sali*, the *w* is pronounced unvoiced (like an *f*) because the following consonant is unvoiced. The examples in **Table 3.5.b.** illustrate this.

Whether *rz* is voiced depends on the preceding consonant. When preceded by an unvoiced consonant it is pronounced as *sz* [ʃ] (note the example *trzy grzyby* [tʃɨ gʒɨbɨ]). However, this dependence does not apply at the beginnings of words, where *rz* will determine the voicing of the previous consonant: (*w Rzymie* [v ʒɨmjɛ]). The best way to learn it is to read aloud, together with native speakers of Polish – too much theory does not help.

The rules for pronouncing the nasal vowels *ę* and *ą* are somewhat complex, and are summarised in **Table 3.5.c.**

Table 3.5.c. Pronunciation vs. spelling of nasal vowels *-ę, -ą*

Example PL		Example ENG	comments[23]			
spelling	IPA					
zęby 'teeth'	zɛmbɨ	me**m**ber	ɛ / ɔ	+ m	+ p / b	
wąwóz 'ravine'	vɔ̃vus	like 'bon' in French	ɛ̃/ ɔ̃		+ f / v	
mądry 'wise'	mɔndrɨ	bo**nd**	ɛ / ɔ	+ n	+ t / d	
wąsy 'moustache'	vɔ̃sɨ	like 'bon' in French	ɛ̃/ ɔ̃		+ s / z	
ręce 'hands'	rɛntsɛ	he re**nts** it	ɛ / ɔ	+ n	+ t͡s / d͡z	
księżyc 'moon'	kɕɛ̃ʒɨts	like 'vin' in French	ɛ̃/ ɔ̃		+ ʃ / ʒ	
Węgry 'Hungary'	vɛŋgrɨ	Be**ng**al	ɛ / ɔ	+ ŋ	+ k / g	
wąchać 'to sniff'	vɔ̃xatɕ	like 'bon' in French	ɛ̃/ ɔ̃		+ x	

---

[22] Lipińska 1999 is worthy of mention here.

[23] A schematic look at how *ę* and *ą* are pronounced in various contexts.

3

Pronunciation and spelling: *wymowa i ortografia*

23

Before a plosive or an affricate consonant, one hears a nasal consonant (*n*, *m*, *ŋ*) pronounced, the place of articulation of which depends on the following plosive or affricate. Thus, *piątek* 'Friday' is pronounced as if it were spelled *piontek*. Before fricative consonants the nasal vowels are pronounced in the standard way. At the end of a word, *-ę* is often pronounced as *-e*, so *piszę* 'I write' and *pisze* 'he/she writes' sound the same. The other nasal vowel *-ą* is pronounced normally at the end of a word.

3.6. Alternations and spelling rules

Polish is a language with a rich inflectional system in which word stems may take various endings. This often leads to alternations – stem consonants may change depending on the ending, e.g. *bogat-y mężczyzn-a* : *bogac-i mężczyźn-i* 'a rich man' : 'rich men'.

Table 3.6.a. shows some typical alternations that occur in Polish inflectional forms. Notice that in some forms there are two different alternants. Which groups of consonants undergo alternations? What do you think determines the choice of alternants? Consult the depiction of the consonant articulations in **Table 3.2.a.** to try to come up with an explanation.

Table 3.6.a. Alternations: Adjectives, Adverbs, Nouns[24]

ADJ NOM ●		ADV Comparative		NOUNS SG		Consonant in Stem	Alternants
MASC SG ♀	PL (+MP 🐜)	Positive	Comparative	NOM ●	LOC ● + e		
łakomy	łakomi	słabo	słabiej	sklep	sklepie	p, b, m	pi, bi, mi
ciekawy	ciekawi	żwawo	żwawiej	szafa	szafie	f, w	fi, wi
bogaty	bogaci	zimno	zimniej	weekend	weekendzie	t, d, n	ci, dzi, ni
łysy	łysi	bardzo	bardziej	kasa	kasie	s, dz	si, dzi
mały	mali	miło	milej	masło	maśle	ł	l
stary	starzy	staro	starzej	teatr	teatrze	r	rz
duży lepszy	duzi lepsi[25]	—	—	—	—	sz, ż	si, zi
wysoki	wysocy	szybko	szybciej	sekretarka	sekretarce	k	c / ci
drogi	drodzy	długo	dłużej	droga	drodze	g	dz / ż
głuchy	głusi	cicho	ciszej	mucha	musze	ch	si / sz

Many of the alternations in the table can be understood in terms of a process called assimilation, by which the consonant sound changes to become more like the vowel that follows it[26]. In English, the vowel alternations are quite common, cf. the verb forms 'begin, began, begun'.

---

[24] 'ADJ: greedy; interesting; rich; bald; small; old; large / better; tall; expensive/dear; deaf; ADV: weakly; briskly; cold; very; nice; old; fast; long; quiet; NOUNS: shop; wardrobe; weekend; cash register; butter; theatre; secretary; way; fly'

[25] The masculine personal of adjective forms is the only grammatical area in which *sz*, and *ż* may have 'soft' alternants.

[26] There is another series of commonly encountered alternations (particularly in verb conjugations) that are not explicable entirely in terms of articulation. Over the course of the book these may be referred to as 'historical' alternations. Some of the most common examples are ***t/ci - c, s/si - sz, d/dzi - dz, z/zi - ż***: e.g. *wypłata : płacić : płacę* 'salary : to pay : I pay'.

Table 3.6.b. shows the tongue positions for **t**, **ć/ci**, and **i**. Can these drawings help you explain the alternation between *bogaty – bogaci*?

Table 3.6.b. Tongue positions for *t, c/a* and *i*.

| t [t] | ć/ci [tɕ] | i [i] |

Before the vowel *i*, which is produced with the tongue body raised toward the palate, the tongue position for preceding consonants will 'anticipate' that of the vowel. In the case of the dental consonants, this produces a series of systematic changes by which *n* changes into *ń/ni*, *s* into *ś/si*, *z* into *ź/zi*, *t* into *ć/ci*, and *d* into *dź/dzi*. Notice the parallels in each of these alternations – the consonant changes to the closest soft consonant, spelled either as a *kreska* consonant (with the diacritic mark), or as a regular consonant letter followed by the letter *i*.

Looking at the phonetic description in § 3.2. we may note that the alternations may be explained in terms of tongue position – the vowel *i* requires an articulation that is similar to the soft consonants in that the body of the tongue is raised toward the palate. At the same time, non-palatal (hard) consonants are incompatible with the vowel *i*.

Alternations can be found in many grammatical categories. **Table 3.6.c.** shows some examples of diminutives.

Table 3.6.c. Alternations in diminutive forms

Adj	Adv	Noun	
mały: malutki, maleńki, malusieńki	trochę: troszkę, troszeczkę, troszeńkę	córka: córeczka, córunia, córusia	stół: stolik, stoliczek
'small' Dim ⊘	'a little' Dim ⊘	'daughter' Dim ⊘	'table' Dim ⊘

Verb conjugations are also full of alternations. Can you explain what you observe in **Table 3.6.d.**?

Table 3.6.d. Alternations: Present tense verbs

'I …'		'go'	'wear'	'take'	'ask for'	'threaten'	'tear'	'can'
1 Sg		idę	niosę	biorę	proszę	grożę	drę	mogę
2 Sg		idziesz	niesiesz	bierzesz	prosisz	grozisz	drzesz	możesz
Alterna-tion	Conso-nant	d↔dzi	s↔si	r↔rz	sz↔si	ż↔zi	r↔rz	g↔ż
	Vowel		o↔e	o↔e				

When learning these alternations, it is helpful to consult the phonetic descriptions in § 3.2. A little technical familiarity with the phonetic and phonological fundaments of the alternations will go a long way in helping to make them automatic for the learner. For learners, reconstructing these alternations can be the key to successful oral communication. Familiarity with this phonological system will help learners see connections among words which might at first seem unrelated, which will greatly ease the learning process.

4 Verbs: *czasowniki*

4.1. Verbs are something else

4.1.1. Translation difficulties

Language learners typically employ word lists in order to master new words: 'table' is *stół*, 'aeroplane' *samolot*, etc. Occasionally a word in one language may have two different translations in the other. For example, the Polish word *palce* is used for both 'fingers' and 'toes' (in Polish to refer explicitly to toes, you have to say 'fingers on your feet'). However, in the case of nouns the list method is generally not problematic, since nouns generally have an equivalent in the other language. Verbs on the other hand, are different in many ways. It is relatively rare for there to be a one-to-one correspondence in meaning between a verb in English and its "equivalent" in Polish. If you look up a verb in a large dictionary, you will often find numerous translations for the verb you look up, and it is often difficult to choose the appropriate form. If you make use of a small dictionary you will find of course significantly fewer translations, but the chances are high that the most appropriate one for your purposes is simply not listed.

 Table 4.1.a. shows some typical equivalents of English 'pay', which most often would translate as *płacić* in Polish. Note that in some cases there is parallel usage of the two verbs, while in others Polish uses completely different verbs than English does.

Table 4.1.a. Parallel vs. idiomatic usage of 'pay' *płacić*

Parallel usage of 'pay' and *płacić*	
Ile za to **płaciłeś**? (za + Acc)	How much did you **pay** for it?
Można **płacić** kartą? (Inst)	Can I **pay** with a credit card?
Dobrze mi **płacą**. (Dat)	They **pay** me well.
Idiomatic expressions with 'pay' that do not translate with *płacić*	
Nie **zwracałem** uwagi.	I wasn't **paying** attention.
Odwiedziłem rodziców.	I **paid** my parents a visit.
Składamy hołd poległym żołnierzom.	We **pay** tribute to the fallen soldiers.

4.1.2. Use in various constructions

 In the case of 'leave' the connections between the Polish and English are even more complicated. What are the equivalents of 'leave' in Polish? **Table 4.1.b.** shows various examples.

Table 4.1.b. Polish equivalents of English 'leave'

A.	There was nothing **left** for us.	Nic nam nie **zostało**.
B.	Ewa **left** her husband.	Ewa **rzuciła** męża.
C.	**Leave** him alone!	**Daj** mu spokój!
D.	We're **leaving** at 4.	**Wyjeżdżamy** o czwartej.
E.	I **left** home very early today.	Dziś bardzo wcześnie **wyszedłem** z domu.
F.	Some things are better **left** unsaid.	O niektórych sprawach lepiej nie **wspominać**.
G.	Ten minus seven **leaves** three.	Dziesięć odjąć siedem **równa się** / jest trzy.

As we see in **Table 4.1.b.**, for the English verb 'leave' there are many different possibilities for translation into Polish. In some cases we might notice how a certain equivalent might depend upon the grammatical construction or context. **Table 4.1.c.** summarizes the constructions and contexts employed in the examples in the previous table.

Table 4.1.c. Constructions and contexts for equivalents of 'leave'

A.	leave	for	zostawać	+ Dat ➽
B.	leave	someone, something	rzucić	+ Acc ♥
C.	leave	someone alone	dać spokój	+ Dat ➽
D.	leave	(by vehicle)	wyjeżdżać	kiedy? skąd? + Adv
E.	leave	(on foot)	wyjść	kiedy? skąd? + Adv
F.	leave	unsaid	nie wspominać	+ Loc ☁
G.	leave	(subtraction)	równać się	+ Numeral

The examples in **A.**, **B.**, **D.** and **E.** show how the equivalent can depend on the grammatical construction. For example the usage in **A.** shows an indirect object in the dative case, in **B.** we have a direct object in the accusative, while in **D.** and **E.** we have an intransitive verb used without an object.

4.1.3. Verbal aspect

The Polish verb system is characterized by a fundamental distinction that is quite foreign to English speakers, namely the notion of **verbal aspect**. Look at the first two examples in **Table 4.1.d.** that are formed from the Polish verb *budować* 'to build'. What is the difference in meaning between 'was building' in the example in row **A.** and 'built' in the example in row **B.**? If you can see this difference, you have taken a significant step in learning what Polish verbal aspect is all about.

Table 4.1.d. Illustration of verbal aspect

A.	Pan Nowak długo **budował** swój dom.	Mr Nowak **was building** his house for a long time.
B.	**Zbudowali** swój dom w 2004.	They **built** their house in 2004.
C.	Marcin **podpisał** umowę.	Marcin **signed** the contract.
D.	Cały dzień **podpisywałem** dokumenty.	I was **signing** documents all day.

A.   **B.**

The most basic distinction in Polish verbal aspect is that of completeness. Thus, all Polish verbs are either **imperfective** ↔ (and refer to an action that is ongoing, repeating, or without completion), or **perfective** ↓ (and refer to an action that is complete). In row **A.**, the example states that Mr Nowak 'was building' his house for a long time, but does not explicitly state that he completed the building. In the example in row **B.**, the opposite is true, and we assume that Mr Nowak has finished building his house. When looking at the Polish sentences in rows **A.** and **B.**, notice how the aspect is expressed – the imperfective verb uses the standard form *budować*, while the perfective form has a prefix *z-*, *zbudować*. Thus, in this case one forms a perfective verb by adding a prefix to an imperfective verb. In the case of 'build', one might say that the verb is by nature imperfective, since 'building' describes an ongoing process without explicit reference to completion. In other cases however, we may assume that a verb is by nature perfective, and the perfective form serves as a base from which imperfective verbs are derived by means of a suffix. Rows **C.** and **D.** show just such a case. The verb *podpisać* 'to sign'[1] can be thought of as being inherently perfective, since putting a signature on something implies an action that is complete. If we want to express the process of signing something, we create an imperfective verb from a perfective one by means of a suffix, in this case *-yw-*.

    These examples show that most Polish verbs come in imperfective-perfective pairs, which, although in dictionaries occupy the same entries, in some sense represent different words in English. Thus, *podpisać* translates as 'to sign', while *podpisywać* means 'to be signing' or 'to sign repeatedly or habitually'. In the other example, *budować* means 'to be building' or 'to build (habitually)', while *zbudować* means 'to build (and finish building)'. Although occasionally meanings will be transparent from the word formation of these verbal pairs, in many cases learners will simply have to learn 'two verbs in one'. These cases will be discussed in further detail in § 4.6.

    An additional element of verbal aspect to remember concerns its relationship to tense. Since the perfective aspect expresses an action that is complete, it follows logically that it can

---

[1] This verb is itself formed from the imperfective *pisać* 'to write'. The prefix *pod-*, with the meaning 'under' is added, producing a new verb that is perfective.

not exist in the present tense – either something has already been completed, or it will be completed at some point in the future. If something is in the process of being completed or is completed regularly, the situation is inherently imperfective and expressed by an imperfective verb. Although perfective verbs do not exist in the present tense, some of their forms LOOK as though they exist in the present tense (they have endings resembling those of present tense verbs). For example, *podpiszę* 'I will sign' has an identical conjugated form to *piszę* 'I am writing, I write'. Notice, however, that the perfective verb has a future meaning.

4.1.4. Multifunctionality of verb endings

Because the verb endings in Polish express person, number, and tense, the personal pronouns will often disappear. For example, to say 'I understand' one simply says *rozumiem*. If you say *ja rozumiem*, that will give special emphasis to the pronoun, implying that 'I understand (perhaps someone else does not)'. This is true in all of the tenses, and is especially true in the 1st and 2nd persons. The dropping of pronouns in Polish provides an additional challenge for foreign learners trying to understand spoken Polish, since there are simply fewer clues for the listener to watch out for. For example ***daj** mi to* means '***give** that to me*', but ***dał** mi to* means '**he gave** it to me'. Thus we can see that a very small phonetic difference can completely change the meaning of the sentence.

Table 4.1.e. shows the conjugation of the common Polish verb *być* 'to be'.

Table 4.1.e. Person and number in the conjugation of *być* 'to be'

			Pronouns		być	Context [2]
Sg	1	'I'		ja	jestem	w domu
	2	'you'		ty	jesteś	w Warszawie
	3	'he'		on ♀		w Londynie
		'she'		ona ♂		
		'it'		ono ⚲	jest	
		'you' polite form for a man		pan		
		'you' polite form for a woman		pani		
Pl	1	'we'		my	jesteśmy	w Hiszpanii
	2	'you'		wy	jesteście	w Stanach
	3	+Mp	'they' (at least one man in group)	oni		w szkole
			'you' plural polite form 'ladies and gentlemen' 'gentlemen'	państwo panowie	są	
		−Mp	'they' (no men in group)	one		
			'ladies'	panie		

[2] *jestem w domu, jesteś w Warszawie, ona jest w Londynie, jesteśmy w Hiszpanii, jesteście w Stanach, oni są w szkole* 'I am at home, you are in Warsaw, she is in London, we are in Spain, you are in the States, they are in school'

| panowie | panie | państwo |

The past tense is also marked according to gender. In the singular they can be feminine, masculine or neuter. In the plural there are only two categories: **masculine personal** (+Mp 🖐) and **non-masculine personal** (−Mp ✕).

Table 4.1.f. Polish verbal categories: dialogue

Anna	Co robi**liście** 🖐 ↔ wczoraj?	What did you do yesterday?
Konrad	By**łem** ♀ ↔ w kinie, a Marek coś czytał ♀ ↔. Potem pisa**liśmy** 🖐 ↔ referat, a co słychać u ciebie i u Ewy?	I was at the cinema, but Marek was reading something. Then we were writing a paper. And what's new with you and Ewa?
Anna	Już przedwczoraj napisa**łyśmy** ✕ ♁ referat. Wczoraj uczy**łyśmy** się ✕ ↔ matematyki.	The day before yesterday we finished writing the paper. Yesterday we studied maths.
Konrad	A co robi**ą** ↔ Piotr i Paweł?	And what are Piotr and Paweł doing?
Anna	Oni dzisiaj pracu**ją** ↔. Referat będą pisa**li** 🖐 ↔ jutro. A Ewa i ja będziemy jutro odpoczywa**ły** ✕ ↔.	Today they are working. Tomorrow they will will be writing the paper. And Ewa and I will rest tomorrow.

Since the verb endings can carry a lot of information, it is advised that they be mastered early in the learning process, especially when one wants to understand spoken Polish.

4.2. The present tense: conjugation types

4.2.1. Regular conjugations

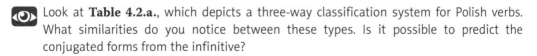 Look at **Table 4.2.a.**, which depicts a three-way classification system for Polish verbs. What similarities do you notice between these types. Is it possible to predict the conjugated forms from the infinitive?

Table 4.2.a. Present tense 👆: regular conjugations

Pronouns		Type 1		Type 2				Type 3	
		-ę, -esz		**-ę, -isz**		**-ę, -ysz**		**-m, -sz**	
Infinitive[3]		studiować		myśleć		liczyć		mieszkać	
Sg	ja	studiuj	-ę	myśl	-ę	licz	-ę	mieszka	-m
	ty	studiuj	-esz	myśl	-isz	licz	-ysz	mieszka	-sz
	on, ona, ono	studiuj	-e	myśl	-i	licz	-y	mieszka	
Pl	my	studiuj	-emy	myśl	-imy	licz	-ymy	mieszka	-my
	wy	studiuj	-ecie	myśl	-icie	licz	-ycie	mieszka	-cie
	oni, one	studiuj	-ą	myśl	-ą	licz	-ą	mieszka	-ją

As we see in the table, the three types of conjugation classes are determined by the present tense endings, and are listed as follows:[4]

$$(1.) \text{ -ę, -esz, } (2.) \text{ -ę, -isz/ysz, } (3.) \text{ -m, -sz}$$

Notice that the two forms to memorize are the first-person singular and the second-person singular. Once you know these forms and you know the pattern, you should be able to figure out the rest of the forms. In Type 2, the choice of vowel in the endings (except for first-person singular and third-person plural) depends on the last consonant of the stem – if it is hard we see the vowel *-y-*, and if it is soft we get *-i-*. Section 3.6. on alternations provides an explanation of this phenomenon.

In these regular verbs, the stem remains the same throughout each conjugated form (although it is often different from that of the infinitive forms). The endings that are added to these stems are shown in **Table 4.2.b.**

Table 4.2.b. Present tense endings 👆

1 Sg	2 Sg	3 Sg	1 Pl	2 Pl	3 Pl
-ę / -m	**-sz**	**-e, -i, -y, ø[5]**	**-my**	**-cie**	**-ą**

As you can see in **Table 4.2.a.**, the fact that these conjugations are regular does not always mean that you can predict the conjugated forms on the basis of the infinitive (cf. *studiować* 'to study (be a student)'. Thus, unfortunately, when learning verbs it will often be necessary to memorize two stems, an infinitive stem and a conjugated stem.[6] However, there are many patterns that can be observed. The verb *studiować* illustrates one of the most common patterns. When the infinitive ends in *-ować*, the present stem will show *-uj-* instead and then conjugate regularly. There is a very large number of verbs that behave this way; very often they are formed from

---

[3] 'to study (be a student), to think, to count, to live'

[4] There are other possible ways of analysing the Polish verb system. The present work chooses the three type system due to pedagogical considerations (see Kaipio 1997 or Mędak 2005a, 2005b).

[5] In the third type, there is no ending in the third-person singular; ø represents this lack of an ending.

[6] The present stem is used to form the perfective future, the imperative, and present active participles and gerunds. The infinitive stem is used to form the past tense, past active participles, past passive participles, as well as verbal nouns.

stems which resemble English words, e.g. *dyskutować, eksperymentować, cytować*, 'to discuss, experiment, cite'.

Only in the third type (*-m, -sz*) does the 1ˢᵗ person singular have the ending *-m*, and only in this type is the 3ʳᵈ person plural form longer than the 1ˢᵗ singular by one syllable. Almost all the verbs in this type end in *-am* in the 1ˢᵗ person singular, although there are a few with *-em*, e.g. *wiem, jem, umiem* and *rozumiem*[7].

4.2.2. Irregular conjugations

 Compare **Table 4.2.c.** below with **Table 4.2.a.** What differences do you notice between regular and irregular conjugations in the present tense?

Table 4.2.c. Present ✋: Conjugations with alternations in the verb stem

Pronouns		Type 1 -ę, -esz		Type 2 -ę, -isz[8]			Type 3 -m, -sz	
Infinitive		*iść* 'go'		*stać* 'be standing'		*nosić* 'wear'	*jeść* 'eat'	
Sɢ	ja	id	-ę	stoj	-ę	nosz	-ę	je	-m
	ty	**idzi**	-esz	**sto**	-isz	**nos**	-isz	je	-sz
	on, ona, ono	**idzi**	-e	**sto**	-i	**nos**	-i	je	
Pʟ	my	**idzi**	-emy	**sto**	-imy	**nos**	-imy	je	-my
	wy	**idzi**	-ecie	**sto**	-icie	**nos**	-icie	je	-cie
	oni, one	id	-ą	stoj	-ą	nosz	-ą	**jedz**	-ą

The alternations affect the following forms: in the first and second conjugation types the first-person singular and third-person plural forms are always the same except for the ending (the last letter *-ę* or *-ą*). In the third type of conjugation only the third-person plural form shows any type of alternation.

For irregular verbs of the first and second types, one should learn the first- and second-person singular forms. For verbs of the third type, one should learn the first-person singular and third-person plural forms.

4.3. The present tense: modal verbs

4.3.1. Translation difficulties

Modality expresses the relationship between the speaker, what he/she says, and reality. Modal verbs thus generally go with other verbs, e.g. 'I can go, I must go'. Polish has many unusual looking modal forms that do not have standard verbal endings. Such forms are impersonal and thus will not have a subject in the nominative case. These include *można* 'one can', *należy* 'one should', *trzeba* 'one must' *wolno* 'one may'. These forms do not conjugate so it is worth learning them early. The relationship between Polish and English modals is not a simple one. There are many idiomatic expressions which must be learned. **Table 4.3.a.** shows some of the differences between Polish and English modals.

---

[7] *wiedzieć* 'to know', *jeść* 'to eat', *umieć* 'to know how to', *rozumieć* 'to understand'

[8] Type 2 verbs with *-ę, -ysz* are not subject to any alternations.

Table 4.3.a. Polish and English modal verbs

English modal forms	Polish modal forms	Examples	
can (be able to)	umieć, móc, potrafić[9], można	**Umiem** pływać, ale teraz nie **mogę**, bo nie mam czasu.	I can swim (I know how to), but now I can't because I have no time.
		On **potrafi** czarować.	He knows how to charm / to work charms / to perform marvels.
		Czy **można** tu płacić kartą?	Can I pay by debit card here?
should	mieć, powinien, należy	Co ona **ma** zrobić?	What should she do?
		Powinna zrobić porządek.	She should tidy up.
		Latem **należy** dużo pić.	In the summer you should drink a lot.
may	móc, wolno	Czy **mogę** już wstać?	May I get up now?
		W lesie **nie wolno** krzyczeć.	You are not allowed to scream in the forest.
must, have to	musieć, trzeba	**Musisz** mi to powiedzieć.	You must tell me this.
		Trzeba dużo czytać.	You have to read a lot / One has to read a lot.
want (would like)	chcieć	**Chcę** ci pomóc.	I want to help you.
		Chciałbym ♀ / **chciałabym** ♂ zapłacić.	I would like to pay.
prefer	woleć	**Wolę** kawę niż herbatę. / **Wolę** kawę od herbaty.	I prefer coffee to tea.

The above examples show how important it can be to learn a verb in context.

4.3.2. Conjugation

Compare the examples in **Tables 4.2.a.**, **4.2.c.** and **4.3.b.** What is similar? What is different?

Table 4.3.b. Conjugation of modal verbs: present tense ☝

Modal forms	want	can	prefer	can	must	can
Infinitive	**chcieć**	**móc**	**woleć**	**potrafić**	**musieć**	**umieć**
Conjugation	-ę, -esz		-ę, -isz / -ysz			-m, -sz
ja	chcę	mogę	wolę	potrafię	muszę	umiem
ty	chcesz	możesz	wolisz	potrafisz	musisz	umiesz
on, ona, ono	chce	może	woli	potrafi	musi	umie
my	chcemy	możemy	wolimy	potrafimy	musimy	umiemy
wy	chcecie	możecie	wolicie	potraficie	musicie	umiecie
oni, one	chcą	mogą	wolą	potrafią	muszą	umieją

---

[9] *Potrafić* and *umieć* are very close in meaning, the former implying a capability to do something while the latter is more associated with knowledge.

The verbs *chcę* and *mogę* belong to the first conjugation type; *wolę, potrafię* and *muszę* are of the second type; *umiem* represents the third conjugation type. Some modal verbs are regular (*chcę, wolę, potrafię, umiem*); two of these verbs (denoted with: *mogę, muszę*) show stem alternations.

4.3.3. Moral obligation: *powinienem / powinnam*

The modal found under the dictionary entry *powinien* (*powinna, powinno* 1 PSG) is generally translated as 'should'. It has no infinitive form. In modern Polish only the present form is used regardless of whether the present, past, or future is referred to[10]. The forms are shown in **Table 4.3.c.** below.

Table 4.3.c. Conjugation: *powinien, powinna, powinno*

Person	Present form (representing present, past, and future)		
	SG		
	MASC ♀	FEM ♂	NEUT ♀
ja	powinienem	powinnam	
ty	powinieneś	powinnaś	
on, ona, ono	powinien	powinna	powinno
	PL		
	+MP 🙍		−MP ✂
my	powinniśmy		powinnyśmy
wy	powinniście		powinnyście
oni, one	powinni		powinny

Try to say the following in Polish: 'I should have helped my mother yesterday/I should help my mother tomorrow'.

These constructions are quite unusual, though not terribly difficult to learn.

Table 4.3.d. Examples of: *powinien, powinna, powinno*

Comments		Examples		
A man says:	**Powinienem**	wczoraj (teraz / jutro) pomóc matce.	I should	help my mother now / tomorrow. or: have helped my mother yesterday.
A woman says:	**Powinnam**			
To a man:	**Powinieneś**		You should	
To a woman:	**Powinnaś**			
One says about a child:	**Powinno**		He/she should	

---

[10] Constructions like *powinna była przyjść* 'she should have come' are archaic and only rarely used. Generally the tense is understood from the context.

Muszę przyznać, że nie lubię dużo pracować. Mogę nawet nic nie robić przez cały dzień. Teraz powinienem naprawić rower, ale mi się nie chce. Wolę tak sobie siedzieć. Umiem wprawdzie zrobić wszystko, ale przecież nie należy przesadzać z wysiłkiem. Trzeba się szanować. Po co mam się męczyć?

4.4. The past tense

 Read the short dialogue in **Table 4.4.a.** and note how the forms of the verbs *kupić, być, rozmawiać*[11] change depending on who the subject is.

Table 4.4.a. Past tense ➡: dialogue

Ewa	1. Kupił**eś** ♀ gazety?	Have you bought / did you buy the newspaper?
Adam	2. Nie, nie kupił**em** ♀. A ty, kupił**aś** ♂ chleb?	No, I haven't. And you, have you bought / did you buy bread?
Ewa	3. Tak, kupił**am** ♂. Był**eś** ♀ u dentysty?	Yes, I have / did. Have you been / did you go to the dentist?
Adam	4. Tak, był**em** ♀. A dziecko był**o** ♀ w szkole?	Yes, I have / did. And was your child at school?
Ewa	5. Tak, był**o** ♀. A ja był**am** ♂ u siostry. Rozmawia**łyś**my ✂ o przyjaciółkach.	Yes, he / she was. And I was at my sister's. We talked about friends. (female)
Adam	6. O, a ja był**em** ♀ u brata i my też rozmawia**liś**my 🐾 o przyjaciółkach.	Oh, I was at my brother's and we also talked about friends. (female)

Verb forms indicating past action are generally derived from the infinitive stem of the verb (although there is one very common exception). In the place of the infinitive ending (most frequently *-ć*) the past endings are added. These endings are made up of a past suffix (*-ł* or *-l*) followed by indicators of the person, number, and gender of the subject.

---

[11] 'to buy, to be, to talk'

Table 4.4.b. Past tense endings ➥

GENUS SG	ja	ty	onᵃ·ᵒ	GENUS PL	my	wy	oni/one
MASC ♀ SG	-łem	-łeś	-ł	+Mp 👥 PL	-liśmy	-liście	-li
FEM △ SG	-łam	-łaś	-ła	−Mp ✂ PL	-łyśmy	-łyście	-ły
NEUT ♀ SG	—	—	-ło				

The neuter ending is used for example when referring to a single child (*Moje dziecko było w szkole* 'My child was at school'). When one speaks of a group of children, the non-masculine personal form is used, as for a group of women, objects, animals, or any group without at least one man. When children speak for themselves, however, they will use their appropriate gender form.

Table 4.4.c. shows which verb forms are used, and in each case designates who is speaking about/to whom. Try to conjugate the verb before reading the table.

Table 4.4.c. Verb forms and gender in the past tense: *być*.

	FEM △		MASC ♀		NEUT ♀	
SG	ja by**łam**	a woman about herself	ja by**łem**	a man about himself		
	ty by**łaś**	X to a woman	ty by**łeś**	X to a man		
	ona by**ła**	X about a woman	on by**ł**	X about a man	ono by**ło**	X about a child
PL	my by**łyśmy**	women about a group without men	my by**liśmy**	X about a group with at least one man		
	wy by**łyście**	X to a group without men	wy by**liście**	X to a group with at least one man		
	one by**ły**	X about a group without men	oni by**li**	X about a group with at least one man		

X: an unspecified third person

Look at **Table 4.4.d.** and compare the past tense conjugations of the verbs *z/robić* 'to do' and *mieć* 'to have'. What similarities and/or differences do you notice?

Table 4.4.d. Past tense ➥: of: *z/robić* and *mieć*

Infinitive	**z/robić**			**mieć**		
			SG			
Pronouns	MASC ♀	NEUT ♀	FEM △	MASC ♀	NEUT ♀	FEM △
ja	z/robi**łem**		z/robi**łam**	mia**łem**		mia**łam**
ty	z/robi**łeś**		z/robi**łaś**	mia**łeś**		mia**łaś**
ona			z/robi**ła**			mia**ła**
on	z/robi**ł**			mia**ł**		
ono		z/robi**ło**			mia**ło**	
			PL			
Pronouns	+Mp 👥	−Mp ✂		+Mp 👥	−Mp ✂	
my	z/robi**liśmy**	z/robi**łyśmy**		mie**liśmy**	mia**łyśmy**	
wy	z/robi**liście**	z/robi**łyście**		mie**liście**	mia**łyście**	
one		z/robi**ły**			mia**ły**	
oni	z/robi**li**			mie**li**		

The past tense endings are always the same.

The verb **z/robić** shows forms of both aspects: imperfective ↔ *robić* and perfective ⅃ *zrobić*. The sentence *On* **robił** *zadanie domowe,* with an imperfective verb, would translate as 'he was doing his homework' (but we don't know if he finished). The perfective version *On* **zrobił** *zadanie domowe* means that 'he did (and finished) his homework'.

The verb **mieć** exists only as an imperfective verb. Notice that in this verb we can see one of the historical vowel alternations (see § 3.6.), giving us *miel-* for masculine personal plural forms, and *miał-* for all the other forms.

You should notice certain regularities. For example, *-a* occurs in all feminine singular forms, *-o* in neuter singular, *-i* in masculine personal plural, *-y* in non-masculine personal plural, and a zero-ending for 3rd person singular forms.

Table 4.4.e. shows the complete conjugations for *być* in the past tense. Try to conjugate the verbs yourself before looking at the table.

byłe[a]m:	(1) by**łe**m	MASC ♀	(2) by**ła**m	FEM △			'I was'
byłe[a]ś:	(1) by**łe**ś	MASC ♀	(2) by**ła**ś	FEM △			'you were'
był[a,o]:	(1) by**ł**	MASC ♀	(2) by**ła**	FEM △	(3) by**ło**	NEUT ♀	'he/she/it was'

In the plural: **li ↔ ty**

byli[ty]śmy:	(1) by-**li**-śmy	+MP 🐾		(2) by-**ty**-śmy		−MP ✂	'we were'

Verbs like *mówić, chodzić* and *pojechać*[12] have regular past conjugations. Verbs with infinitives ending in **-ąć** (e.g. *zacząć*[13]) show an **ą/ę** alternation. Read **Tables 4.4.f.** and **4.4.g.** and try to figure out some patterns for yourself.

Table 4.4.f. Past tense verbs ➡: regular conjugations

	A.			B.	
	mówić	chodzić	po/jechać	zacząć	
				MASC ♀	FEM △, NEUT ♀
ja	mówiłe[a]m	chodziłe[a]m	pojechałe[a]m	zacz**ą**łem	zacz**ę**łam
ty	mówiłe[a]ś	chodziłe[a]ś	pojechałe[a]ś	zacz**ą**łeś	zacz**ę**łaś
on[a,o]	mówił[a,o]	chodził[a,o]	pojechał[a,o]	zacz**ą**ł	zacz**ę**ła[o]
my	mówili[ty]śmy	chodzili[ty]śmy	pojechali[ty]śmy	zacz**ę**li[ty]śmy	
wy	mówili[ty]ście	chodzili[ty]ście	pojechali[ty]ście	zacz**ę**li[ty]ście	
oni 🐾 one ✂	mówili[ty]	chodzili[ty]	pojechali[ty]	zacz**ę**li[ty]	

---

[12] 'to speak, to go/walk, to go (by vehicle)'

[13] 'to begin'

- The verbs in column **A.** have regular past tense conjugations. Here it does not matter whether a perfective or imperfective is used; the stems are the same (*jechałe^am* ↔ / *pojechałe^am* ⬇).

- In **B.** ending all verbs with infinitives, in *-ąć* show the same alternation of *-ę* and *-ą*. Generally we have *-ę*, except in the masculine singular forms, where we have *-ą*: *wziąć*: *wziął* ↔ *wzięła*; *zdjąć*: *zdjął* ↔ *zdjęła*[14].

  In past tense forms before *-ł*, the vowels *-ę-*, *-ą-* are generally pronounced like *-e-*, *-o-* (without nasality).

Verbs with infinitives ending in *-eć* conjugate according to a different model. Look at **Table 4.4.g.** and see if you can figure out the pattern.

Table 4.4.g. Past tense ➡: Verbs ending in *-eć*

	A. widzieć		**B.** myśleć	
	Sg			
ja	wiedziałe^am		myślałe^am	
ty	wiedziałe^aś		myślałe^aś	
on^{a,o}	wiedział^{a,o}		myślał^{a,o}	
	Pl			
	oni +Mp 🚹	one –Mp ✂	oni +Mp 🚹	one –Mp ✂
my	widzieliśmy	widziałyśmy	myśleliśmy	myślałyśmy
wy	widzieliście	widziałyście	myśleliście	myślałyście
oni, one	widzieli	widziały	myśleli	myślały

Verbs like ***widzieć, myśleć*** show a historical vowel alternation (*-el-* ↔ *-ał-*) with *-e* occurring before the consonant *-l*. Thus, the vowel *-e* appears only in the male personal plural forms and the infinitive. Otherwise the vowel *-a* occurs.

4.5. The future tense

4.5.1. Imperfective future

As was mentioned earlier, the relationship in Polish between tense and aspect can be somewhat complex. To express future actions, both aspects can be used, but they have very different meanings. The imperfective future will carry a meaning along the lines of 'will be doing something' while the perfective future forms would translate as 'will do something (finish doing it)'. Thus, an imperfective future construction of the type *będę pisać list* 'I will be writing a letter' makes no explicit statement about whether that letter will actually be completed.

---

[14] 'to take; to take off'

There are two possibilities for forming the imperfective future, both of them use future forms of the verb *być* 'to be'. Compare the examples in **Table 4.5.a.** and try to describe the differences between the two constructions.

Table 4.5.a. Imperfective Future I and II: *pisać* → 'to write'

	A. FUT I		**B. FUT II**				
SG			**MASC ♂**		**FEM △**		**NEUT ♀**
ja	będę		będę		będę		
ty	będziesz		będziesz		będziesz		
on, ona, ono	będzie	pisać	on będzie	pisał	—	pisała	—
			—		ona będzie		—
			—		—		ono będzie pisało
PL			**+MP 👥**		**−MP ✂**		
my	będziemy		będziemy		będziemy		
wy	będziecie		będziecie	pisali	będziecie		pisały
oni, one	będą		oni będą		one będą		

- **A.** The first and somewhat simpler construction uses future forms of **być** (*będę, będziesz,* etc.) followed by the infinitive form of an imperfective verb[15].

- **B.** The second construction, instead of using the infinitive, employs past tense forms of imperfective verbs. However, the forms with *ł* used in the future do not designate person, only gender and number (thus you say *będę czytał* and not *będę czytałem for 'I will be reading', since the first person is already marked by *będę*).

Table 4.5.b. The future

	FUT ☞ *być* (specifies the category 'person')	**IMP ↔ PAST FORM ➍ 3 SG or PL**
(ty)	będziesz	pisał[a,o]
(my)	będziemy	pisali[ły]

In most cases it does not matter which of the two future constructions is used. They have the same meaning. With modal verbs, however, you must use the second construction, thus *będę musiał* (and not: *będę musieć) 'I will have to'. The imperfective future II is also used when two future verbs are used in a row: *będę próbował[a] za/dzwonić* 'I will try to phone' (and not: **będę próbować za/dzwonić*).

---

[15] It is an error to use these forms of *być* with a perfective verb: *będę napisać, **będę napisał[a]* are impossible in Polish.

4.5.2. Perfective future

 Compare **Table 4.5.c.** with the tables in § 4.2. The present tense: conjugation types. What similarities do you notice?

Table 4.5.c. Perfective future ↓ / imperfective present ↔ : regular conjugation[16]

		Type 1		Type 2				Type 3	
		-ę, -esz		-ę, -isz		-ę, -ysz		-m, -sz	
	Inf	s/próbować		po/dzielić		na/uczyć na/uczyć się		po/czekać	
Sg	ja	s/próbuj	-ę	po/dziel	-ę	na/ucz	-ę (się)	po/czeka	-m
	ty	s/próbuj	-esz	po/dziel	-isz	na/ucz	-ysz (się)	po/czeka	-sz
	on[a,o]	s/próbuj	-e	po/dziel	-i	na/ucz	-y (się)	po/czeka	
Pl	my	s/próbuj	-emy	po/dziel	-imy	na/ucz	-ymy (się)	po/czeka	-my
	wy	s/próbuj	-ecie	po/dziel	-icie	na/ucz	-ycie (się)	po/czeka	-cie
	oni, one	s/próbuj	-ą	po/dziel	-ą	na/ucz	-ą (się)	po/czeka	-ją

Notice that aspect is independent of the verb conjugation. In the cases above, a prefix makes the verb perfective. However, the conjugations are the same. The difference is that the perfective verbs carry FUTURE meaning. These differences in meaning are summed up in **Table 4.5.d.**

Table 4.5.d. From present imperfective to future perfective

	A. Pres Imp ↔ *teraz* 'now'	**B.** Fut Perf ↓ *jutro* 'tomorrow'	Eng
1	uczę się wiersza	**na**uczę się wiersza	1A. I am learning the poem. 1B. I will learn the poem.
2	uczę córkę wiersza	**na**uczę córkę wiersza	2A. I am teaching my daughter the poem. 2B. I'll teach my daughter the poem.
3	próbujemy dzwonić do Australii	**s**próbujemy zadzwonić do Australii	3A. We're trying to phone Australia. 3B. We will try to phone Australia.
4	czekamy na was	**po**czekamy (**za**czekamy)[17] na was	4A. We are waiting for you. 4B. We'll wait for you.

Table 4.5.e. shows more verb conjugations for present imperfective/future perfective pairs. This time we may note some alternations in the verb stems.

---

[16] 'to try; to divide; to teach; to learn; to wait'

[17] There are two possible perfectives for this verb.

Table 4.5.e. Perfective future ↓ / imperfective present ↔: conjugation with alternations[18]

		Type 1 -ę, -esz		Type 2 -ę, -isz/-ysz				Type 3 -m, -sz	
		Alternations							
Infinitive		po/jechać		z/robić		po/prosić		powiedzieć; wiedzieć	
Sᴳ	ja	po/jad	-ę	z/robi	-ę	po/prosz	-ę	po/wie	-m
	ty	po/jedzi	-esz	z/rob	-isz	po/pros	-isz	po/wie	-sz
	on[a,o]	po/jedzi	-e	z/rob	-i	po/pros	-i	po/wie	
Pʟ	my	po/jedzi	-emy	z/rob	-imy	po/pros	-imy	po/wie	-my
	wy	po/jedzi	-ecie	z/rob	-icie	po/pros	-icie	po/wie	-cie
	oni, one	po/jad	-ą	z/rob	-ią	po/prosz	-ą	po/wiedz	-ą

As far as learning the conjugations is concerned the same principles apply to the verbs in these tables as to those in Section 4.2. For Types 1 and 2, one need only memorize the 1ˢᵗ and 2ⁿᵈ person singular, while in the case of Type 3 one should learn the 1ˢᵗ person singular and 3ʳᵈ person plural forms.

Occasionally, adding prefixes to imperfective verbs will produce a perfective verb with a significantly different meaning. This is the case for *wiem* 'I know' and *powiem* 'I will say'. There is no perfective equivalent of *wiedzieć*, since knowing is seen as an ongoing state. *Powiedzieć* is a different verb from *wiedzieć*, even if they look very similar. In some cases perfective/imperfective pairs will form from different verb stems (see **Table 4.6.c.**). The imperfective 'equivalent' of *powiedzieć* is *mówić*, which of course looks completely different. The following sentence shows how these two verbs form an imperfective/perfective pair: *On będzie trzy godziny mówić, ale nic konkretnego nie powie* 'he will speak for three hours, but he won't say anything in particular'.

4.6. Aspectual forms

Although both English and Polish employ the notion of aspect, they express it in different ways – Polish uses prefixes and suffixes with standard verb tenses and conjugations, while English uses a more complex tense system, along with **-ing** forms of verbs. This section takes a closer look at how these notions are expressed in Polish.

Look at the examples in **Table 4.6.a.** What functions do the prefixes on the verbs fulfil?

Table 4.6.a. Aspectual forms in Polish and their English equivalents

z/jeść 'eat'	△ **Jadła i jadła** ↔, aż wszystko **zjadła** ↓.	She ate and ate, until she had finished everything.
	☷ Długo **jedliśmy** ↔, jednak nie wszystko **zjedliśmy** ↓.	We ate for a long time, however we didn't finish everything.
z/budować 'build'	Ten dom **budowano** ↔ 5 lat. Hotel Forum **zbudowano** ↓ w 2002 roku.	They were building this house for 5 years. The Forum Hotel was built in 2002.
prze/czytać 'read'	**Będę czytać** ↔ tę książkę tak długo, aż ją **przeczytam** ↓ do końca.	I will be reading the book for a long time, until I finally finish reading it.

---

[18] 'to drive; to do; to request; to say; to know'

Imperfective verb forms (in these examples without prefixes) thus express an action without specific reference to whether that action is complete, or express a process or a regularly repeating action. Schematically represented on a timeline, imperfective verbs would be expressed with a horizontal line. Perfective verbs, on the other hand, can be placed at a specific point on a timeline. **Table 4.6.b.** illustrates this difference:

Table 4.6.b. Temporal relations and aspect

Telefon **za**dzwonił ⌁, kiedy pisałeᵃm ↔ list.	Telefon dzwonił ↔ i dzwonił ↔, ale ja spałeᵃm ↔.	Kiedy byłeᵃm ↔ na wakacjach, **na**pisałeᵃm ⌁ do ciebie list.
The telephone rang while I was writing a letter.	The telephone rang and rang, but I was sleeping.	When I was on holiday I wrote you a letter.

Kiedy byłeᵃm ↔ na wakacjach, codziennie pisałeᵃm ↔ listy do przyjaciółki.	Jeżeli pojadę ⌁ na wakacje, **na**piszę ⌁ raz do mamy. Do ciebie będę pisać ↔ codziennie.
When I was on holiday, I wrote letters to my friend every day.	If I go on holiday, I will write once to my mother. To you I will write every day.

The sentences in the table above present relatively straightforward examples of which aspect to choose. However, the choice of aspect is not always clear. In general, it is worth considering the imperfective as a sort of default form, which is used unless you want to express the fact that the action is complete or took place at a very specific point in time.

Read the examples in **Table 4.6.c.** Notice that in the three rows, there are three different ways in which the form of the aspectual pair is constructed. How can you describe them?

Table 4.6.c. Formation of aspectual pairs: examples[19]

	Examples	Infinitive IMP ↔ – PERF ⊥
A.	1. Może **myłeś** ręce, ale dobrze nie **umyłeś**. 2. **Budziłam** go długo, ale był tak pijany, że go nie **obudziłam**. 3. **Czyścił** buty, ale wszystkich nie **wyczyścił**.	myć – umyć budzić – obudzić czyścić – wyczyścić
B.	4. Często **kupowałam** „Wprost", ale wczoraj **kupiłam** „Forum". 5. Nie **dawaj** mi codziennie po dwa euro, **daj** mi raz sto euro. 6. Nasz pies zawsze **trafiał** do domu, ale wczoraj nie **trafił**.	kupować – kupić dawać – dać trafiać – trafić
C.	7. Często **brał** prysznic rano, ale wczoraj nie **wziął**. 8. Nie **mów** godzinami, tylko **powiedz**, o co chodzi. 9. **Oglądaliśmy** ten film, ale nie **obejrzeliśmy** do końca.	brać – wziąć mówić – powiedzieć oglądać – obejrzeć

A. Prefixation

Prefixes are used to form perfective verbs from imperfective verbs. In these cases, the action associated with the verb tends to be imperfective by nature, so the imperfective is the 'base' form. Many different prefixes are used to build aspectual pairs. Unfortunately, learners generally will just have to memorise which prefix to use for a given verb: **na**/pisać 'to write', **u**/gotować 'to cook', **s**/chować 'to hide, to put away', **wy**/prać 'to wash clothes', **z**/organizować 'to organise'.

Table 4.6.d. presents the relationship between tense and the prefixed aspectual pairs.

Table 4.6.d. Aspect and Tense: z/robić 'to do'[20]

	Infinitive	PAST 🗩	PRES ✋	FUT ◖
			1 SG	
IMP ↔	robić	robiłe^am	robię	będę robić
PERF ⊥	zrobić	zrobiłe^am	—	zrobię

B. Suffixation

In some cases, an action can be perfective by nature. 'To buy' might serve as an example. Once you have bought something it is yours; the process is over. Thus, this is an example where the perfective forms the 'base'. In these cases, imperfective verbs are formed by adding suffixes. In the case of 'to buy' we observe the pair *kupować – kupić*, presented in **Table 4.6.e.**

---

[19] '**A.** (1) Maybe you washed your hands, but you didn't get them clean.; (2) I was trying to wake him up for a long time, but he was so drunk that I didn't manage to do it.; (3) He was cleaning shoes, but he didn't manage to clean them all.; **B.** (4) I used to buy "Wprost" but yesterday I bought "Forum".; (5) Don't give me 2 euro a day, but rather give me 100 all at once.; (6) Our dog used to find his way home, but yesterday he didn't.; **C.** (7) He often took a shower in the morning, but yesterday he didn't.; (8) Don't just go on for hours, say what's on your mind.; (9) We saw the film, but we didn't watch it through to the end.'

Notice that what is expressed with different aspectual forms of the same verb in Polish, is sometimes expressed with completely different verbs in the English translation.

[20] 'I did (for some time), I do / I am doing, I'll do (for some time); I did (and finished), I'll do (and finish)'

Table 4.6.e. Tense and aspect with suffixes, *kupować – kupić* 'to buy'

	Infinitive	Past ⬛	Pres ✋	Fut ⬅
			1 Sg	
Imp ↔	kupować	kupowałeªm	kupuję	będę kupować
Perf ⬇	kupić	kupiłeªm	—	kupię

The suffixes used to form imperfective verbs from perfectives generally follow the stem and precede the infinitive ending: *kup+owa+ć, pod+pis+ywa+ć, da+wa+ć kupować, podpisywać, dawać* 'to buy, to sign, to give'.

C. Aspectual pairs formed from different stems

There is a small number of aspectual pairs that are formed from completely different verb stems. This notion, referred to as suppletion, occurs in English as well; consider the past tense of the verb 'to go'. Suppletion often occurs with very commonly used verbs which must be memorized.

Table 4.6.f. shows one of the more common suppletive aspectual pairs in Polish. What verb does the perfective 'to say' resemble?

Table 4.6.f. Tense and aspect with unrelated stems, *mówić – powiedzieć* 'to speak – to say'

	Infinitive	Past ⬛	Pres ✋	Fut ⬅
			1 Sg	
Imp ↔	mówić	mówiłeªm	mówię	będę mówić
Perf ⬇	powiedzieć	powiedziałeªm	—	powiem

Table 4.6.g. shows some other common pairs including *brać – wziąć* 'to take', *kłaść – położyć* 'to put', *oglądać – obejrzeć* 'to watch' and *widzieć – zobaczyć* 'to see'.

Table 4.6.g. Aspectual pairs from unrelated verbs

Imp ↔	brać	oglądać	kłaść	mówić	widzieć
Perf ⬇	wziąć	obejrzeć	położyć	powiedzieć	zobaczyć
	to take	to watch, look at	to place, put	to speak, say	to see

4.7. Verbs of motion

The verb *pojechać* is conjugated in **Table 4.5.e.** and translated as 'go'. However, the English 'go' can be expressed in many different ways in Polish. For example, there is a distinction between *jechać* and *jeździć*.

Read the examples in **Table 4.7.a.** What does the choice of verb in Polish depend on?

Table 4.7.a. Aspect and verbs of motion: *jechać, jeździć, pojechać, pojeździć*

A. Kiedy **jechałem** ↔ do Krakowa, spotkałem Basię.	When I was on my way to Krakow, I met Basia.
B. Latem często **jeździłem** ⇄ do Krakowa.	In summertime I used to go to Krakow.
C. **Pojechałem** ⊥ do Krakowa, żeby **spotkać** ⊥ Basię.	I went to Krakow to meet Basia.
D. **Pojeździłem** (sobie) trochę po Krakowie.	I went for a little ride around Krakow.

- **A. + B.** Both verbs are **imperfective**. *Jechać* implies being on one's way to a destination, while *jeździć* implies going regularly to a destination, or riding around without a specific destination:

  *Często (od czasu do czasu / tylko w poniedziałki) **jeździliśmy** ⇄ do Warszawy.*

  'Often (from time to time / only on Mondays) we went to Warsaw.'

- **C. + D.** Both verbs, ***pojechać*** and ***pojeździć***, are **perfective**; implying complete actions.

- **D.** The prefix ***po-*** can have a specific function in Polish, namely to do something for a short time, and can be used with verbs of motion or other verbs: *pojeździłem, pospacerowałem, potańczyłem, popisałem* 'I went for a ride, I went for a little walk, I danced for a little while, I wrote a bit'.

A notion closely related to aspect is that of repetition or regularity, which is generally expressed with the imperfective aspect. However, there is an additional class of verbs that makes explicit use of this notion of regularity: verbs related to going, often referred to as verbs of motion. In the imperfective aspect, verbs of motion divide into two categories, one of which implies being on one's way to a specific destination (destinational), the other expresses either going somewhere regularly (iterative) or going without a specific destination (non-destinational) **Table 4.7.a.** illustrates these notions with the example of the verbs ***jechać*** and ***jeździć*** ⇄ 'to go by vehicle', both of which are imperfective verbs that can form perfectives with the prefix ***po-***.

 Polish verbs of motion present a real difficulty for English speakers. There are a large number of ways to say 'go', depending on the mode of transport, regularity of the journey, etc. **Table 4.7.b.** shows a number of Polish equivalents of the English verb 'to go'. The forms presented are all destinational, and each verb has an iterative/non-destinational form as well.

Table 4.7.b. Polish equivalents of 'go'

		Comments
I go (I am going)	jadę ↔ jechać / jeżdżę ⇄ jeździć	riding (a car, bicycle, horse)
	lecę ↔ lecieć / latam ⇄ latać	in the air
	płynę ↔ płynąć / pływam ⇄ pływać	on/in the water
	idę ↔ iść / chodzę ⇄ chodzić	on foot

Table 4.7.c. summarises the most common verbs of motion in Polish in their three aspectual forms.

Table 4.7.c. Aspectual forms of verbs of motion

Verbs of motion	Aspect		
	Perfective ⊥	Imperfective ↔	Iterative ⇄
to go on foot	pójść	iść	chodzić
to go by vehicle	pojechać	jechać	jeździć
to run	pobiec	biec	biegać
to fly	polecieć	lecieć	latać
to swim	popłynąć	płynąć	pływać
to carry (to take on foot)	zanieść	nieść	nosić
to transport (to take by vehicle)	zawieźć	wieźć	wozić

We have observed many times that the most commonly used words in a language are often irregular in their grammatical formation. Probably the most common of the verbs in **Table 4.7.c.**, *iść* and *pójść*, have irregular past tense forms (parallel to English 'go – went'), see **Table 4.7.d.**

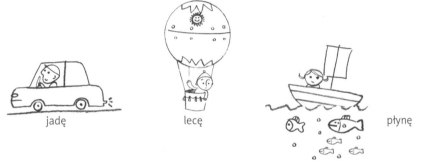

jadę   lecę   płynę

 How are the past tense forms of *iść* and *pójść* 'to go', as well as related verbs like *odejść* 'to go away' conjugated?

Table 4.7.d. Past tense: *iść*, *pójść* and *odejść*

	pójść / iść		odejść	
ja	po/szedłem	po/szłam	od/szedłem	ode/szłam
ty	po/szedłeś	po/szłaś	od/szedłeś	ode/szłaś
on	po/szedł		od/szedł	
ona, ono		po/szłaº		ode/szłaº
my	po/szli[ty]śmy		ode/szli[ty]śmy	
wy	po/szli[ty]ście		ode/szli[ty]ście	
oni, one	po/szli[ty]		ode/szli[ty]	

The past tense of *iść* has two separate conjugation stems in the singular (compare masculine *szedłem* and feminine *szłam*). The perfective form *pójść* is also conjugated according to this model, as are other perfectives formed by adding prefixes to *iść*: *odejść* : *odszedłem / odeszłam* 'to go away', *wyjść* : *wyszedłem / wyszłam* 'to go out', *wejść* : *wszedłem / weszłam* 'to enter', 'to go in'.

(◉) **Table 4.7.e.** shows some typical examples of verbs of motion. Try to translate the English examples into Polish.

Table 4.7.e. Verbs of motion: dialogue

Ewa	Może pójdziemy ↓ ⬅ do kina?	Shall we go to the cinema?
Adam	Idź ↔ sama.	Go by yourself.
Ewa	Myślałam, że lubisz chodzić ⇄ do kina.	I thought you liked going to the cinema.
Adam	Lubię, ale dzisiaj wolę iść ↔ popływać.	I do, but today I'd rather go swimming.
Ewa	Czy możesz zawieźć ↓ psa do babci?	Can you take the dog to grandmother's?
Adam	Czemu ja zawsze muszę go wozić ⇄?	How come I always have to take him?
Ewa	No dobrze, ja go zawiozę ↓. A czy możesz pójść ↓ po zakupy?	OK, I will take him. But can you go shopping?
Adam	Czemu ja mam iść ↔ po zakupy? Wiesz, że nie lubię chodzić ⇄ po sklepach.	How come I have to go shopping? You know I don't like going to the shops.
Ewa	No dobrze, to ja pójdę ↓. A może zaniesiesz ↓ listy na pocztę?	OK, I'll go. But can you take the letters to the post office?
Adam	Już raz zaniosłem ↓. A ty nie możesz zanieść ↓?	I've already done that once. Can't you take them?
Ewa	Hmmm... Mogę. A ty możesz się wynieść ↓ (COLL).	Hmmm ... I can. And you can move out.

4.8. Prefixation and change of meaning

(◉) Read the examples in **Table 4.8.a.** Try to describe how the prefixes affect the meanings of the verbs.

Table 4.8.a. Prefixes on verbs: *pisać* 'write'

pisać	**na**pisać	**o**pisać	**pod**pisać	**roz**pisać	**w**pisać	**do**pisać
to write	to describe	to sign	to announce	to write in	to add

While we have already seen how prefixes may be used to build the aspectual pairs of Polish verbs, they may also create new verbs, whose meanings may not be transparent.

Thus, prefixes generally have two different roles in the Polish verbal system. A closer look at these prefixes reveals that in appearance (and often in meaning) they are quite similar to prepositions. Therefore, by learning the prepositions, a student can go a long way in building his or her inventory of verbs, since the verbs will become easier to remember. For example, the prefix *o-* in *opisać* is apparently the same as the preposition *o* 'about', thus the meaning of *opisać* becomes transparent – 'write about' or 'describe'.

In the examples in **Table 4.8.a.**, each prefixed verb derived from *pisać* is perfective. Thus, as they are perfective, none of these new verbs can exist in the present tense. This is illustrated in **Table 4.8.b.**

When we want to create an imperfective verb from these new prefixed verbs that altered the meaning of *pisać*, we do so with the help of a suffix, in this case *-ywa*. This suffix may give an iterative meaning to the verb, or simply be used to show that the action is in progress. Examples are given in **Table 4.8.c.**

Table 4.8.b. Tense and aspect: *na/pisać, opisać, podpisać, wpisać, dopisać*[21]

Aspectual pair		PAST ☞	PRES ✋	FUT ☜
Aspectual pair	IMP ↔	pisałe[a]m	piszę	będę pisać
	PERF ↧	**na**pisałe[a]m	—	**na**piszę
Modification of meaning	PERF ↧	**o**pisałe[a]m	—	**o**piszę
		podpisałe[a]m	—	**pod**piszę
		wpisałe[a]m	—	**w**piszę
		dopisałe[a]m	—	**do**piszę

Table 4.8.c. Verbal prefixes and aspect forms: *-pisywać*

↧	**(na)**pisać	**o**pisać	**pod**pisać	**roz**pisać	**w**pisać	**do**pisać
⇄	pisywać	**o**pisywać	**pod**pisywać	**roz**pisywać	**w**pisywać	**do**pisywać
ENG	to write	to describe	to sign	to announce	to write in	to add

Present: The utterances 'I describe, I sign, I add (in writing)' would translate into Polish as *ja opisuję, podpisuję, dopisuję*. Notice the alternation in stem between the infinitive and the conjugated forms.

Past: Polish sentences like *ja opisywałem, podpisywałem, dopisywałem* might have two different translations in English. Either such forms express that the action was in progress:

Kiedy zadzwoniłe[a]ś, właśnie podpisywałe[a]m umowę 'When you called me, I was signing a contract'. or that the action was regularly repeated: *Często / długo / zawsze w piątek / tylko wieczorem / czasami podpisywałe[a]m ⇄ umowy* 'I often / sometimes used to sign contracts on Fridays / in the evening'.

The corresponding perfective constructions: *ja opisałem, podpisałem, dopisałem,*[22] express that the action took place only once and was completed.

Future: The Polish *będę opisywać, podpisywać, dopisywać* (imperfective future), expresses that these actions will be in progress or will be repeated. Although in English such structures are probably best translated as 'I will be describing, signing, adding (in writing)', the distinction between this and 'I will write, sign, add (in writing)' is not so important in English. **Table 4.8.d.** shows some of the most important prefixes that may be used to change the meaning of a verb.

Często / zawsze / w piątek / wieczorem podpisywałem umowy.

---

[21] 'to write, to describe, to sign, to write in, to add (in writing)'

[22] 'I described, signed, added (in writing)'

Table 4.8.d. Meaning change using prefix verbs

	Prefix	PERF ↧	ITERATIVE ⇄ (1. right now ... 2. regularly ...)	ENG
do-	**to, towards**	dojechać	dojeżdżać	to reach
		dopisać	dopisywać	to add to (in writing)
na-	**on, upon, in**	nałożyć	nakładać	to set, put on
o(b)-	**of, about**	objechać	objeżdżać	to go around, detour
		opisać	opisywać	to describe
od(e)-	**from**	odjechać	odjeżdżać	to drive away/depart
		odpisać	odpisywać	to respond, write back
po-	**after, over, through**	pojechać	pojeździć	to go / to go for a ride
pod(e)-	**below, under**	podłożyć	podkładać	to place under
		podkreślić	podkreślać	to underline, emphasize
		podpisać	podpisywać	to sign
prze-	**across, through**	przejechać	przejeżdżać	to drive through
		przepisać	przepisywać	to rewrite, copy
przy-	**by, close to, near**	przyjechać	przyjeżdżać	to arrive
		przynieść	przynosić	to bring
		przywieźć	przywozić	to bring (with a vehicle), transport
roz(e)-	**dis-**	rozejść (się)	rozchodzić (się)	to disperse
		rozdać	rozdawać	to distribute
w(e)-	**in**	wejść	wchodzić	to enter
wy-	**out**	wyjść	wychodzić	to go out, leave
		wynieść	wynosić	to take out
z(e)- **s-**	**down, with**	zjechać	zjeżdżać	to drive down, exit (the motorway)
		spaść	spadać	to fall down

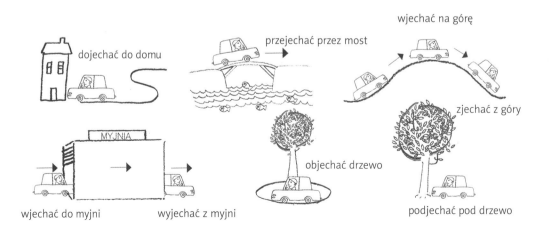

dojechać do domu

przejechać przez most

wjechać na górę

zjechać z góry

objechać drzewo

wjechać do myjni   wyjechać z myjni

podjechać pod drzewo

Verbs: czasowniki

Try to translate the dialogue in **Table 4.8.e.**

Table 4.8.e. Verbal prefixes: dialogue

Mama	Syneczku, kiedy przyjedziesz, żeby zobaczyć nasz nowy dom?	Son, when will you come to see our new house?
Syn	A jak do was dojechać? Możesz mi opisać drogę?	How do I get there? Can you give me directions?
Mama	Najpierw musisz jechać prosto, aż dojedziesz do leśniczówki. Najlepiej objechać ją z prawej strony. Potem będzie rzeka, musisz przejechać przez przez most i jechać dalej, aż dojedziesz do nowego osiedla. Mieszkamy na rogu głównej ulicy, możesz podjechać pod samą bramę.	First go straight until you get to the forest lodge. Best to go around from the right side. Then there is a river, you have to cross the bridge and drive until you get to the new housing estate. We live on the corner of the main street. You can drive right up to the gate.
Syn	A co mam ci przywieźć?	And what shall I bring?
Mama	Co mówisz? Nic nie słyszę, malarze wchodzą i wychodzą, jakieś drabiny wnoszą i wynoszą, ciągle jeszcze mamy remont w domu...	What did you say? I can't hear a thing. Painters are going in and out, carrying in and out ladders and the like; we're still renovating the flat ...
Syn	Babcia mi napisała, że przepisała testament. Podobno tym razem mnie też dopisała.	Grandma wrote that she has rewritten her will. Apparently this time she's included me.
Mama	No widzisz, syneczku, mówiłam ci, żebyś odpisywał babci na listy.	You see my son, I told you you should answer grandma's letters.

4.9. The imperative

4.9.1. Formation of 2ⁿᵈ person singular imperative

👁 Read the list of common commands to a child below. The **imperative forms** are printed in bold. Compare these imperative forms with the present conjugations and the past tense conjugations (**Tables 4.2.c.** and **4.5.e.**). Which conjugations are the imperatives based on?

*Nie **stój** tak! **Idź** do kuchni! **Jedz** śniadanie! **Powiedz**, co było w szkole! **Zrób** lekcje! **Daj** mi spokój!* [23]

As in many other languages, Polish imperative forms are generally short. For most verbs they are built from the present tense stem. When the conjugation is marked by an alternation, it is the altered form that serves as the base for forming the imperative.

👁 Before looking at **Table 4.9.a.** try yourself to form imperatives from *pisać, myśleć, brać, po/prosić, z/robić, powiedzieć, jeść, ciągnąć* and *być*.

Table 4.9.a. Imperative: Formation of the 2ⁿᵈ Person Singular

	A.		B.			C.		D.	E.
	-ę, -esz; -ę, -isz without alternation		-ę, -esz; -ę, -isz with alternation			-m, -sz with alternation		Stem ending in 2+ cons.	Exceptions
	pisać	myśleć	brać	po/prosić	z/robić	powiedzieć	jeść	ciągnąć	być
1 Sɢ	piszę	myślę	biorę	po/proszę	z/robię	powiem	jem	ciągnę	jestem
3 Sɢ	**pisze**	**myśli**	**bierze**	**po/prosi**	**z/robi**	powie	je	**ciągnie**	jest
3 Pʟ	piszą	myślą	biorą	po/proszą	z/robią	**powiedzą**	**jedzą**	ciągną	są
Imperative[24]	pisz!	myśl!	bierz!	po/proś!	z/rób!	powiedz!	jedz!	ciągnij!	bądź!

- **A.** Verbs in this column simply take the consonantal stem for the imperative. The 2ⁿᵈ person singular imperative has 'no ending'. The final vowel letter in the conjugation is simply deleted, leaving the base imperative. In other words, take the third person singular, chop off the last sound, and you are left with the imperative form.

- **B.** In § 4.2. it was mentioned that for verbs with stem alternations, one alternant is found in the 1ˢᵗ person singular and 3ʳᵈ person plural forms, while the other occurs in the rest of the forms (the 'middle' of the paradigm). With these verbs, as with those in column **A.**, the third person singular forms the base for the imperative. In some sense the same instructions apply to the verbs in column **A.** However, the multiple functions of the letter *-i-* (see **Table 3.5.a.**) in Polish must be considered here. For **B.** verbs such as *prosić* (3ʳᵈ person singular *prosi*) the letter has two functions, to indicate the sound /i/ and to show that the consonant is the 'soft partner' of /s/ (equivalent to the letter *-ś*). In such cases, to form the imperative you chop off the last sound, leaving you with *-ś* and the form *proś!* The same happens to Type 1.

---

[23] 'Don't stand there! Go to the kitchen! Eat your breakfast! Tell me what happened at school! Do your homework! Leave me alone!'

[24] 'write!, think!, take!, ask for!, do!, say!, eat!, pull!, be!'

- **A.** Verbs such as *iść* (3rd sing. *idzie*). When you take off the last sound you are left with the soft partner of /d/, which is spelled *dź* at the end of a word or before a consonant. Thus we have the correct imperative form *idź!* The historical alternation *o ↔ ó* (see § 3.6.) is often found in these imperatives on *kroi ↔ krój!, on stoi ↔ stój!, on się boi ↔ bój się!*.[25]

- **C.** For verbs with 1st person singular ending in *-m* (C), one generally uses the 3rd person plural form as the base for the imperative. For these you simply drop the final *-ą* and you are left with the imperative: *oni powiedzą – powiedz!, oni jedzą – jedz!, ja kocham / oni kochają – kochaj!, ja śpiewam / oni śpiewają – śpiewaj!, ja szukam / oni szukają – szukaj!*.[26] The verb *rozumieć* (*rozumiem – rozumieją*) 'to understand' does not quite fit this pattern. Its imperative form is *zrozum!*.

- **D.** When the present tense stem of the verb ends in two or more consonants, the last of which is a nasal consonant (*n, m*)[27] the imperative will be formed with *-ij, on zamknął – zamknij!, on biegnie – biegnij!, on zdejmie – zdejmij!*.[28]

- **E.** There are some other exceptions to these patterns, including verbs in *-awać*, such as *wstawać – wstają – wstawaj!*, as well as others: *być – bądź grzeczny!, mieć – miej cierpliwość!*, or *widzieć – patrz!*.[29]

4.9.2. Formation of the other imperative forms

Look at **Table 4.9.b.** and try to spot the patterns in the formation of the imperative forms. The third person forms generally translate as 'Let/may he/she/they/it …' (i.e. 'let it be'), the first person plural forms translate as 'Let's …'.

Table 4.9.b. Imperative: 2nd, 3rd Person Singular and 1st, 2nd, 3rd Person Plural

	pisać	**z/robić**	**powiedzieć**	**być**
2 Sg	pisz!	z/rób!	powiedz!	bądź…!
3 Sg	niech on[a,o] pisze!	niech on[a,o] z/robi!	niech on[a,o] powie!	niech on[a,o] będzie…!
1 Pl	pisz**my**!	z/rób**my**!	powiedz**my**!	bądź**my**…!
2 Pl	pisz**cie**!	z/rób**cie**!	powiedz**cie**!	bądź**cie**…!
3 Pl	niech oni/one piszą!	niech oni/one z/robią!	niech oni/onepowiedzą!	niech oni/onebędą…!

The first and second person plural imperatives are formed by adding *-my* or *-cie* to the second singular imperative.

The 3rd person imperative is formed with the word *niech* and is not followed by a standard imperative, but by the appropriate 3rd person conjugated form of the verb.

---

[25] 'slice!, stand!, be afraid!'

[26] 'say!, eat!, love!, sing!, look for!'

[27] Stems with **l, r** may also fit this pattern, but they don't have to: *wysłać-wyśle-wyślij!* 'to send', but *myśleć-myśli-myśl!* 'to think'.

[28] 'close!, run!, take it off!'

[29] 'get up!, be polite!, have patience!, look, see!'

Notice that when addressing someone politely (using *pan, pani*, etc.) you must use the 3rd person singular. Thus this construction is quite important. **Table 4.9.c.** illustrates it in more detail.

Table 4.9.c. Imperative: use of the third-person construction[30]

		Masc ♀ +Mp 🏛	Fem Δ −Mp ✂
A. Sg		(Proszę) niech pan spróbuje wina.	(Proszę) niech pani spróbuje wina.
B. Pl		(Proszę) niech panowie usiądą.	(Proszę) niech panie usiądą.
		(Proszę) niech państwo usiądą.	—
C. officially		Dzień dobry państwu. Proszę siadać. Proszę otworzyć podręcznik na stronie trzydziestej. Proszę przeczytać tekst o letnich kursach językowych w Polsce.	

It is customary and polite to say *proszę* before an imperative form. Remember the polite forms of the pronouns: *pan, panowie* for men, *pani, panie* for women and *państwo* for a group with at least one man.

The construction *proszę* and the **infinitive** (as in C) is another formal construction in Polish. It is often used when one person is addressing a group.

---

[30] 'A. (Please) try the wine.; B. (Please) sit down.; C. Good day. Please sit down. Please open your textbooks at page thirty. Please read the text about summer language courses in Poland.'

4.9.3. Imperative and aspect

Table 4.9.d. shows a few examples of positive and negative imperatives. Do you notice how the choice of aspect can depend on whether the command is positive or negative?

Table 4.9.d. Imperative and aspect

		Positive imperative		Negative imperative ↔
		Pres 👆 ↔	Fut 👉 ↓	
A.[31]	1.	**Rób** lekcje!	**Zrób** to jutro!	Nie **rób** tego!
	2.	**Pisz** do mnie czasami!	**Napisz** do niej list!	Nie **pisz** do niej listu!
B.[32]	1.	**Wracaj** szybko!	**Wróć** za tydzień!	Nie **wracaj** tu nigdy!
	2.	**Kupuj** tylko świeży chleb!	**Kup** mi piwo!	Nie **kupuj** tego piwa!
C.[33]	1.	**Mów** zawsze prawdę!	**Powiedz** to wreszcie!	Nie **mów** tego!
	2.	**Bierz** regularnie lekarstwa!	**Weź** jutro moją torebkę!	Nie **bierz** mojej torebki!

With positive imperatives both aspects can be used.[34] However, when you tell someone not to do something, you should use the imperfective form.

4.9.4. Emphatic particle

In informal speech one may often hear the particles *-że* and **no** added to imperative forms, generally expressing impatience on the part of the speaker, *daj no!, chodźże tu!, róbże!*[35]

Nie bójże się!

---

[31] 'A1. Do your homework!; Do it tomorrow!; Don't do this!; A2. Write to me sometimes!; Write her a letter!; Don't write any letters to her!'

[32] 'B1. Come back soon!; Come back in a week!; Don't ever come back!; B2. Always buy fresh bread!; Buy me a beer!; Don't buy this beer!'

[33] 'C1. Always tell the truth!; Say it finally!; Don't say that!; C2. Take your medicine regularly!; Take my handbag tomorrow!; Don't take my handbag!'

[34] In the imperative, the relationship between perfective and imperfective is not quite as clearly defined as in other contexts. Thus, there is a tendency to use the imperfective even in cases where one might think the speaker is referring to a completed action.

[35] 'give it here!, come here now!, do it now!'

4.10. The conditional

 Read the dialogue in **Table 4.10.a.** Conditional forms, expressing a wish or possibility are printed in bold. Try to spot the patterns in the formation of the conditionals.

Table 4.10.a. Functions of the conditional

A.	Ewa	**Mógłbyś** ze mną porozmawiać?	Could you have a word with me?
B.	Adam	A o czym **chciałabyś** rozmawiać?	And what would you like to talk about?
C.	Ewa	**Chciałabym** iść do kina.	I would like to go to the cinema.
D.	Adam	**Moglibyśmy** pójść do kina, gdyby nie padało.	We could go to the cinema if it weren't raining.
E.	Ewa	**Gdybyśmy pojechali** taksówką, to **byśmy** nie **zmokli**. (= Jakbyśmy pojechali taksówką, to nie **zmoklibyśmy**.)	If we were to take a taxi, we would not get wet.
F.	Adam	**Gdybyśmy** nie kupili domu, to **mielibyśmy** pieniądze na samochód i nie **musielibyśmy** jeździć taksówkami. (= ... **tobyśmy mieli** pieniądze na samochód i **byśmy** taksówkami jeździć nie **musieli**.)	If we hadn't bought the house, we would have money for a car and we would not have to take taxis.
G.	Ewa	**Można by** sprzedać dom i kupić samochód...	We could sell the house and buy a car ...
H.	Adam	Najpierw **sprzedawałbym** ⇄ twoją biżuterię, zanim **sprzedałbym** ↧ ten dom.	I would sell your jewellery before I would sell this house.

Conditionals in Polish may express a hypothetical state of affairs (as in **D.** or **F.**), an invitation or a wish (as in **A.**). They can refer to the past (as in **F.**), the present (as in **C.**) or the future (as in **E.**). They can also be tenseless, having no reference to time, expressing general beliefs or statements (as in **H.**). The modal particle *by* (with personal endings) combines with a past tense form of the verb (not marked for person) to express the conditional in Polish. The particle *by* is marked by personal endings:

Table 4.10.b. Personal forms and the modal particle *by*

SG		PL	
ja	**bym**	my	**byśmy**
ty	**byś**	wy	**byście**
on, ona, ono	**by**	oni, one	**by**

As can be seen in the dialogue in **4.10.a.** (F. *mieli**byśmy*** = ***byśmy*** *mieli; nie musieli**byśmy*** = ***byśmy*** *nie musieli*), the conditional particle ***by*** can attach to the verb or precede the verb (the last construction would be more frequently encountered in the spoken language). Notice as well that the conditional particle can attach to a conjunction to form a dependent clause (as in E. *gdy**byśmy*** *pojechali*; see § 11.3.). When they attach to the verb, the particles are not supposed to count when it comes to assigning the stress on the word, i.e. they remain unstressed; for example, *mo**glibyśmy*** should be stressed on the first syllable, as if the particle were not there at all. When connected with impersonal forms, the conditional particles are written as separate words, ***można by***; ***warto by***; ***kto by nam pomógł?***.[36]

 Table 4.10.c. shows the conditional forms of the verbs *z/robić* and *mieć*. How is this table similar to **Table 4.4.d.**? Do you notice what would remain if you were to remove the ***by*** that is printed in bold?

Table 4.10.c. Conditionals of: *z/robić* and *mieć*

Infinitive	**z/robić**			**mieć**		
		Sɢ				
Pronouns	Masc ♀	Neut ♀	Fem ♀	Masc ♀	Neut ♀	Fem ♀
ja	z/robił**by**m		z/robiła**by**m	miał**by**m		miała**by**m
ty	z/robił**by**ś		z/robiła**by**ś	miał**by**ś		miała**by**ś
on	z/robił**by**			miał**by**		
ona			z/robiła**by**			miała**by**
ono		z/robiło**by**			miało**by**	
		Pʟ				
Pronouns	+Mp	−Mp		+Mp	−Mp	
my	z/robili**by**śmy	z/robiły**by**śmy		mieli**by**śmy	miały**by**śmy	
wy	z/robili**by**ście	z/robiły**by**ście		mieli**by**ście	miały**by**ście	
oni	z/robili**by**			mieli**by**		
one		z/robiły**by**			miały**by**	

The conditional forms are based on the past tense stem of the verb. In essence you take the past tense form, and add *-by-* after the indicator for number/gender and before the personal endings.

 Table 4.10.d. shows the conditional forms for the verbs *chcieć* and *móc*, which are probably the most frequently used verbs in the conditional in Polish. Before reading the table, try to build these forms yourself.

---

[36] 'one could; it would be worth it; who could help us?'

Table 4.10.d. Conditional forms of: *chcieć* and *móc*

Infinitive	**chcieć**			**móc**		
	S_G					
Pronouns	MASC ♀	NEUT ♀	FEM ♦	MASC ♀	NEUT ♀	FEM ♦
ja	chciał**bym**		chciała**bym**	mógł**bym**		mogła**bym**
ty	chciał**byś**		chciała**byś**	mógł**byś**		mogła**byś**
on	chciał**by**			mógł**by**		
ona			chciała**by**			mogła**by**
ono		chciało**by**			mogło**by**	
	P_L					
Pronouns	+M_P 👥	–M_P ✂		+M_P 👥	–M_P ✂	
my	chcieli**byśmy**	chciały**byśmy**		mogli**byśmy**	mogły**byśmy**	
wy	chcieli**byście**	chciały**byście**		mogli**byście**	mogły**byście**	
oni	chcieli**by**			mogli**by**		
one		chciały**by**			mogły**by**	

When starting a polite conversation the conditional forms are extremely useful *Chciałabym zapytać...*; *Czy mogłaby mi pani pomóc...*; *Czy mógłbym / mogłabym zapytać...*[37]

4.11. Reflexive constructions

Reflexive constructions in English are those that include the words 'myself, yourself, himself, ourselves, etc'. These types of sentences in Polish are made in a quite different way. Instead of many different 'self' words, Polish only has one *się* that can occur in three different forms. Furthermore, this reflexive *się* is used in a lot of constructions where English would not use a reflexive. Thus, this type of sentence in Polish is quite difficult and foreign for English-speaking learners.

👁 **Table 4.11.a.** shows a number of Polish reflexive sentences. Which of these translate into English reflexives?

Table 4.11.a. Reflexive constructions

Acc ♥ się	A.	Umyj **się**!	Wash yourself!
		Rozbierz **się**!	Get undressed! (undress yourself)
	B.	Koncert zaczyna **się** za 5 minut.	The concert begins in 5 minutes.
		Cieszę **się**, że przyszedłeś. Nasz pies też **się** cieszy. Wszyscy **się** cieszymy.	I'm glad you came. Our dog is also glad. We're all glad.
		Nasze dzieci boją **się** psów.	Our kids are afraid of dogs.
	C.	Ewa nazywa **się** Kowalska.	Ewa's surname is Kowalska.
		Ona **się** często śmieje.	She often laughs.
	D.	Moi rodzice często **się** całują.	My parents often kiss (each other).
		Czy my **się** znamy?	Do we know each other?
	E.	Mówi **się**, że kiedyś tu był kościół.	They say there used to be a church here.
	F.	Myj **siebie**, a nie tylko lalkę!	Wash yourself, not just only the doll!

[37] 'I would like to ask ...; Could you help me ...; Could I ask you ...'

DAT ➡ sobie	G.	Zrób **sobie** herbatę.	Make yourself tea.
		Wymyjcie **sobie** ręce.	Wash your hands.
	H.	Jak **sobie** dajesz radę?	How do you manage?

• In row **A.**, we see verbs that have reflexive equivalents in English. In these cases we might say that *się* is the direct object of the verb, and *się* is thus in the accusative (see § 7 on pronouns). These verbs can take other objects as well, *umyj dziecko* 'wash the child'. These examples also feature the long form reflexive pronoun *siebie*, actually emphasizing the reflexivity of the construction.

• The examples in row **B.** show how constructions with *się* can translate as English intransitive verbs. A literal English translation of *koncert zaczyna się za 5 minut* would be 'the concert begins itself in 5 minutes'. However, English speakers do not say this, they just say the concert begins.

• Row **C.** shows verbs that always have reflexive forms in Polish, with no transparent explanation for English speakers.

• Row **D.** contains examples where *się* gives verbs a reciprocal meaning, translatable into English as 'one another' or 'each other'.

• Row **E.** shows an example where *się* can make a sentence impersonal.

• **F.** shows the reflexive pronoun in the accusative case, where the object referred to is an indirect object.

• **G.** gives dative examples where the object of the sentence is also an indirect object.

• The example in **H.** is an idiomatic expression.

These examples do not exhaust all the possibilities of reflexive constructions. As we will see in the next two sections, the reflexive pronoun may also be used in passive and impersonal constructions. To gain real intuition of how *się* and *sobie* are used can take quite a long time.

4.12. The passive

Read the dialogue in **Table 4.12.a.** How are passive constructions formed? What roles do the auxiliary verbs *być* and *zostać* play?

Table 4.12.a. Passive sentences

A.	**Byłem** długo **badany** ↔ w centrum zdrowia, więc myślę, że **zostałem** dobrze **zbadany** ⅃, a ty?	I was (being) examined for a long time at the health centre, so I think I was well examined, and you?
B.	Też **chciałabym być** solidnie **zbadana** ⅃. **Będę badana** ↔ dopiero za miesiąc, za to **zostanę zbadana** ⅃ przez zespół specjalistów.	I too would like to be examined well. I won't be examined for another month, but then I will be examined by a team of specialists.
C.	Każdy człowiek powinien **być** regularnie **badany** ↔, tak jak nasi rodzice. Oni **są** co roku dokładnie **badani** ↔.	Everyone should be examined regularly like our parents. They are examined thoroughly every year.

Passive constructions are used to express that something was done to the subject of the sentence, *byłem badany* 'I was examined'. While passive constructions such as those in the above dialogue are generally limited to the written language, many passive participles (passive participles end in *-ny* or *-ty* see § 14.3.) may become used as common adjectives in the spoken language (and thus the participles decline like adjectives). **Table 4.12.b.** shows this connection: *męczony* 'tormented' is a participle, while *zmęczony* 'tired' is a commonly used adjective.

Table 4.12.b. Tense forms: passive of: *być na/karmionym*

	PAST ⮑ / PRES 👆 / FUT ⬅	PART PAST ⮑ passive				
		MASC ♀	FEM △	NEUT ⚲	+MP 👥	−MP ✂
ja	byłeᵃm / jestem / będę	na/karmiony	na/karmiona	—	—	—
ty	byłeᵃś / jesteś / będziesz			—	—	—
onᵃ'ᵒ	był^{a,o} / jest / będzie			na/karmiona	—	—
my	byli^{iy}śmy / jesteśmy / będziemy	—	—	—	na/karmione	na/karmieni
wy	byli^{iy}ście / jesteście / będziecie	—	—	—		
oniᵉ	byli^{iy} / są / będą	—	—	—		

Polish passive constructions are somewhat complex because in addition to tense, there is also the aspect distinction:

* Constructions of the type '*jest* + imperfective past passive participle' (e.g. *on jest karmiony*; *list jest pisany*; *dom jest budowany*)[38] would generally be expressed in English as 'is being'.

* A present form of the verb **być** with a perfective past passive participle has a present meaning, but implies that the verb which forms the participle is complete: *jestem nakarmiony*; *list jest napisany*; *dom jest zbudowany*.[39]

The verb **zostać** (literally 'become') is used to form perfective passive constructions in the future or in the past (*zostać* is a perfective verb that cannot exist in the present). Thus, these constructions imply the result of the verb that forms the participle. **Table 4.12.c.** shows how such passive constructions are formed.

Table 4.12.c. Passives with *zostać zbadanym*

	PAST ⮑ / FUT ⬅	PART PAST ⮑ passive				
		MASC ♀	FEM △	NEUT ⚲	+MP 👥	−MP ✂
ja	zostałeᵃm / zostanę	zbadany	zbadana	—	—	—
ty	zostałeᵃś / zostaniesz			—	—	—
onᵃ'ᵒ	został^{a,o} / zostanie			zbadane	—	—
my	zostali^{iy}śmy / zostaniemy	—	—	—	zbadani	zbadane
wy	zostali^{iy}ście / zostaniecie	—	—	—		
oniᵉ	zostali^{iy} / zostaną	—	—	—		

Notice how aspectual pairs may behave in passive constructions, as well as prefixed verbs with altered meaning, see **Table 4.12.d.**

---

[38] 'he is being fed; the letter is being written; the house is being built'

[39] 'I have been fed; the letter is written; the house is built'

Table 4.12.d. Passives: aspectual pairs and other prefixed verbs

	Ta książka...	This book ...
Aspectual pair	była długo **pisana** ↔.	was being written for a long time.
	została **napisana** ⊥ w 1999 roku.	was written in 1999.
Altered meaning	jest **opisana** ⊥ w katalogu.	is described in the catalogue.
	została **podpisana** ⊥ przez autora.	was signed by the author.
	została **wpisana** ⊥ na listę lektur.	was added to the reading list.

Passive sentences may also be formed with 3rd person forms of a verb with *się*, *już się robi* 'it is already being done'; *tu się buduje nowe osiedle* 'a new housing estate is being built here' (see also § 4.13.).

4.13. Impersonal constructions

Polish is full of what are referred to as impersonal constructions. In the case of Polish this means that the sentence has no grammatical subject. This is quite a foreign concept for English speaking learners. However, one example does come to mind in English. Consider the English sentence 'It is raining'. Grammatically speaking the subject of this sentence is 'it', but what does 'it' refer to? The sky? The clouds? Linguists generally agree that the 'it' in these sentences is a 'dummy', inserted to fill the subject position in a sentence, but it does not refer to anything in the real world. Thus, the sentence 'it is raining' is impersonal. Other examples of impersonal constructions in English include sentences with 'one', 'One shouldn't play ball in the house', with 'you' 'You can't smoke in an aeroplane', or with 'they', 'They say it's going to rain tomorrow'. In each of these cases the pronouns used do not refer to anyone or anything in particular.

While English impersonal sentences have what might be referred to as a 'pseudo-subject', Polish impersonal sentences have no grammatical subject at all. Such sentences in Polish can take a number of different forms.

• The forms *słychać* and *widać* translate to something along the lines of 'one can see' and 'one can hear'. These forms look like infinitive verbs. However, they do not conjugate at all; they have no other forms. The common question *co (u pana / u pani) słychać* is used to ask 'What's new with you?', although it literally means something like 'What is to be heard with you'? *Widać* might be used in examples like *nic nie widać* 'I can't see anything' (lit. 'nothing is to be seen') or *widać, że ona jest zdenerwowana* 'you can see she's upset' (lit. 'it is to be seen that she is upset').

• Modal verbs form impersonal sentences as well. *Można już zaczynać?* 'May we begin?' (lit. 'Is it allowed to begin?'). *Nie wolno używać windy w czasie pożaru* 'it is not permitted to use the lift during a fire'. *Należy myć owoce przed jedzeniem.* 'one should wash fruit before eating it'. *Trzeba wreszcie skończyć ten rozdział* 'It's about time I finished this chapter' (lit. It is necessary to finish this chapter').

• Many Polish impersonal constructions are formed with a 3rd person singular verb form and the reflexive pronoun *się*. These constructions frequently translate into English with impersonal 'one' or 'you' sentences, *tu się nie pali* 'you can't smoke here' (lit. 'one does not smoke here'). However, some of the notions expressed by these constructions may translate into English completely differently. *Dobrze się czyta tę książkę* literally means 'one reads this book well' or 'this book reads well'. However, in such situations English speakers would more likely say that the book is well written, easy to read, a page turner, etc.

• The common English construction 'There is/are' translates into Polish using the verb **być**, *czy jest piwo z beczki?* 'Is there beer on draught'?; *Tu są ładne dziewczyny.* 'There are pretty girls here'.

• Another impersonal construction, this one found almost exclusively in the written language, is formed with a past passive participle with the endings **-no, -to** (see § 14.3.)[40] *Tu zbudowano pierwszy kościół; Amerykę odkryto w 1492 roku.* 'The first church was built here; America was discovered in 1492'.

4.14. Polish verb forms: an overview

 Table 4.14.a. presents the twenty most common Polish verbs (see Zgółkowa 1983). Can you conjugate and translate all of these verbs? Which verb from the table has not been mentioned in this chapter? Where can you find the information you need on how to conjugate the most common Polish verbs?

Table 4.14.a. The most common Polish verbs [41]

Rank	Verb	Rank	Verb	Rank	Verb	Rank	Verb
1	być	6	móc	11	zrobić	16	myśleć
2	mieć	7	musieć	12	można	17	pójść
3	wiedzieć	8	chcieć	13	chodzić	18	przyjść
4	mówić	9	robić	14	widzieć	19	zacząć
5	powiedzieć	10	znaczyć	15	trzeba	20	iść

• Only **znaczyć** 'to mean' has not yet been mentioned in this chapter. One can say *ty dużo dla mnie znaczysz* 'you mean a lot to me'. However, this verb is most often used in the third person singular, *to znaczy, że...* 'this means that ...' or *co to znaczy?* 'what does this mean?'.

• In § 15 you will find tables with the conjugations of over two hundred of the most common Polish verbs.

Table 4.14.b. provides an overview of the verbal categories of tense and aspect in Polish. Participles (adjectives and adverbs formed from verbs) are included in the table (they are discussed in detail in § 14).

The verb *z/rozumieć* 'to understand' serves as an example. Notice that the English translations in the footnote do not always maintain the same distinctions as the Polish forms.

---

[40] These constructions are somewhat peculiar for two reasons: (1) the endings *-no, -to* are not the standard neuter singular endings one would expect, and (2) since the object of the participle is used in the accusative case, *Amerykę odkryto*, it seems that these constructions are not really passive. The standard passive sentence would be *Ameryka została odkryta*.

[41] '(1) to be; (2) to have; (3) to know; (4) to speak; (5) to say; (6) to be able; (7) to have to; (8) to want; (9) to do; (10) to mean; (11) to do (perfective); (12) one can; (13) to go (on foot) (iterative, non-destinational); (14) to see; (15) one must; (16) to think; (17) to go (perfective); (18) to come; (19) to begin; (20) to go (on foot) (destinational)'

Table 4.14.b. Summary: tense and aspect [42]

	Tense	IMP ↔	PERF ⫣
A.	PRES ✋	rozumiem	—
B.	PAST ⇨	rozumiałe[a]m	zrozumiałe[a]m
C.	FUT I ⇐	będę rozumieć	zrozumiem
	FUT II ⇐	będę rozumiał[a]	
D.	PARTICIPLE present	rozumiejąc	
E.	PARTICIPLE past	—	zrozumiawszy
F.	PARTICIPLE PRES ✋ Active	rozumiejący[a]	—
G.	PARTICIPLE PAST ⇨ Passive	rozumiany[a]	zrozumiany[a]
H.	Imperative	—	zrozum!
I.	Conditional form	rozumiał[a]bym	zrozumiał[a]bym

- **A.** Only imperfectives can be used in the present tense, *wszystko rozumiem* 'I understand everything'.
- **B.** In the past tense both aspects are possible. The imperfective simply names the action, often implying process or repetition, while the perfective emphasizes completion of the action, *Długo nie rozumiałe[a]m matematyki, ale w końcu ją zrozumiałe[a]m* 'For a long time I didn't understand mathematics, until finally I understood it (I got it)'.
- **C.** The future examples present a similar distinction to the past examples. The imperfective merely states the action, implying a process. The perfective expresses completion. Thus, in the case of the perfective, one might interpret the English equivalent of *zrozumieć* as 'to get it', *Jeśli będziesz dużo czytać, to będziesz coraz więcej rozumieć (rozumiał[a]). Nie szkodzi, że wszystkiego nie zrozumiesz.*[43]
- **D.** The present imperfective adverbial participle generally translates into English using '*-ing*' forms, *Rozumiejąc niemiecki, możesz czytać Thomasa Bernharda w oryginale.*[44]
- **E.** Past active participles are formed from perfective verbs, and their English equivalent is found in phrases like 'Having understood …', *Zrozumiawszy swój błąd, przeprosiła córkę.*[45]
- **F.** Present active adjectival participles are formed from imperfective verbs and replace an English relative clause such as 'who understands', *Osoba rozumiejąca (człowiek rozumiejący) podstawy gramatyki łatwiej się uczy języków obcych.*[46]
- **G.** Passive constructions are formed with a past passive participle, which can exist in both aspects, *Biblia była rozumiana na różne sposoby, ale nie została zrozumiana do końca.*[47]
- **H.** Normally imperatives can form from both aspects, although in the case of *rozumieć* only the perfective imperative is formed.[48] *Zrozum wreszcie, że nie mam teraz czasu.*[49]
- **I.** Polish conditionals are formed with the help of the particle *by* and express notions such as possibilities, wishes, hypotheses, etc. Generally, one needs the context to determine whether a Polish conditional construction refers to the past, present, or future.[50] *Nie rozumiał[a]bym po niemiecku, gdybym się nie nauczył[a] tego języka. Może bym cię lepiej zrozumiał[a], gdybyś mi dokładniej wytłumaczył[a], o co ci chodzi.*[51]

---

[42] 'A. I understand; B. I understood, I have understood; C. I will understand, I will understand; D. understanding; E. having understood; F. understanding; G. understood, understood; H. (Please) understand; I. I would understand, I would have understood'

[43] 'If you read a lot, you will understand more and more. It doesn't matter if you don't get everything.'

[44] 'Being able to understand German, you can read Thomas Bernhard in the original.'

[45] 'Having understood her mistake, she apologized to her daughter.'

[46] 'A person who understands the basics of grammar will have an easier time learning foreign languages.'

[47] 'The Bible has been understood in different ways, but it hasn't been understood completely.'

[48] In the case of an imperative with *z/rozumieć*, the speaker wants the listener to 'get it', so only the perfective *zrozum* makes sense.

[49] 'Understand that I have no time.'

[50] Forms like *byłbym zrobił* 'I would have done it' exist, but are quite archaic and rarely found.

[51] 'I wouldn't understand German if I hadn't studied it. Maybe I would understand you better if you explained to me precisely what you are talking about.'

5 Nouns: *rzeczowniki*

5.1. The function of case

The notion of case plays a crucial role in Polish grammar. In general terms case refers to the role a noun, pronoun, or adjective may play in a sentence. Familiar notions such as 'subject' and 'direct object' fall under the category of case – in the English sentence 'John knows Mary', 'John' is the subject and 'Mary' is the direct object. We know this because John comes first, before the verb, whereas Mary follows the verb. English speakers unconsciously know that the subject comes before the verb. We see that in English, case is 'marked' most frequently by the word's position in the sentence. Polish, on the other hand, uses inflectional endings to denote case. Indeed, if we were to translate 'John knows Mary' into Polish, either name could precede the verb depending on the emphasis. Word order does not determine case the way it does in English. In addition, Polish uses cases to express a large number of functions – Polish uses 7 cases, and some cases have many possible roles. Many of these roles are quite important for everyday communication, so those learning Polish must familiarize themselves with the cases and their functions as soon as possible.

Profesor sprezentował student**owi** książk**ę**.   Student sprezentował profesor**owi** książk**ę**.

Case endings can be found in Polish in many different parts of speech (those that are declinable[1]), and denote the role in the meaning of a sentence. Compare the following two sentences: *Ewa kupiła auto Piotrowi* 'Ewa bought Piotr a car', or *Ewa kupiła auto Piotra* 'Ewa bought Piotr's car'. The three nouns in the sentence, *Ewa, Piotr*, and *auto*, are all designated for case. In both examples, *Ewa* plays the role of the subject of the sentence (the nominative case), and *auto* plays the role of the direct object (the thing that is bought, the accusative case). However, in the first example *Piotr* is the recipient of the car (*Piotr* is the indirect object – expressed by the dative case), while in the second it is *Piotr's* car that has been bought (*Piotr* is the possessor – expressed by the genitive case). We may notice that the ending in the name Piotr changes according to its grammatical role in the sentence.

---

[1] In Polish, nouns, pronouns, numerals, adjectives and adjectival participles all decline.

Since it makes no sense to memorize tables of endings before one knows the functions of the cases, here we simply have an introduction into the topic of cases. It is suggested that learners first learn the roles of the cases – endings will be learned parallel to learning the language.

Table 5.1.a. shows the names of the Polish cases, along with questions associated with them[2], and a communicative context (abbreviated CONTEXT 🖂) for using them.

Table 5.1.a. Inventory of cases in Polish

	Abbreviation, Symbol	Name	Questions	Name	Questions	CONTEXT 🖂[3]
1	NOM ◉	Nominative	who? what?	mianownik	kto? co?	to jest / to są
2	GEN ◉	Genitive	whose?	dopełniacz	kogo? czego?	nie lubię
3	DAT ◉	Dative	to whom / for whom?	celownik	komu? czemu?	dzięki
4	ACC ♥	Accusative	whom? what?	biernik	kogo? co?	lubię
5	INST ◉	Instrumental	with whom / what?	narzędnik	(z) kim? czym?	interesuję się
6	LOC ◉	Locative	about what / whom?	miejscownik	(o) kim? czym?	mówię o
7	VOC ◉	Vocative	form of address	wołacz		o!

The choice of case forms generally depends on the verb. For example, the verb *kupić* 'buy' can have (in Polish as well as in English) a direct object (the thing that is bought, *co?* 'what') and an indirect object (the recipient, *komu?* 'for whom'). Polish speakers generally associate cases with the appropriate forms of the question words.

As was mentioned earlier, Polish has 7 cases, many of which have multiple grammatical roles. **Table 5.1.b.** summarizes the most frequent functions for each of the cases.

Table 5.1.b. Common functions of the Polish cases.

	Function (short description)[4]	Example
NOM ◉[5]	Subject of a sentence	**pan Kowalski** dobrze gotuje
	Predicative noun after ***to*** (categorization)	**Mateusz** to **dobry syn**
	Comparisons (***jak***)	zdrowy jak **koń**; głupi jak **but**

---

[2] When Polish speakers actively try to explain case endings, they usually use the question words to bring the proper context and endings to mind.

[3] The dative most often expresses an indirect object, which in English is frequently expressed with the help of the prepositions 'to' or 'for'. We might think of this context in terms of 'thanks to something/someone', and thus the dative case; 'this is / these are …; I don't like …; thanks to …; I like …; I'm interested in …; I'm talking about …; hey!/oi!'

[4] A comprehensive presentation of the functions of the cases can be found in Pyzik 2006.

[5] 'NOM: Mr Kowalski cooks well; Mateusz is a good son; healthy as a horse; dumb as a shoe'

	Function (short description)	Example
Gen ☹[6]	Possession ('s)	dom **ojca**; Hamlet **Szekspira**
	Negation[7]	nie mam **czasu**; nie ma **jej** tu; nie znam **tej pani**
	The absence of something	brakuje mi **pieniędzy**; szukam **klucza**
	Time expressions (dates)	urodzony **drugiego** maja; od **piątej** do **ósmej**
	Quantities	pół **chleba**; dużo **ludzi**; pięć **osób**[8]
	Wishes and needs	życzę wam **szczęścia**; chcę / potrzebuję **spokoju**
	As objects of specific verbs	uczę się **polskiego**, boję się **pająków**
	After the prepositions	bez, blisko, dla, do, dookoła ≈ dokoła, koło ≈ obok, naprzeciw(ko), niedaleko, od, około, oprócz, podczas, sprzed, u, w czasie, w ciągu, w razie, wśród, z, z powodu, zza
Dat ☞[9]	Recipient (indirect object)	kup **mi** / **sobie** / **mu** / **jej** coś; daj **dziecku** pić
	Subject of subjectless (impersonal) sentences[10]	miło **mi**; **dziecku** jest za ciepło; dobrze **mu** tam
	With specific verbs and phrases[11]	przeszkadzasz **ojcu**; zazdroszczę **wam**; pomagam **przyjacielowi**, wierzę **ci**
	After the prepositions	dzięki, na przekór, przeciw(ko), wbrew
Acc ♥[12]	Direct object	kupił **nowy komputer**; daj **spokój**
	Time expressions (durations)	spała **całą noc**; przyszedł **na chwilę**
	Constructions ACC ♥+ ACC ♥ ...	lubię **Ewę** za **jej poczucie humoru**; zapraszam **was** na **obiad**; wybrali **go** na **skarbnika** za **uczciwość**
	Prepositions used only with: ACC ♥	przez, bez względu na, ze względu na, w zamian za, z uwagi na
	Prepositions used not only with ACC ♥[13]	między, na, nad, o, po, pod, ponad, poza, przed, w, za

[6] 'GEN (also called the possessive case) father's house; Shakespeare's Hamlet; I have no time; she isn't here; I don't know this woman; I don't have money; I am looking for the key; born on the 2nd of May; from 5 to 8; half a loaf of bread; a lot of people; five people; I wish you luck; I need peace; I learn Polish; I'm afraid of spiders' The translation of prepositions can depend on context, so they are not translated here.

[7] Direct objects, when negated go into the genitive: *lubię sok, piwo i kawę / nie lubię soku, piwa ani kawy* 'I like/don't like juice, beer, and/or coffee'.

[8] With numerals 5 and above the genitive plural is used: *tu są dwa małe koty / tu jest pięć małych kotów* 'here are two / five little cats', see § 8.

[9] 'DAT: buy / me / yourself / him / her something; give the child something to drink; a pleasure for me; the child is too hot; he feels good there'

[10] These types of constructions are VERY common in Polish. Poles say 'For me it's cold' – *Zimno mi* for 'I'm cold'. A literal Polish equivalent of 'I'm cold' – *Jestem zimny* – would mean 'I am a cold person'.

[11] 'You're bothering your father; I envy you (PL); I help my friend; I believe you'

[12] 'ACC: he bought a new computer; give me peace; she slept the whole night; he has come for a little while; I like Ewa for her sense of humour; I invite you for lunch; they elected him as treasurer for his honesty'

[13] Many prepositions are used with more than one case: *idę na wykład* ACC / *byłam na wykładzie* LOC 'I am going to the lecture / I was at the lecture'.

	Function (short description)	Example
INST ①[14]	Nouns as predicates with the verb *być*	on jest **policjantem**, a ona jest **bibliotekarką**
	The instrument used to do something	pisz **ołówkiem**; jadę **rowerem / taksówką**[15]
	Accompaniment	pani **z psem** rozmawia **z taksówkarzem**
	Specific verbs of authority and power: 'manage, rule'	babcia kieruje **dużą firmą** i rządzi **całą rodziną**
	After the prepositions	między, (po)nad, pod, poza, przed, z, za, w porównaniu z, w związku z, zgodnie z…
LOC ◎[16]	Location, time, cause, purpose, manner, etc.	będę **w domu o / po dwunastej**; mam urodziny **w maju**; masz plamę **na spodniach**; dyskutujemy **o waszych problemach**; nie przeklinaj **przy dzieciach**
	With the prepositions	na, o, po, przy, w
VOC ▪[17]	To address someone[18] (in plural: VOC= NOM)	Szanowna **Pani Profesor**! Drogi **Dziadku**! Kochana **Mamo**! Proszę **Państwa**! **Aniu**!

5.2. Nouns: grammatical categories

In addition to playing various grammatical roles expressed by cases, nouns and all other declinable words in Polish are categorized according to gender and number. In Polish there are three basic genders: masculine ♀, feminine ♟, and neuter ♀. These grammatical genders are related to the meaning of the noun (e.g. nouns referring to men are masculine, nouns referring to women are feminine). Often, however, you cannot predict a noun's gender from its meaning. On the other hand, most of the time you can tell the gender of a noun by its ending.

 Table 5.2.a. shows an overview of the genders in the singular, with some examples of nouns that fit the common patterns for determining gender from the ending of a noun. See if you can make a generalization as to what noun endings are associated with each gender.

---

[14] 'INST: he is a policeman and she is a librarian; write with a pencil; I go by bicycle / by taxi; the woman with a dog is speaking with the taxi driver; grandmother manages a large firm and rules the whole family'

[15] See *jadę rowerem* 'I am going by bicycle'; *jadę z rowerem* means 'I am travelling, and I have taken my bicycle with me' (e.g. on the train or underground).

[16] The locative is always used with a preposition (and sometimes referred to as the prepositional case). 'LOC: I'll be home at/after twelve; my birthday's in May; you have a stain on your trousers; we are discussing your problems; don't swear in the presence of (the) children'

[17] 'VOC: Distinguished Professor! (FEM); Dear Grandfather!; Dear Mother!; Ladies and Gentlemen!; Anna!'

[18] The vocative is being used less and less frequently in Polish, often replaced by the nominative; it is still obligatory in formal letters.

Table 5.2.a. Gender and endings of nouns[19]

Typical endings	A. MASC ♂ -ø		B. FEM △ -a		C. NEUT ♀ -o, -ę, -e	
	1.	**2.**	**1.**	**2.**	**1.**	**2.**
	Mateusz	teatr	Maria	opera	dziecko	nazwisko
	syn	film	córka	poezja	niemowlę	imię
	ojciec	brzuch	matka	głowa	prosię	słońce
	brat	nos	siostra	ręka	cielę	serce
Less common endings	dentyst**a**	—	sprzedawczyn**i**	miło**ść**	—	muze**um**

- **A.** Masculine nouns (in the nominative case) often end in a consonant. Since endings are generally thought to consist of vowels, it might be said that masculine singular nominative nouns have a zero-ending (or no ending at all, **-ø**). A small number of masculine nouns end in **-a**, including those with the suffix **-ysta** (**-ista**), more or less equivalent to English (**-ist**): *ten dentysta, artysta, pianista, gitarzysta* (but: *ta dentystka, ta artystka* for the female equivalents).

- **B.** The majority of feminine nouns end in **-a**. A few end in **-i**, such as *pani* 'woman' and there is a relatively small group of feminine nouns that end in a consonant (soft or functionally soft): *miłość, kość, mysz* 'love, bone, mouse'.

- **C.** Neuter nouns most frequently end in **-o**, and **-e**, but can also end in **-ę**, and in **-um** (in words of Latin origin like *liceum, centrum*).

As we see above, masculine nouns typically end in consonants, feminine nouns in **-a**, and neuter in **-o, -ę** and **-e**. Most of the time the sex of a person will determine the grammatical gender. This is also true of first names. The young of people and animals are often neuter. For other types of nouns, gender can seem somewhat arbitrary.[20] All other declinable words going with a noun will have to 'agree' in gender (and in number and case) with the noun they modify, *twój duży nos* ♂ 'your big nose', *twoja piękna głowa* △ 'your beautiful head', *twoje nowe auto* ♀ 'your new car'.

 There is an additional subcategory of masculine singular nouns that is important in the accusative case. In **Table 5.2.b.** we see this contrast presented. Can you figure out what the subcategory is based on?

Table 5.2.b. Animate and inanimate[21]

lubię...	**A.**	Piotr**a** i Pawł**a**	nasz**ego** mał**ego** brat**a**	moj**ego** kot**a**	twoj**ego** ps**a**
	B.	teatr, cyrk i sport	twój nowy samochód	sok pomidorowy	nasz dom

- Category **A.** is made up of things that are alive or animate: people and animals (+AN 🐂); The typical endings for this category in the accusative singular are **-ego** (adjectives, pronouns) and **-a** (nouns). These endings are the same as the genitive singular forms. There are also a large number of 'facultative animates': nouns which are technically inanimate, but

---

[19] 'A1. Mateusz, son, father, brother, dentist; A2. theatre, film, belly, nose; B1. Maria, daughter, mother, sister, salesclerk FEM; B2. opera, poetry, head, hand, love; C1. child, infant, piglet, calf; C2. surname, name, sun, heart, museum'

[20] E.g. *auto* and *samochód* both mean 'car', but *auto* is neuter and *samochód* masculine.

[21] 'A. I like: Piotr and Paweł; our little brother; my cat; your dog; B. I like: the theatre, the circus and sport; your new car; tomato juice; our house'

are treated grammatically as animates. These include brand names, food and drinks, and names of dances and games, *mam forda* 'I have a Ford (car)', *zjadłem hot-doga* 'I ate a hot dog', *zamówiłem Żywca* 'I ordered a Żywiec (beer)', *gramy w brydża* 'we're playing bridge'.

- **B.** Other masculine nouns fall into the category of inanimate nouns (–AN ☠) and have the same form in the accusative as in the nominative. Plants are treated as inanimate, *mam duży, czerwony kwiat* 'I have a big, red flower'.

👁 In the nominative plural there is an additional gender category not found in the singular. **Table 5.2.c.** shows pronouns, adjectives and nouns in the nominative plural. Can you figure out what these categories depend on? What property do the nouns in column **A.** share?

Table 5.2.c. Masculine personal and non-masculine personal[22]

+ Mp 👫	– Mp ✄		
A. Masc ♀	**B.** Masc ♀	**C.** Neut ☕	**D.** Fem ⚲
ci mili panowie	te miłe koty	te miłe dzieci	te miłe panie
nasi nowi sąsiedzi	nasze nowe kwiaty	nasze nowe biurka	nasze nowe sąsiadki
twoi starzy rodzice	twoje stare domy	twoje stare auta	twoje stare ciotki
ładni chłopcy	ładne samochody	ładne drzewa	ładne dziewczynki

- **A.** These nouns refer to groups of people in which there is at least one male person. This category will be referred to as **masculine personal** (+MP 👫). For this group, the accusative plural will be the same as the genitive plural.

- **B., C.** and **D.** These nouns refer to groups in which there are no male persons, labelled **non-masculine personal** (–MP ✄). For this group, the accusative plural forms will be the same as the nominative plural forms. When in a language course there are 10 female students, the **non-masculine personal** form is used, *te studentki są zdolne i pracowite* 'these students are talented and hard-working'. However, add one man to the group, and you must use the masculine personal form, *ci studenci są zdolni i pracowici*.

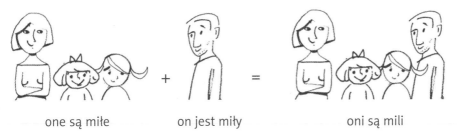

one są miłe   on jest miły   oni są mili

5.3. Case endings: overview

👁 Before sitting down to try to memorize large tables of case endings, it is worth looking at some general tendencies in declension. On the basis of **Tables 5.3.a.** and **5.3.b.** you can learn these tendencies and general patterns. What do you notice at first sight?

---

[22] 'these nice **A.** men, **B.** cats, **C.** children, **D.** women; our new **A.** neighbours MASC, **B.** flowers, **C.** desks, **D.** neighbours FEM; your old **A.** parents, **B.** houses, **C.** cars, **D.** aunts; beautiful **A.** boys, **B.** cars, **C.** trees, **D.** girls'

Table 5.3.a. Case endings: singular

Case	Examples[23] (Pron + Adj + Noun)			
	Masc ♂		Neut ⚲	Fem △
	+An ✈	−An ☠		
Nom ⬭	ten ciekawy człowiek, temat		to ciekawe miejsce	ta ciekawa osoba
Gen ⊗	tego ciekawego człowieka, tematu, miejsca			tej ciekawej osoby
Dat ➮	temu ciekawemu człowiekowi, tematowi, miejscu			tej ciekawej osobie
Acc ♥	= Gen ⊗	= Nom ⬭		tę ciekawą osobę
Inst ①	tym ciekawym człowiekiem, tematem, miejscem			tą ciekawą osobą
Loc ☕	o tym ciekawym człowieku, temacie, miejscu			o tej ciekawej osobie
Voc 📣	o, ciekawy człowieku, temacie!		= Nom ⬭	o, ciekawa osobo!

- The endings for the pronouns and adjectives will almost always be the same or only slightly different.[24] Thus, mastering them together in the learning process will save you a lot of time and effort.

- In feminine nouns, the dative and locative forms are identical (the locative will always be used with a preposition).

- The category ± animate is relevant in the accusative: animate masculine nouns will have the same endings as the genitive, inanimate nouns will look like the nominative forms. (see **Table 5.5.b.**).

- The vocative is used more and more rarely. Very often it is replaced by the nominative.

Table 5.3.b. Case endings: plural

Case	Masc ♂		Neut ⚲	Fem △	Nouns: shared endings
	+Mp 👥	−Mp ✂			
Nom ⬭	ci ciekawi ludzie	te ciekawe filmy, miejsca, osoby			—
Gen ⊗	tych ciekawych ludzi, filmów, miejsc, osób				—
Dat ➮	tym ciekawym ludziom, filmom, miejscom, osobom				**-om**
Acc ♥	= Gen ⊗	= Nom ⬭			—
Inst ①	tymi ciekawymi ludźmi, filmami, miejscami, osobami				**-ami**
Loc ☕	o tych ciekawych ludziach, filmach, miejscach, osobach				**-ach**
Voc 📣	Plural: Voc 📣 = Nom ⬭				

---

[23] 'this interesting person; this interesting topic; this interesting place; this interesting person'

[24] Only in the accusative singular feminine of the demonstrative pronoun do the pronouns have different endings than the adjectives. The pronoun shows *-ę*, while the adjective has *-ą*. However, in the spoken language, one hears *widzę tą kobietę* even though *widzę tę kobietę* is the correct written form for 'I see that woman'.

- In the plural the pronouns and adjectives have the same endings.

- In the dative all nouns end in **-om**; in the instrumental almost all nouns end in **-ami** (the few exceptions have a closely related ending **-mi**: *ludźmi, braćmi, przyjaciółmi*)[25]; and in the locative in **-ach** (with some exceptions in **-ech**, see *w Niemczech, we Włoszech*, 'in Germany, in Italy'). The vocative is always the same as the nominative in the plural.

- The most important category distinction in the plural is ±MP, as the case forms in the nominative and accusative depend on whether the group contains a male person or not.[26] The accusative of +MP forms will be the same as the genitive, for −MP forms the accusative is the same as the nominative.

- Animals count as masculine animate in the singular, but group with feminine and neuter nouns in the plural (e.g. they are +AN, but −MP):

masculine singular								
Lubię	**tego**	nowego	sąsiada,	**tego**	dużego	psa	i	**ten**	nowy	komputer.

masculine plural								
Lubię	**tych**	nowych	sąsiadów,	**te**	duże	psy	i	**te**	nowe	komputery.

5.4. Nouns: word formation

 Look at **Table 5.4.a.** and notice how word-building suffixes may have transparent meanings.

Table 5.4.a. Word formation with suffixes[27]

A.	księgar**nia**	kwiaciar**nia**	pral**nia**	pracow**nia**	siłow**nia**
B.	mur**arz**	pis**arz**	kontrol**er**	tren**er**	dyrekt**or**
	nauczyc**iel**	german**ista**	polon**ista**	psycho**log**	neuro**log**
C.	czyt**anie**	pis**anie**	mówi**enie**	bic**ie**	pic**ie**
D.	dom**ek**	stol**ik**	syn**uś**	syn**eczek**	brac**iszek**
	drzew**ko**	ocz**ko**	usz**ko**	siostr**zyczka**	mam**usia**
E.	prezent**acja**	publik**acja**	agre**sja**	komun**izm**	socjal**izm**
F.	**pod**tytuł	**pra**dziadek	**auto**portret	**wice**prezydent	**super**market

- **A.** Place names may be formed with the suffix **-nia** (*portier* → *portiernia* 'door-keeper's lodge').

- **B.** Words denoting professions may end with: **-arz, -er, -or, -ciel, -ista, -log**.

---

[25] '(with the) people, brothers, friends'

[26] The word *osoba*, however, as in *te ciekawe osoby* 'these interesting persons' is grammatically feminine, so the plural form belongs to the category Non-Masculine Personal.

[27] 'A. bookshop, flower shop, laundrette, workroom, fitness club; B. bricklayer, writer, ticket inspector, coach, director, teacher, Germanist, Polish studies teacher, psychologist, neurologist; C. reading, writing, speaking, beating, drinking; D. little house, little table, son, little son, little brother, little tree, little eye, little ear, little sister, mummy; E. presentation, publication, aggression, communism, socialism; F. subtitle, great grandfather, self-portrait, vice-president, supermarket'

- **C.** One can make nouns from verbs with the suffixes *-anie, -enie, -cie*. They often have similar meanings to English nouns ending in *-ing*.

- **D.** There are numerous suffixes used for diminutives. Masculine *-ek, -ik, -uś*; neuter *-ko,* feminine *-usia, -ka* (see **Table 5.4.b.**). Often alternations come with diminutive formation, *ucho → uszko* 'little ear', *oko → oczko* 'little eye' (see § 3.6.).

- **E.** Many suffixes for abstract nouns and sciences resemble suffixes found in English, *-cja* '-tion', *-sja* '-sion', *-izm* '-ism'. It can be useful to look in a backwards dictionary[28] to check what nouns may be formed with which suffixes.

- **F.** Prefixation is often used in Polish. Frequently the prefixes are derived from prepositions, or they could be of foreign origin: *podtytuł, podpis, pradziadek, Prasłowianie, autoportret, autobiografia, wiceprezes, wiceprezydent*.[29] More than two thirds of the 30 most common noun prefixes are foreign in origin, e.g. **anty**faszysta, **de**centralizacja, **hiper**poprawność, **mini**golf, **post**modernizm, **eks**mąż, **super**market.[30]

One of the most commonly encountered suffixes is **-ka**. What functions does it fulfil?

Table 5.4.b. The suffix **-ka**[31]

A.	aktor	aktor**ka**	student	student**ka**	dentysta	dentyst**ka**
B.	Polak	Pol**ka**	Niemiec	Niem**ka**	Austriak	Austriacz**ka**
C.	szafa	szaf**ka**	Ewa	Ew**ka**	ręka	rącz**ka**
D.	sałata	sałat**ka**	kanapa	kanap**ka**	woda	wód**ka**

The suffix *-ka* has many different functions; it can form feminine professions (see Row **A.**); it can denote a woman of a given nationality (Row **B.**). It can form diminutives as in **C.** Diminutive forms of women's names are especially common: *Barbara → Basia → Baśka; Katarzyna → Kasia → Kaśka; Liliana → Lila → Lilka.* Note the tendency for the suffix to spark alternations, *ręka → rączka* 'little hand or 'handle'; *noga → nóżka* 'little leg' (see § 3.6.).

For masculine nouns the suffixes *-ek / -ik* play a similar role (*kot → kotek* 'kitty'; *fotel → fotelik* 'little armchair'), and with neuters *-ko* (*piwo → piwko* 'beer').

Sometimes the suffix will play two roles, one with transparent meaning, the other without, as in **D.** *sałata* 'lettuce', *sałatka* 'small head of lettuce' or 'salad'; *kanapa* 'sofa', *kanapka* 'little sofa' or 'sandwich', but *woda* 'water', *wódka* 'vodka'.

As far as feminine professions are concerned, there is a tendency to not use the feminine endings, especially with newer or more prestigious professions, where the masculine form will be used with *pani* and feminine modifiers (*pan/pani doktor*, but not **doktorka*). In such cases, the masculine form is neutral as far as gender is concerned. Thus, we observe the following in

---

[28] E.g. Bańko et al. 2003.

[29] 'subtitle, signature, great grandfather, proto-Slavs, self-portrait, autobiography, vice-chairman, vice-president'

[30] 'anti-fascist, decentralisation, hypercorrectness, mini-golf, post-modernism, ex-husband'

[31] 'A. actor, actress; student MASC; student FEM; dentist MASC; dentist FEM; B. Pole MASC; Pole FEM; German MASC; German FEM; Austrian MASC; Austrian FEM; C. wardrobe, small wardrobe (cupboard); Ewa, Ewa (DIM); hand, little hand'

the case of *dyrektor: ten nowy (pan) dyrektor* if it is a man, *ta nowa (pani) dyrektor* if it is a woman. When such profession words refer to women, they are not declined. However, they are declined when they refer to men: *Panie profesorze, czy mógłbym z panem* (profesorem) *porozmawiać po wykładzie?* versus *Pani profesor, czy mógłbym z panią* (profesor) *porozmawiać po wykładzie?*[32]

Table 5.4.c. Declension: profession words[33]

Case	Masc ♀		Fem ♀	
			with feminine endings	without feminine endings
Nom ●	pan profesor	nauczyciel	nauczyciel**ka**	pani dyrektor
Gen ☺	pana profesor**a**	nauczyciel**a**	nauczyciel**ki**	pani dyrektor
Dat ➡	panu profesor**owi**	nauczyciel**owi**	nauczyciel**ce**	pani dyrektor
Acc ♥	pana profesor**a**	nauczyciel**a**	nauczyciel**kę**	panią dyrektor
Inst ①	panem profesor**em**	nauczyciel**em**	nauczyciel**ką**	panią dyrektor
Loc ●	panu profesor**ze**	nauczyciel**u**	nauczyciel**ce**	pani dyrektor
Voc ✿	panie profesor**ze**!	nauczyciel**u**!	nauczyciel**ko**!	pani dyrektor!

5.5. Declension: singular

5.5.1. Introduction

Table 5.5.a. shows declensions for several nouns in the singular. What similarities and differences do you notice among the endings?

Table 5.5.a. Declension: singular nouns, examples[34]

Case	Masc ♀				Neut ♀	Fem ♀		
Nom ●	kolega	człowiek	kot	problem	piwo	siostra	Basia	miłość
Gen ☺	kolegi	człowiek**a**	kot**a**	problem**u**	piw**a**	siostr**y**	Bas**i**	miłoś**ci**
Dat ➡	koledze	człowiek**owi**	kot**u**	problem**owi**	piw**u**	siostr**ze**	Bas**i**	miłoś**ci**
Acc ♥	koleg**ę**	człowiek**a**	kot**a**	problem	piwo	siostr**ę**	Bas**ię**	miłość
Inst ①	koleg**ą**	człowiek**iem**	kot**em**	problem**em**	piw**em**	siostr**ą**	Bas**ią**	miłoś**cią**
Loc ●	koledze	człowiek**u**	ko**cie**	problem**ie**	piw**ie**	siostr**ze**	Bas**i**	miłoś**ci**
Voc ✿	koleg**o**	człowiek**u**	ko**cie**	problem**ie**	piw**o**	siostr**o**	Bas**iu**	miłoś**ci**

One will find tables of declensions in many grammar books. **Table 5.5.b.** presents such a table for the endings in the singular. What does this table actually show? What does the choice of ending for a given case or grammatical category depend on? Can the meaning of the noun play a role? Are the forms predictable?

---

[32] 'Professor, could I speak with you after the lecture?'

[33] 'professor, teacher, teacher (FEM), director (FEM)'

[34] 'colleague, person, cat, problem, beer, sister, Basia (DIM of Barbara), love'

Table 5.5.b. Declensional endings: Singular nouns[35]

Case	I		II	III		
	A.	**B.**	**C.**	**D.**	**E.**	**F.**
	Masc ♀		Neut ♀	Fem △		
	+An 🐴	–An 🐿		–soft	+soft	consonant -ø
Examples	człowiek, kot	dom	słowo	siostra (kolega)	Basia	noc
Nom ●[36]	ø[37] (-o)		**-o, -e, -ę**	**-a**	**-a,** (-i)	(ø)
Gen ☹	-a	-u / -a	-a	-y / -ki, -gi	-i, -y	
Dat ➹	-owi (-u)	-owi	-u	Alternation + (i)e		
Acc ♥	=Gen ☹	=Nom ●		-ę		=Nom ●
Inst ①	-em, (-kiem, -giem)			-ą		
Loc ●	Alternation + -(i)e; -(i)u			=Dat ➹		
Voc 🎺	=Loc ●		=Nom ●	-o	-u, -o, (-i)	-i, -y

The choice of ending depends upon a number of different factors:

- gender: masculine, feminine, neuter (masculines in **-a** take the same endings in the singular as feminines),
- phonetic features: the final sound of the stem,
- semantic features: animate vs. inanimate, masculine personal,
- usage: the genitive singular of inanimate masculine nouns is generally not predictable,
- the word's origin.

5.5.2. Masculine

In the nominative singular, masculine nouns generally end in a consonant which can affect the choice of ending in a given case. In Polish declension we need not only concern ourselves with the choice of ending, but also alternations. Thus, some common alternations are shown in **Table 5.5.c.**

---

[35] 'person, cat, house, word, sister, (colleague), Basia (DIM of Barbara), night'

[36] Uncommon endings (**-o** for masculines and **-i** for feminines in the nominative singular) are italicised and placed in parentheses.

[37] Masculines tend to end in a consonant in the nominative singular. One can also say that such nouns have a null or zero ending, presented here as ø.

Table 5.5.c. Singular nouns: masculine, examples[38]

Case	Masc ♀							-a
	+An 🐕					−An ☠		like Fem △
Nom ●	ojciec	aktor	mąż	Jasio	koń	chleb	stół	mężczyzna
Gen ⊗	ojca	aktora	męża	Jasia	konia	chleba	stołu	mężczyzny
Dat ➨	ojcu	aktorowi	mężowi	Jasiowi	koniowi	chlebowi	stołowi	mężczyźnie
Acc ♥	Acc ♥ = Gen ⊗					Acc ♥ = Nom ●		mężczyznę
Inst ①	ojcem	aktorem	mężem	Jasiem	koniem	chlebem	stołem	mężczyzną
Loc ●	ojcu	aktorze	mężu	Jasiu	koniu	chlebie	stole	Loc ● = Dat ➨
Voc 📣	ojcze!	Voc 📣 = Loc ●						mężczyzno!

The most common endings are genitive *-a* / *-u*, dative *-owi*, instrumental *-em* and locative *-e* / *-u*.

- The **genitive** singular of inanimate nouns is not predictable. The most common ending is *-u* (*bez adresu, telefonu, biletu, celu*).[39] A few nouns can take either *-a* or *-u*, e.g. *krawata / krawatu* 'tie'. Often abstract nouns, foreign words, uncountable nouns, and abbreviations take *-u*, *sens, uniwersytet, cukier, PAN – bez sensu, uniwersytetu, cukru, PAN-u*.[40] You find the ending *-a* on names of currencies, fruits, months, games, tools, brands of cars, dances, body parts, and nouns ending in *-or, -er, -ik, -ek*, *bez dolara, banana, marca, tenisa, młotka, mercedesa, komputera, znaczka, tanga, języka*.[41]

- In the **genitive** and **accusative** the choice of ending depends on whether the noun is animate or inanimate, see **Table 5.5.d.** Remember also the so-called 'facultative animates' (see § 5.2.), including brand names, *mam nowy samochód* (inanimate), but *mam nowego mercedesa*.

Table 5.5.d. Animate and inanimate masculine nouns[42]

Masc ♀	+An 🐕: Acc ♥ = Gen ⊗	−An ☠: Acc ♥ = Nom ●
Nom ●	to jest pan Adam, kot i krasnoludek	tu jest prezent, alkohol i kwiat
Acc ♥	widzę pana Adama, kota i krasnoludka	widzę prezent, alkohol i kwiat

- In the **dative** almost all nouns take the ending *-owi*. A few nouns (some of which are relatively common words) take *-u*, e.g. *daj to bratu, ojcu, chłopcu, panu, diabłu, Bogu*.[43]

- In the **instrumental** we find the ending *-em*. After *-k, -g* you get *-iem* due to a spelling rule (see § 3.6.).

---

[38] 'father, actor, husband, Jasio (DIM of Jan), horse, bread, table, man'

[39] 'without an address, telephone, ticket, goal'

[40] 'without sense, university, sugar, Polish Academy of the Arts and Sciences (*Polska Akademia Nauk*)'

[41] 'without a dollar, banana, March, tennis, hammer, Mercedes, computer, stamp, tango, tongue' (*język* means both 'tongue' and 'language')

[42] 'this is/I see Adam, a cat and a dwarf; here/there is/I see a present, alcohol and a flower'

[43] 'give it to the brother, father, dog, boy, gentleman, devil, God'

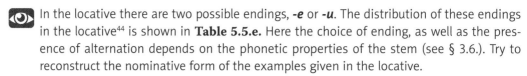 In the locative there are two possible endings, **-e** or **-u**. The distribution of these endings in the locative[44] is shown in **Table 5.5.e.** Here the choice of ending, as well as the presence of alternation depends on the phonetic properties of the stem (see § 3.6.). Try to reconstruct the nominative form of the examples given in the locative.

Table 5.5.e. Locative masculine singular, examples[45]

Case	A. Nom ● hard / Loc ● -e with hard-soft alternations			B. Nom ● soft / Loc ● -u without alternations	
Nom ●	hard consonants: -p, -b, -m, -f, -w, -t, -d, -n, -s, -z ↓ -pi, -bi, -mi, -fi, -wi, -ci, -dzi, -ni, -si, -zi		-r, -ł ↓ -rz, -l	soft consonants: -ś, -ź, -ć, -dź, -ń	functionally soft consonants: -sz, -rz, -ż, -cz, -dż, -c, -dz and -k, -g, -ch as well as -l, -j
Loc ●	**-ie**		**-e**	**-iu**	**-u**
	w skle**pie**	w instytu**cie**	o reżyse**rze**	o tatu**siu**	o leka**rzu**
	o grzy**bie**	w listopa**dzie**	o kompute**rze**	o śle**dziu**	w gara**żu**
	o telegra**mie**	o telefo**nie**	w tea**trze**	o go**ściu**	na koń**cu**
	o sze**fie**	w no**sie**	w artyku**le**	w Pozna**niu**	o Pola**ku**
	o moty**wie**	o wyra**zie**	na sto**le**	o mi**siu**	o przyjacie**lu**

If the stem ends in a hard consonant, you add the ending **-e**, which causes the hard-soft alternation (*t → ci, d → dzi* etc, see § 3.6.). In other cases (soft stems, functionally soft stems, and stems in **-k, -g, -ch**), the ending **-u** is used. In the case of soft stems, remember the spelling rules regarding softness and the letter **-i** (**Table 3.5.a.**).

- In the **vocative**[46] masculine nouns have the same endings as the locative.

- Masculines in **-a** are declined like feminine nouns[47].

- Masculine diminutives in **-o**, e.g. *dziadzio* 'Grandpa', and forms of first names such as *Jan – Jasio (Jasiu), Tadeusz – Tadzio (Tadziu), Kazimierz – Kazio (Kaziu)* decline like other masculine nouns in all cases but the nominative, that is: genitive + accusative *Tadzia*, dative *Tadziowi*, instrumental *Tadziem*, locative + vocative *Tadziu*.

Typical Stem Alternations:

- ą : ę,   Nominative: *mąż, ząb, dąb, gołąb*;
  Genitive: *męża, zęba, dębu, gołębia*[48]
- e : ø,   Nominative: *ojciec, Niemiec, chłopiec, pies, wujek, uczeń, Paweł, sen*;
  Genitive: *ojca, Niemca, chłopca, psa, wujka, ucznia, Pawła, snu*[49]

---

[44] Exceptions: *pan* 'sir', *dom* 'house', *syn* 'son': LOC *o panu, domu, synu*.

[45] 'A. in a shop, about a mushroom, about a telegram, about the boss, about a motive, in the institute, in November, about a telephone, in the nose, about a word, about a film director, about a computer, in a theatre, in an article, on a table; B. about dad, about a herring, about a guest, about Poznań, about a teddy bear, about a doctor, in the garage, in the end, about a Pole, about a friend'

[46] There are a couple of exceptions: *pan* 'sir', *Bóg* 'God' and *chłopiec* 'boy': VOC *panie, Boże, chłopcze*.

[47] This is also true for the diminutives of 'father', *tata* and *tato* (GEN *taty*, DAT and LOC *tacie*, ACC *tatę*, INST *tatą*, VOC *tato!*).

[48] 'husband, tooth, oak, pigeon'

[49] 'father, German, boy, dog, uncle, pupil, Paweł, dream'

- **ó : o,**   Nominative: *stół, róg, Bóg, Kraków*;

                 Genitive: *stołu, rogu, Boga, Krakowa*[50]

- **a : e,**   Nominative: *sąsiad, anioł*;

  o : e,   Locative: *o sąsiedzie, o aniele*[51]

There are also some words that have two stem alternations simultaneously: a hard-soft alternation and a vowel-zero alternation, producing the following: *dzień → dnia, kwiecień → kwietnia*)[52] see **Table 5.5.j.**

5.5.3. Neuter

The distribution of the case endings in neuter nouns is relatively uncomplicated, see **Table 5.5.f.**

Table 5.5.f. Singular nouns, neuter [53]

Case	-o		-ę; alternate stems		endings
Nom ⬤	słowo	serce	imię	zwierzę	-o, -e, -ę, (-um)
Gen ☹	słowa	serca	imieniu	zwierz**ęcia**	-a
Dat ➥	słowu	sercu	imi**enia**	zwierzęciu	-u
Acc ♥	słowo	serce	imię	zwierzę	= Nom ⬤
Inst ⓘ	słowem	sercem	imieniem	zwierzęciem	-em
Loc ⬤	słowie	sercu	imieniu	zwierzęciu	see Table 5.5.i.
Voc ✦	słowo	serce	imię	zwierzę	= Nom ⬤

- The endings in the neuter declensions are predictable. The *słowo*-type have stems ending in a hard consonant, while the *serce*-type have stems ending in a soft or functionally soft consonsant. This produces different endings in the locative singular (-*e* with hard-soft alternation in the case of hard stems, and -*u* in the case of the non-hard stems).

- In the small group of neuters ending in -*ę*, a different form of the stem appears in four case forms (genitive, dative, instrumental, locative), either with -*eni* or -*ęci* (the second suffix denotes small creatures). Here we have such examples with -*eni*: *imię / imienia, ramię / ramienia*; and -*ęci*: *niemowlę / niemowlęcia, kurczę / kurczęcia, prosię / prosięcia*[54]. In the case of animal young, these neuters are often replaced by masculine nouns with the suffix -*ak*, *kurczę → kurczak; prosię → prosiak*; the meaning is the same. Since the constructions with neuters ending in -*ę* and numerals can be quite complicated, we recommend you learn the forms with -*ak*.

- Words of Latin origin ending in -*um* (*muzeum, centrum, liceum*) are not declined in the singular (locative *jestem w muzeum* 'I'm in the museum' – accusative *widzę muzeum* 'I see the museum'), and are not shown in the table.

- The choice of ending and alternations in the locative are similar to those for masculine nouns, see **Table 5.5.g.**

---

[50] 'table, horn, God, Kraków'

[51] 'neighbour, angel'

[52] 'day, April'

[53] 'word, heart, name, animal'

[54] 'name, arm, infant, chick, piglet'

Table 5.5.g. Locative: neuter singular, examples[55]

Nom ◖ hard consonant/ Loc ◔ -e with hard — soft alternations; sometimes vowel alternations in stem				Nom ◖ soft/functionally soft / Loc ◔ -u without alternations			
hard -p, -b, -m, -f, -w, -t, -d, -n, -s, -z		-r, -ł		soft consonants -ci, -si, -dzi, -zi, -ni		functionally soft -rz, -ż, -sz, -c, -dż, -cz, -dz and -k, -g, -ch or -l, -j	
Nom ◖	Loc ◔ -ie	Nom ◖	Loc ◔ -e	Nom ◖	Loc ◔ -iu	Nom ◖	Loc ◔ -u
słowo	słowie	biuro	biurze	zdjęcie	zdjęciu	morze	morzu
lato	**lecie**	ciało	ci**ele**	szczęście	szczęściu	pole	polu
miasto	mie**ście**	masło	ma**śle**	śniadanie	śniadaniu	cielę	cielęciu

In the case of some nouns whose stems end in a consonant cluster, the hard — soft alternation occurs in both of the consonants. Also, historical vowel alternations can be found in many cases in the stem vowels before the locative singular ending: *ciasto – cieście, ciało – ciele*.[56]

5.5.4. Feminine

The distribution of endings in feminine noun declension depends on the final consonant of the stem. There are three categories, ending in *-a*, *-i* or in a consonant. The most frequently encountered ending is *-a*. Feminines in *-i* are very rare, and those ending in consonants are not terribly numerous (though they include some common words). Examples are given in **Table 5.5.h.**

Table 5.5.h. Singular nouns: feminine, examples[57]

Case	Ending: vowel						Ending: -ø (consonant)	
	hard		soft				soft	funct. soft
	-p, -b, -m, -f, -w, -t, -d, -n, -s, -z, -ch	-k, -g	soft[58]	funct. soft	-i		soft	funct. soft
Nom ◖	dziewczyna	matka	ciocia	Austria	róża		wolność	noc
Gen ✖	dziewczyny	matki	cioci	Austrii	róży	sprzedawczyni	wolności	nocy
Dat ➠	dziewczynie	matce						
Acc ♥	-ę						=Nom ◖	
Inst ①	-ą							
Loc ◔	=Dat ➠							
Voc 📢	dziewczyno	matko	ciociu	Austrio	różo	sprzedawczyni	wolności	nocy

---

[55] 'word, summer, city; office, body, butter; photo, luck, breakfast; sea, field, calf'

[56] 'cake; body'

[57] 'young girl (*moja dziewczyna* 'my girlfriend'), mother, aunt, Austria, rose, saleslady, freedom, night'

[58] Diminutives have the vocative ending *-u*. Other soft-stem nouns have vocatives ending in *-o*, e.g. *kuchnia*, vocative *kuchnio* 'kitchen'; *ekonomia*, vocative *ekonomio* 'economy'. Since vocative forms are most likely found in the diminutives of names, the ending *-u* is emphasized in this chapter. You may find vocative endings for the names of countries in patriotic poems, *Austrio! Rosjo!*

- In the **genitive** we find the endings *-i* and *-y*. After soft consonants as well as after **k-** and **g-** the ending is *-i* (*matki, cioci, sprzedawczyni, wolności*), and after hard (and functionally soft consonants) the ending is *-y*. In the case of words of foreign origin ending in *-ia* or *-ja* (including the names of many countries) the *-a* is replaced by *-i*: *Austria, Dania, Rosja, Francja – jestem z Austrii, z Danii, z Rosji, z Francji* (but *ciocia, Kasia, kuchnia – nie ma tu cioci, Kasi, kuchni*).[59]

- After hard consonants (as well as **k-, g-**), we get the **dative/locative** ending *-e* (*dziewczynie, matce*); causing the hard-soft alternation[60] e.g. *Agata → Agacie, woda → wodzie, Barbara → Barbarze, przyjaciółka → przyjaciółce, droga → drodze, mucha → musze* (see **Table 5.5.h.**).

- The **accusative** ending *-ę* is found in all feminine nouns ending in a vowel (*to mała lalka / widzę małą lalkę*)[61], those feminine nouns ending in a consonant have accusative forms that are identical to the nominative (*miłość – miłość* 'love').

- The **instrumental** for all feminine nouns is *-ą* in the singular.

- The **locative** endings are the same as the dative.

- Feminines ending in a consonant as well as those ending in *-i* have a **vocative** ending in *-i* or *-y*. Diminutives end in *-u*, otherwise the ending is *-o*.

- Masculines ending in *-a* (like *poeta* 'poet') are an important group, including the names of many professions: *dentysta, artysta, pianista, humanista, komunista*, but also *kolega*[62] etc. (the feminine versions feature the suffix *-ka*: *dentystka, artystka, pianistka, poetka, humanistka, komunistka*, but *koleżanka*). Such nouns are declined in the singular like feminines in *-a*.[63] However, adjectives and pronouns referring to such nouns have masculine forms, nominative singular *ten nowy **dentysta** i ta nowa **dentystka*** 'this new dentist (male) and that new dentist (female)'.

- Many feminine declensions also feature alternations in the stem, see nominative *wieś, sól, gałąź*; genitive *wsi, soli, gałęzi*[64].

5.5.5. Alternations in the locative singular

 Understanding the phonetic and phonological processes behind the Polish alternations not only helps one master the declensional system, but contributes to one's overall knowledge of Polish. Thus, we refer the reader to Chapter 3. **Table 5.5.i.** shows the alternations caused by the ending *-e* in the locative singular. Is it possible to explain many of these alternations with the help of a few simple phonetic tendencies?

---

[59] 'I am from Austria, from Denmark, from Russia, from France; there is no aunt here, no Kasia, no kitchen'

[60] Similar to alternations in the locative singular of masculine nouns (see Table 5.5.h.); in the case of the masculines only the hard consonants: *r* and *ł*; but not *k, g* and *ch*. In the feminine, these consonants have alternants.

[61] 'It is a small doll / I see a small doll'

[62] 'dentist, artist, pianist, humanist, communist, colleague'

[63] In the plural they are declined like masculine personal nouns.

[64] 'village, salt, branch'

Table 5.5.i. Alternations in the locative singular before *-e*

	Fem ♀: **A. + B. + C.**		
	Masc ♂ and Neut ⚲: **A. + B.**		**C.**
	A.	**B.**	
	front consonants	sonorants	back (velar) consonants
Stem consonant	-p, -b, -m, -f, -w, -t, -d, -n, -s, -z	-r, -ł	-k, -g, -ch
Alternate form in Loc ☟ Sg	-pi, -bi, -mi, -fi, -wi, -ci, -dzi, -ni, -si, -zi	-rz, -l	-c, -dz, -sz

- In the case of masculine and neuter, we get the ending *-u* after velar consonants, so *k-*, *g-* and *ch-* do not alternate. All consonants are subject to this alternation in feminine nouns (*ten chłopak/o tym chłopaku; ta matka/o tej matce*).

- **A.** The front consonants are articulated with the lips or the tip of the tongue. In the pronunciation of their softened partners, the tip of the tongue is more or less in the same place. However, at the same time the body of the tongue is raised to the palate (these soft consonants are often called 'palatalised'): in the case of *t, d* their soft partners are *ci, dzi*.

- **B.** In the case of *r* and *ł* the alternations are not quite so transparent as far as a phonetic explanation is concerned. Rather, they reflect the history of the phonological system, which left the alternants *rz* and *l*.

- **C.** In the case of the velar consonants (those articulated with the back of the tongue, *k, g* and *ch*), we are also left with the traces of a historical sound change by which the place of articulation moved toward the front of the mouth in anticipation of a vowel that was also articulated at the front of the mouth[65]: *k → c, g → dz* and *ch → sz*.

- **A. + B. + C.** To put it briefly: from the front the body of the tongue moves up and back towards the middle ➚, and from the back the tongue moves forward ➘. These two tongue motions underlie all of the Polish alternations, including the hard – soft, the historical consonant alternations, and even some of the vowel changes[66].

---

[65] Only in the feminine in the case of the locative singular.

[66] E.g. *lato / w lecie* 'in the summer' features similar tongue movements.

5.6. Declension: plural nouns

biznesmeni

biznesmeny

5.6.1. Masculine plural

 It is in the masculine plural that the category masculine personal (MP) becomes important, referring to occupations, titles, nationalities and various other groups. There need
only be one male person in the group to require the (+MP) forms. Read **Table 5.2.c.**,
which shows examples of the alternations associated with the category.

Table 5.6.a. Nominative plural: hard stemmed masculine nouns[67]

Case		Hard consonant stems					
		Front articulations +MP 👓: **-i**, −MP ✂: **-y**				Back articulations +MP 👓: **-y**, −MP ✂: **-i**	
A.		pi ↗	ci ↗	dzi ↗	ni ↗	cy ↗	dzy ↗
Noм 🔴 PL		**p**	**t**	**d**	**n**	**k**	**g**
B.		py ↘	ty ↘	dy ↘	ny ↘	ki ↘	gi ↘
A. +MP 👓	SG	chłop	student	Szwed	biznesmen	Polak	neurolog
	PL	chło**pi**	studen**ci**	Szwe**dzi**	biznesme**ni**	Pola**cy**	neurolo**dzy**
with alternations		**-i**				**-y**	
B. −MP ✂	SG	sklep	akt	obiad	plan	słownik	pociąg
	PL	skle**py**	ak**ty**	obia**dy**	pla**ny**	słowni**ki**	pocią**gi**
without alternations		**-y**				**-i**	

---

[67] 'A. peasant, student, Swede, businessman, Pole, neurologist; B. shop, act, dinner, plan, dictionary, train'

The distribution of endings for nominative plural masculine nouns depends on both phonetic and semantic factors, as can be seen in **Table 5.6.a.** Stems ending in hard consonants are softened for masculine personal forms before the ending *-i* (*student/studenci*), while the ending *-y* occurs in non-masculine personal forms and there is no softening (*akt/akty*). These endings are reversed, however, in the case of back (velar) articulations (stems in *-k, -g*). The reversal can be explained in terms of the spelling rules introduced in § 3.6. In the case of *-k* and *-g*, their partners are functionally soft, and as such cannot be followed by the letter *-i*. As a result, *-y* occurs (*Polak – Polacy, neurolog – neurolodzy*). The appearance of the ending *-i* for non-masculine personal forms after **k, g** is also due to the spelling rule by which *-y* cannot appear after these consonants and is replaced by *-i*. In the case of **ch-**, an alternate soft partner *-ś* appears, giving *Włoch – Włosi* 'Italian(s).'

Forms without alternations denoting masculine personal groups have a pejorative meaning, *brudas – brudasy, leniuch – leniuchy*,[68] compare *ci sympatyczni Polacy, Szwedzi, Francuzi* (neutral), but *te dumne Polaki, Szwedy, Francuzy* (pejorative; ironic).[69] In such cases they are declined as if they were non-masculine personal.

Teraz na stadion wchodzą młodzi, sympatyczni Francuzi,
za nimi Szwedzi i Polacy.

In addition to semantic and phonological considerations, usage also plays a role. **Table 5.6.b.** shows further examples of plural masculine noun case forms.

---

[68] 'dirty bums, lazy bums'

[69] 'these nice Poles, Swedes, Frenchmen; these proud Poles, Swedes, Frenchmen'

Table 5.6.b. Plural nouns: masculine[70]

CASE	Hard consonants +Mp			Hard consonants −Mp		Soft consonants ± Mp	
	A.	**B.**	**C.**	**D.**	**E.**	**F.**	**G.**
Nom Sg	respected male persons	-k, -g, -c, -r	hard consonants (other than those in **B**: k, g, c, r)	hard consonants (other than those in **E**: k, g)	-k, -g	soft: -ś,-ź,-ć,-dź,-ń, and -l, -j, -anin	functionally soft: -sz, -ż/-rz, -cz, -dż, -c,-dz
	pan syn ojciec profesor	Austriak kolega Niemiec	poeta kuzyn Francuz Włoch	temat melon wyraz dach	ptak parking	kamień nauczyciel Słowianin Amerykanin	lekarz garaż tłumacz koc
Nom Pl	with alternations **-owie**	**-y**	**-i**	without alternations **-y**	**-i**	**-(i)e**	**-e**
	panowie synowie ojcowie profesorowie	Austriacy koledzy Niemcy profesorzy	poeci kuzyni Francuzi Włosi	tematy melony wyrazy dachy	ptaki parkingi	kamienie nauczyciele[71] Słowianie Amerykanie	lekarze garaże tłumacze koce
Gen	**-ów**					**-i, (-ów, -ø)**	**-y, -ów**
	panów synów ojców profesorów	Austriaków kolegów Niemców	poetów kuzynów Francuzów Włochów	tematów melonów wyrazów dachów	ptaków parkingów	kamieni nauczycieli Słowian Amerykanów	lekarzy garaży tłumaczy koców
Dat	**-om**						
	panom synom ojcom profesorom	Austriakom kolegom Niemcom	poetom kuzynom Francuzom Włochom	tematom melonom wyrazom dachom	ptakom parkingom	kamieniom nauczycielom Słowianom Amerykanom	lekarzom garażom tłumaczom kocom
Acc	+Mp = Gen; −Mp = Nom						
	panów synów ojców profesorów	Austriaków kolegów Niemców	poetów kuzynów Francuzów Włochów	tematy melony wyrazy dachy	ptaki parkingi	kamienie nauczycieli Słowian Amerykanów	lekarzy garaże tłumaczy koce
Inst	**-ami**						
	panami synami ojcami profesorami	Austriakami kolegami Niemcami	poetami kuzynami Francuzami Włochami	tematami melonami wyrazami dachami	ptakami parkingami	kamieniami nauczycielami Słowianami Amerykanami	lekarzami garażami tłumaczami kocami
Loc	**-ach**						
	panach synach ojcach profesorach	Austriakach kolegach Niemcach	poetach kuzynach Francuzach Włochach	tematach melonach wyrazach dachach	ptakach parkingach	kamieniach nauczycielach Słowianach Amerykanach	lekarzach garażach tłumaczach kocach
Voc	Voc = Nom						

5

Nouns: rzeczowniki

---

[70] 'A. Lord, son, father, professor; B. Austrian, colleague, German; C. poet, cousin, Frenchman, Italian; D. topic, melon, word, roof; E. bird, car park; F. stone, teacher, Slav, American; G. doctor, garage, translator / interpreter, blanket'

[71] In this group the nouns ending in -l or -j have the ending -e; in other cases we get the ending -ie.

The choice of ending in the **nominative plural** depends on the final stem consonant:

• After soft and functionally soft consonants the ending is *-e*, otherwise it is *-y* or *-i*.

Many masculine personal nouns have the ending *-owie* in the nominative plural. This ending is especially common for male persons that occupy high positions in society or demand respect, but is also frequently used for nationalities: *synowie, ojcowie, mężowie, ministrowie, uczniowie, Belgowie, Persowie, Arabowie*[72]. Some nouns have two possible nominative plural forms: *profesorowie / profesorzy, inżynierowie / inżynierzy*.

When the nominative singular ends in *-ec*, as in *Niemiec, Ukrainiec, mieszkaniec*, we get an *e : ø* alternation, *Niemcy, Ukraińcy, mieszkańcy*[73]; in addition, in masculine forms in *-c(a)* we get the ending *-y*, but without an alternation: *morderca – mordercy* 'murderers'.

The final *-a* in masculine forms does not play a role in the choice of ending; only the final consonant is relevant, *kolega, poeta, przestępca*[74] will be declined like masculine forms in *-g, -t* or *-c*.

In the **genitive plural**, the general rule is that the ending *-ów* occurs after hard consonants, *-i* occurs after soft consonants, and *-y* occurs after functionally soft consonants. However, *-ów* as the most common ending may also occur after stems ending in *-j, -c, -dz, -cz* and also occurs for masculine forms ending in *-a*: *kraje* 'countries' – *krajów*, and some masculine plurals ending in *-anie*: *Amerykanie* 'Americans' – *Amerykanów*.

Masculine forms in *-(i)anie* (inhabitants of places) have either *-ów* (*Amerykanie – Amerykanów*) or no ending at all in the genitive plural *warszawianie* 'Varsovians' – *warszawian*).

Table 5.6.c. provides an overview of nominative and genitive masculine plural endings.

Table 5.6.c. Nominative and genitive masculine plural endings

Ending in Nom ⬭ Sg		Hard consonants		Soft consonants	
		front articulation	back articulation	soft	functionally soft
		p, b, m, f, w, t, d, s, z	k, g	ś, ź, ć, dź, ń	sz, ż/rz, cz, dż
Nom ⬭ Pl	+Mp 🐾	alternations + **-i**	alternations + **-y**	**-ie**	**-e**
	−Mp ✂	**-y**	**-i**		
Gen ⊗ Pl		**-ów**		**-i**	**-y**

The **accusative** is the same as the genitive for masculine personal nouns, while for non-masculine personal nouns it is like the nominative. The **vocative plural** is always the same as the nominative.

The **dative** ending is always *-om*, the **instrumental** ending is *-ami* (except for a few exceptions with *-mi*) and the **locative** ending is *-ach* (with a few exceptions, e.g. *w(e) Włoszech, Niemczech* – 'in Italy, in Germany').

---

[72] Singular: *syn, ojciec, mąż, minister, uczeń, Belg, Pers, Arab* 'sons, fathers, husbands, ministers, pupils, Belgians, Persians, Arabs.'

[73] 'German(s), Ukrainian(s), inhabitant(s)'

[74] 'friend/colleague, poet, criminal'

Note the role of the letter *i* indicating the softness of a consonant before a vowel:

kamień → *kamienie*: *kamieniom, kamieniami, kamieniach;*

cień → *cienie*: *cieniom, cieniami, cieniach;*

niedźwiedź → *niedźwiedzie*: *niedźwiedziom, niedźwiedziami, niedźwiedziach.*[75]

Below we see the nouns with **-mi** instead of **-ami** in the instrumental plural:

Nom ◔ Pl[76]	ludzie	goście	bracia	liście	dzieci	konie
Loc ◕ Pl	ludźmi	gośćmi	braćmi	liśćmi	dziećmi	końmi

5.6.2. Feminine plural

The declension of feminine nouns in the plural is largely dependent on the last consonant in the stem. In the nominative we get the endings **-y**, **-i** or **-e**. In feminine nouns in the plural both the accusative and the vocative are identical to the nominative.

---

[75] 'stone, shadow, bear'

[76] 'people, guests, brothers, leaves, children, horses'

Table 5.6.d. Nominative and genitive plural: feminine

Case	Final position (stems ending)					
	soft		functionally soft		hard	
	-ø	-a	-a, -i	-ø	-p, -b, -t, -d, -f, -w, -s, -z, -m, -n, -r, -ł	-ka, -ga -ść[77]
Nom Sg ●	odpowiedź przyjaźń	babcia lekcja fobia	tablica dusza pani	rzecz mysz podróż	gazeta strona siostra	córka noga miłość
Nom Pl ●	**-i / -e**	**-e**		**-e / -y**	**-y**	**-i**
	odpowiedzi przyjaźnie	babcie lekcje fobie	tablice dusze panie	rzeczy myszy podróże	gazety strony siostry	córki nogi miłości
Gen ☺	**-i**	**-i; -ø**	**-ø**	**-y**	**-ø**	
	odpowiedzi przyjaźni	babć lekcji fobii	tablic dusz pań	rzeczy myszy podróży	gazet stron sióstr	córek nóg miłości
Dat ☞	**-om**					
	odpowiedziom przyjaźniom	babciom lekcjom fobiom	tablicom duszom paniom	rzeczom myszom podróżom	gazetom siostrom stronom	córkom nogom miłościom
Acc ♥	**Acc ♥ = Nom ●**					
	odpowiedzi przyjaźnie	babcie lekcje fobie	tablice dusze panie	rzeczy myszy podróże	gazety strony siostry	córki nogi miłości
Inst ⓘ	**-ami**					
	odpowiedziami przyjaźniami	babciami lekcjami fobiami	tablicami duszami paniami	rzeczami myszami podróżami	gazetami stronami siostrami	córkami nogami miłościami
Loc ◔	**-ach**					
	odpowiedziach przyjaźniach	babciach lekcjach fobiach	tablicach duszach paniach	rzeczach myszach podróżach	gazetach stronach siostrach	córkach nogach miłościach
Voc ♠	**Voc ♠ = Nom ●**					

- In the **nominative plural** feminine nouns are not always predictable. Hard stem feminines ending in *-a* (except *-ka, -ga*) have the ending *-y*. Feminine forms with nominative singular ending in *-i* have the ending *-e*. Soft stem endings are somewhat problematic – most have the ending *-e*. However, many soft stems have *-i*: *gęś : gęsi, sieć : sieci* [78]. All feminine forms with nominative singular in *-ka, -ga* also have *-i*. Feminine forms with functionally soft stems have nominative plural ending in *-e* or *-y*. Feminines ending in *-ść* always have a nominative plural and genitive plural ending in *-i*.

- The **accusative** and **vocative plural** always have identical forms to the nominative plural.

---

[77] Feminine nouns in *-ść* have the nominative/accusative/vocative plural ending *-i* like nouns in *-ka, -ga*. Otherwise they decline like other soft stem nouns.

[78] 'goose, network'

- Most feminine forms have a zero-ending (here: **ø**) in the **genitive plural.** These include all hard stems, functionally soft stem nouns with nominative singular in *-a* as well as those with a nominative singular ending in *-i*. The zero-ending often produces consonant clusters that may be broken up by a vowel – zero alternation. In other words, the insertion of *e* facilitates the pronunciation, see *matki – matek, córki – córek*[79]. The vowel alternation *o : ó* is also quite common in the genitive plural: *drogi – dróg, nogi – nóg, rozmowy – rozmów*.[80] Feminine forms with soft stems have the ending *-i*; however, words of foreign origin often have *-ii* (*kawiarnia – kawiarni*, but *filharmonia – filharmonii, ironia – ironii* [81]). Feminine nouns with stems ending in functionally soft consonants have the ending *-y*.

- In the dative all feminine nouns have *-om*, in the instrumental *-ami*,[82] and in the locative *-ach*.

5.6.3. Neuter plural

Look at **Table 5.6.e.**, which shows the plural declensions of neuter nouns. What do these declensions have in common with the masculine and feminine ones? What is different?

Table 5.6.e. Nouns: neuter plural[83]

Case	-o, -e			-ę		-um
Nom Sg	biurko	serce	stulecie	imię	zwierzę	muzeum
Nom Pl	-a					
	biurka	serca	stulecia	imiona	zwierzęta	muzea
Gen	-ø, (-i)					-ów
	biurek	serc	stuleci	imion	zwierząt	muzeów
Dat	-om					
	biurkom	sercom	stuleciom	imionom	zwierzętom	muzeom
Acc	Acc = Nom					
Inst	-ami					
	biurkami	sercami	stuleciami	imionami	zwierzętami	muzeami
Loc	-ach					
	biurkach	sercach	stuleciach	imionach	zwierzętach	muzeach
Voc	Voc = Nom					

- In the **nominative, accusative** and **vocative**, neuter nouns have the ending *-a*. Other endings: *dative -om, instrumental -ami, locative -ach*.[84]

---

[79] 'mothers, daughters'

[80] 'roads, legs, conversations'

[81] 'café, Philharmonic, irony'

[82] Except for a few in *-mi*: *dłoń – dłońmi, kość – kośćmi* 'palm, bone'.

[83] 'desk, heart, century, name, animal, museum'

[84] After soft consonants the letter *i* appears, see *mieszkania – mieszkaniom* 'flats', but *słowo – słowom* 'words'.

- In the **genitive plural**, neuter nouns almost always have a zero-ending. These zero endings, however, create consonant clusters that may be interrupted with a vowel-zero alternation: *biurko → biurek*; *jabłko → jabłek*, *okno → okien*[85]. We may also witness vowel alternations ***o : ó***, *morze → mórz, pole → pól*.[86]

  In stems with soft consonants the ending *-i* can appear, e.g. *narzędzia → narzędzi* 'tools'; after functionally soft consonants we find the ending *-y: zbocza → zboczy* 'hillside'. The ending *-ów* appears only in neuters ending in *-um*, *centra → centrów* 'centres'.

Neuters ending in *-ę* are marked by an alternative longer form of the stem which is always visible in the plural. Those with *-eni-* in the singular feature *-on-*, and those with *-ęci-* are lengthened with the help of *-ęt*: *ramię – ramiona*; *niemowlę – niemowlęta*.[87]

5.6.4. Plural of nouns: summary

 Try for yourself to make a table of endings for plural noun declensions. Which categories need to be represented? Compare your own table with **Table 5.6.f.** In the case of differences try to think about where these differences come from – have you forgotten something or is your table more precise?

Table 5.6.f. Examples, plural nouns

Case	Context 🖼	Masc ♀ +Mp 🏃	Fem △ −Mp ✂	Neut ♀
Nom ⬤	to są	-owie, -i, -y, -e	-i, -y, -e	-a
Gen ⊗	brakuje	(-ø), -ów, -i, -y	-ø, -i, -y	-ø, -ów, (-i)
Dat ⬅	dzięki	-om		
Acc ♥	lubię	= Gen ⊗	= Nom ⬤	
Inst ①	interesuję się	-ami		
Loc ⬤	mówię o	-ach		
Voc 🗣	o!	= Nom ⬤		

5.7. Declension of names and polite forms

In official situations, one addresses one's interlocutor in the third person, with the help of *proszę pani, proszę pana, proszę państwa*, or with first names in a slightly less official manner: *pani Ewo, panie Adamie* 'miss Ewa, mister Adam'. Such forms as *pan, pani* and *państwo* are in fact necessary and cannot be deleted.

 Table 5.7.a. shows how such forms are declined. *Nowak* is the most common surname in Polish, the second most common being *Kowalski*; the feminine form is *Kowalska*.

How are surnames ending in *-ski* (♀) and *-ska* (△) declined? What differences do you notice between the declensional forms of *Nowak* and *Kowalski*?

---

[85] 'desk(s), apple(s), window(s)'

[86] 'sea(s), field(s)'

[87] 'arm(s), infant(s)'

Table 5.7.a. Singular nouns: names

Case	Masc ♀	Fem ♀
Nom ●	pan Adam / Nowak / Kowalski	pani Ewa / Nowak[88] / Kowalska
Gen ☹	pana Adama / Nowaka / Kowalskiego	pani Ewy / Nowak / Kowalskiej
Dat ☞	pan**u** Adamowi / Nowakowi / Kowalskiemu	pani Ewie / Nowak / Kowalskiej
Acc ♥	= Gen ☹	pani**ą** Ewę / Nowak / Kowalską
Inst ①	panem Adamem / Nowakiem / Kowalskim	panią Ewą / Nowak / Kowalską
Loc ☛	panu Adamie / Nowaku / Kowalskim	= Dat ☞
Voc ✦	o, panie Adamie / Nowak / Kowalski!	o, pani Ewo / Nowak / Kowalska!

- *Pan* and *Nowak* are declined much like masculine nouns ending in *-n* or *-k* (dative: *pan-u*, as with a small number of one-syllable masculine nouns). The vocative of *Nowak* is like the nominative; but actually forms like *panie Nowak* are used infrequently[89], replaced by *proszę pana*. Forms of address with first names, *panie Adamie, pani Basiu* are very common.

- *Pani* has an untypical ending (with *-ą*) only in the accusative singular (all other feminine singular nouns have the ending *-ę*).

- Surnames ending in consonants are not declined when referring to women.

- Surnames ending in *-ski* (♀) and *-ska* (♀), *-cki* and *-cka*, *-dzki* and *-dzka* are declined like adjectives: *mówię o tej miłej pani, Ewie Kowalskiej / Basi Zawadzkiej*[90]. Also, a few other nouns (referring to family relations: *synowa, teściowa*)[91], are declined like adjectives.

Names and polite forms of address may also be used in the plural. **Table 5.7.b.** shows how the forms *szanowni panowie, szanowne panie, państwo Kowalscy*[92], are declined.

Table 5.7.b. Plural nouns: names

Case	+Mp 👥	−Mp ✂	Mixed group (men and women)
Nom ●	szanowni panowie	szanowne panie	państwo Kowalscy
Gen ☹	szanownych panów	szanownych pań	państwa Kowalskich
Dat ☞	szanownym panom	szanownym paniom	państwu Kowalskim
Acc ♥	= Gen ☹	= Nom ●	= Gen ☹
Inst ①	szanownymi panami	szanownymi paniami	państwem Kowalskimi
Loc ☛	szanownych panach	szanownych paniach	państwu Kowalskich
Voc ✦	Voc ✦ = Nom ●[93]		

[88] Other forms, such as *pani Nowakowa* (wife of Nowak) or *Nowakówna* (daughter) are not obligatory and are used more and more infrequently.

[89] They can be seen as arrogant.

[90] 'I am talking about this nice lady, *Ewa Kowalska / Basia Zawadzka*.'

[91] 'daughter-in-law, mother-in-law'

[92] 'distinguished gentlemen, distinguished ladies, Mr and Mrs Kowalski'

[93] Demonstrative pronouns (*ci, te*) do not change in the vocative.

Forms like *pan, pani* will be used by some learners with the second person plural. However, it is correct to use them with the third person, since the 2nd person form is associated with the Communist regime.

5.7.1. Polite forms of address

The importance of mastering polite forms of address and the various forms they may take, are illustrated in **Table 5.7.c.**, where a few examples of questions asked by students talking with their Polish teacher during her consultation hours are given.

Imagine that the questions in **Table 5.7.c.** are questions that a teacher is asked by her student. Which of them are correct, and which are inappropriate in this context?

Table 5.7.c. Examples of questions asked by a student[94]

A.	Jaki słownik może mi pani polecić?
B.	Czy mamy jutro ćwiczenia?
C.	Czy sprawdziłaś już mój esej?
D.	Czy macie w przyszłym tygodniu dyżur?

Examples **A.** and **B.** are neutral and correct. In example **B.** the plural includes in its scope both the student who asks the question and the teacher who gives the class. Example **C.** is correct only if the students address their teacher by her/his first name. In Polish culture, the decision to move onto first-name terms is left to the person who is 'more important' socially, i.e. who occupies a senior position, who is older, etc. Example **D.** is striking in its inappropriateness in this situation.

Some learners of Polish (for instance those who speak languages such as Russian) tend to substitute the Polish forms *pan, pani* with the second person plural, which can lead to misunderstandings. *Wy* instead of *pan, pani* was the official form of address among the members of the Communist Party. Some Poles can therefore be offended when addressed in the second person plural. Consequently, for pragmatic reasons, correct usage of forms of address is crucially important.

5.8. Peculiarities of the declensional system

Plural forms are not always formed from the singular according to patterns presented in the previous sections. Some of the most common examples include *dziecko : dzieci, brat : bracia, człowiek : ludzie, rok : lata, dzień : dni, tydzień : tygodnie*[95], many of which have irregular declensions.

A couple of words referring to paired items can have special plural forms, see *oko : oczy* 'eyes', *oka* 'dots'; *ucho : uszy* 'ears', *ucha* 'handles'.

---

[94] 'A. What dictionary can you recommend me?; **B.** Do we have classes tomorrow?; **C.** Have you (SG) marked my essay yet?; **D.** Do you (PL) have office hours next week?'

[95] 'child, brother, person, year, day, week'

Some nouns are only used in the singular (**singularia tantum**). The nouns *złoto, mleko, woda* have no plural form, nor do *rodzeństwo, młodzież* or abstract nouns like *zło, duma*.[96]

A number of nouns have only plural forms (**pluralia tantum**), including *drzwi, imieniny, wakacje, odwiedziny*, and those that indicate paired objects such as *nożyczki, okulary* or *spodnie*.[97]

Some nouns, especially foreign surnames, have complicated declensions that share features of both nouns and adjectives, see *sędzia* 'judge'. This topic will not be addressed further here. Interested readers are advised to consult the *Słownik odmiany rzeczowników polskich* by Mędak (2003).

There are also nouns which have different stems in the nominative than they do in the other case forms. **Table 5.8.a.** shows a few examples of some of the most common such nouns.

Table 5.8.a. Nouns with irregular declensions (stem alternations)

Case	Singular examples				Plural examples		
	day	week	April	pigeon	hands	friends	money
Nom ⬤	dzień	tydzień	kwiecień[98]	gołąb	ręce	przyjaciele	pieniądze
Gen ☹	dnia	tygodnia	kwietnia	gołębia	rąk	przyjaciół	pieniędzy
Dat ➡	dniowi	tygodniowi	kwietniowi	gołębiowi	rękom	przyjaciołom	pieniądzom
Acc ♥	dzień	tydzień	kwiecień	gołębia	ręce	przyjaciół	pieniądze
Inst ⓘ	dniem	tygodniem	kwietniem	gołębiem	rękami, rękoma	przyjaciółmi	pieniędzmi
Loc ☁	dniu[99]	tygodniu	kwietniu	gołębiu	rękach	przyjaciołach	pieniądzach
Voc 📢	dniu	tygodniu	kwietniu	gołębiu	ręce	przyjaciele	pieniądze

Many nouns (in particular foreign words ending in *-o*), *euro, kakao, Tokio*, but also *guru, kamikadze, hobby, Monachium* and many abbreviations, particularly those ending in a vowel, like *USA* or *UE* (*Unia Europejska* 'European Union'), are not declined.

5.9. Nouns: summary

Polish nouns are grouped into three gender categories: masculine, feminine, and neuter. In the masculine singular there is an additional categorization between animate and inanimate nouns, which plays a role in the choice of endings in the genitive and accusative cases. In the plural, nouns are grouped into masculine personal and non-masculine personal, relevant for determining nominative and accusative endings. These subcategories affect not only the choice of ending in the noun, but also the choice of other declinable words, see **Table 5.9.a.**

---

[96] 'gold, milk, water; siblings, youth; evil, pride'

[97] 'door, name day, holidays, visit, scissors, glasses, trousers'

[98] similar: *grudzień* : *grudnia* 'December'

[99] *we dnie*: an archaic form (possible in the phrase *we dnie i w nocy* 'day and night')

How can you learn all this? It takes time and a lot of work, reading and analysing constructions found in texts. It is not advisable to try to learn declensional endings in isolation, since the relationships between the whole elements of speech are more important than the endings themselves.

It is best to find a few examples, including names of familiar people, places, hobbies, foods, etc., to form short sentences to learn. **Table 5.9.b.** shows some examples of such constructions for the singular. We have chosen phrases connected with acting: *dobry aktor, dobry teatr, dobre kino, dobra opera.*[100]

Table 5.9.a. Nouns in combination with other declinable words[101]

	Sɢ			
	Masc ♀		Neut ♀	Fem ♠
	+Aɴ 🐕	–Aɴ ☠		
Noᴍ ◔ to jest...	mój nowy partner, **pies**	mój nowy plan	moje nowe mieszkanie	moja nowa koleżanka
Acc ♥ lubię...	moj**ego** nowego partnera, **psa**	mój nowy plan	moje nowe mieszkanie	moją nową koleżankę
	Pʟ			
	Masc ♀		Neut ♀	Fem ♠
	+Mᴘ 🧑‍🤝‍🧑	–Mᴘ ✂		
Noᴍ ◔ to są...	moi nowi partnerzy	moje nowe plany, **psy**	moje nowe mieszkania	moje nowe koleżanki
Acc ♥ lubię...	mo**ich** nowych partnerów	moje nowe plany, **psy**	moje nowe mieszkania	moje nowe koleżanki

Table 5.9.b. Examples: *dobry aktor, dobry teatr, dobre kino, dobra opera*

Case	Context 📺	Masc ♀		Neut ♀	Fem ♠
		+Aɴ 🐕	–Aɴ ☠		
Noᴍ ◔	to jest	dobry aktor, teatr		dobre kino	dobra opera
Gᴇɴ ⊗	brakuje	dobrego aktora, teatru		dobrego kina	dobrej opery
Dᴀᴛ ➔	dzięki	dobremu aktorowi, teatrowi		dobremu kinu	dobrej operze
Acc ♥	lubię	dobrego aktora[102]	dobry teatr	dobre kino	dobrą operę
Iɴsᴛ ⓘ	interesuję się	dobrym aktorem, teatrem		dobrym kinem	dobrą operą
Loc ☁	mówię o	dobrym aktorze, teatrze		dobrym kinie	dobrej operze
Voc 🗣	o!	dobry aktorze, teatrze!		dobre kino!	dobra opero!

---

[100] 'good actor, good theatre, good cinema, good opera'

[101] 'my new partner, dog, plan; my new flat, friend (FEM)'

[102] Only in the accusative are two examples necessary: one animate (person or animal) and one inanimate.

Can you fill out **Table 5.9.c.** with your own examples?

Table 5.9.c. Your examples

Case	Context 🖳	Masc ♀ +An 🐎 / +Mp 👥	Masc ♀ −An 💀 / −Mp ✂	Neut ♀	Fem △
Nom ●	to jest / to są				
Gen ☹	brakuje				
Dat ☞	dzięki				
Acc ♥	lubię				
Inst ①	interesuję się				
Loc ☕	mówię o				
Voc 🎙	o!				

5.10. Is grammar necessary?

If a tourist wants to say a few words in the language of the country he/she is visiting, it is not necessary to learn the entire grammatical system. Young children are able to master new languages without explicit grammatical instruction. However, this is not true for adults.

It is very important to consider the structure of the target language.

 In **Table 5.10.a.** we show you an authentic letter written by a Polish learner, without accurate application of English grammatical and idiomatic norms. Are you able to understand this message?

Table 5.10.a. The importance of basic grammar

> *Honourable State!*
>
> *It appears you drive a fare of English Language. If there is still for me a space? How much cost the lessons in your school? I am from Poland and I have 19 years.*
>
> *I am in London from several months and I much understand, but I can not very well write. I can go to lessons after midday or in the evening. Before midday I am helping by the children, because I have many patience. From which hour begin the lessons and to which hour they remain?*
>
> *How I will go to school, this I will need a testimonial for Home Office, that I am a student. When I will write myself to you school, if you can put out for me testimonial, that I am student in the school? Please answer me yes or not, because I must quick to find a school. How I will not find a school, this I will must to lower London.*
>
> *Thank you from the mountain,*

6 Adjectives: *przymiotniki*

6.1. Declension

Adjectives are used to characterize or describe a person, place, thing, event, or situation. In other words, they attribute some property to a noun or describe some property of a noun. Therefore, like nouns they are marked with inflections for gender, number and case.

👁 Compare the examples in **Table 6.1.a.** How can you describe the main differences between Polish and English?

Table 6.1.a. Phrases: nominative forms of adjectives

Masc Sg	To jest sympatyczn**y**	aktor.	This is a nice actor.
Fem Sg	To jest sympatyczn**a**	aktorka.	This is a nice actress.
Neut Sg	To jest sympatyczn**e**	dziecko.	This is a nice child.
+Mp	To są sympatyczn**i**	aktorzy.	These are nice actors.
−Mp	To są sympatyczn**e**	aktorki.	These are nice actresses.
Masc Sg	Ten aktor jest	sympatyczn**y.**	This actor is
Fem Sg	Ta aktorka jest	sympatyczn**a.**	This actress is
Neut Sg	To dziecko jest	sympatyczn**e.**	This child is nice.
+Mp	Ci aktorzy są	sympatyczn**i.**	These actors are
−Mp	Te aktorki i dzieci są	sympatyczn**e.**	These actresses and children are

Adjectives can be used as attributes (cf. the top half of **Table 6.1.a.**), in which case they appear adjacent to the nouns they modify. They can also be used as predicates (cf. the bottom half of the table) in the nominative case in conjunction with the verb *być*.

In Polish the adjectival endings agree in gender and number with the nouns they modify.

Notice that in the singular, adjectives may be masculine, feminine, or neuter. In the plural, there are two genders: masculine personal for groups containing male persons (+Mp 👪), non-masculine personal for groups not containing male persons (−Mp ✂).

👁 Read the examples in **Table 6.1.b.** What else can be affected by the choice of declension endings?

Table 6.1.b. Adjectives: case forms, singular

Case	Verbal context	Masc		Neut	Fem
		+An (animate: persons and animals)	−An (inanimate: things)		
Nom	to jest	nowy student		now**e** auto	now**a** studentka
Gen	nie ma	now**ego** studenta, auta			now**ej** studentki
Dat	dzięki	now**emu** studentowi, autu			now**ej** studentce
Acc	lubię	now**ego** studenta	now**y** komputer	now**e** auto	now**ą** studentkę
Inst	interesuję się	now**ym** studentem, autem			now**ą** studentką
Loc	mówię o	now**ym** studencie, aucie			now**ej** studentce
Voc	o!	now**y** studencie!		now**e** auto!	now**a** studentko!

In the genitive, dative, instrumental and locative cases, the masculine and neuter forms have identical endings. In the accusative case of masculine nouns and adjectives, Polish distinguishes between **animate** (referring to persons or animals +An 🐕) and **inanimate** (for objects and abstract concepts −An 💀).[1] Masculine animate accusative forms are identical to the genitive (*mam nowego kota* 'I have a new cat'), while the inanimate forms are identical to the nominative (*mam nowy komputer* 'I have a new computer').

Table 6.1.c. shows the case forms of a possessive pronoun (or possessive adjective) and a comparative adjective. Are there any differences between the inflectional endings of standard and comparative adjectives? Is there parallelism between the inflectional endings of adjectives and pronouns?

Table 6.1.c. Possessive pronouns with comparative adjectives: case forms, singular

Case	Verbal context 🖵	Masc ♀		Neut ♀	Fem ♀
		+An 🐕 (animate: persons and animals)	−An 💀 (inanimate: things)		
Nom ●	to jest	mój starszy brat, komputer		moje starsze dziecko	moja starsza siostra
Gen ☹	nie ma	mojego starszego brata, komputera, dziecka			mojej starszej siostry
Dat ➜	dzięki	mojemu starszemu bratu, komputerowi, dziecku			mojej starszej siostrze
Acc ♥	lubię	mojego starszego brata	mój starszy komputer	moje starsze dziecko	moją starszą siostrę
Inst ①	interesuję się	moim starszym bratem, komputerem, dzieckiem			moją starszą siostrą
Loc ◐	mówię o	moim starszym bracie, komputerze, dziecku			mojej starszej siostrze
Voc ✦	o!	mój starszy bracie, komputerze		moje starsze dziecko	moja starsza siostro

As far as declension is concerned, there are no differences between the standard and comparative adjectives. Also, notice that many possessive pronouns are also declined according to the adjectival model.[2]

---

[1] These categories are somewhat flexible. Many types of inanimate nouns are in fact used as animates, including brand names, and names of food or drinks, e.g. *Zamówiłem dużego Żywca* – 'I ordered a large *Żywiec* (a brand of beer)'.

[2] This also applies to numerals and adjectival participles. See the following chapters in this book.

Adjectives: *przymiotniki*

95

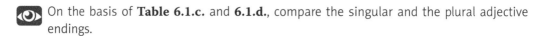 On the basis of **Table 6.1.c.** and **6.1.d.**, compare the singular and the plural adjective endings.

Table 6.1.d. Adjectives: case forms, plural

Case	Context 🖼	+Mp 👥 (at least one male person in the group)	−Mp ✂ (no male person in the group)
Nom 😐	to są	now**i** studenci	now**e** studentki, koty, dzieci
Gen 😵	nie ma	now**ych** studentów ani studentek	
Dat 🐾	wierzę	now**ym** studentom i studentkom	
Acc ♥	lubię	now**ych** studentów	now**e** studentki
Inst ①	interesuję się	now**ymi** studentami i studentkami	
Loc 😮	mówię o	now**ych** studentach i studentkach	
Voc 🐱	o!	now**i** studenci!	now**e** studentki!

The plural adjectival endings are simpler than the singular.

Notice that in the genitive, dative, instrumental, and locative cases there is only one form for both genders. In the nominative, accusative, and vocative cases the choice of endings depends on the MP distinction. If there is at least one male person in the group, the +Mp 👥 form is used. Otherwise, the −Mp ✂ form should be used. For example, if in a university lecture hall there are only female students, you say *nowe studentki*. However, even if you have a number of female students and just one male student, the masculine personal form must be used: *nowi studenci*.

Remember that while the accusative singular distinguishes animate from inanimate (animals would be included in the animate category), in the plural the distinction is between **male human** and **non male human** (so in the plural animals are grouped together with female persons and objects).

👁 Compare the masculine and feminine nominative singular forms with those of the masculine personal and non-masculine personal nominative plural. Which consonants undergo alternation? Can you explain these alternations in terms of the motions of the speech articulators (see § 3.6.)? What are the columns **A. – E.** based on?

Table 6.1.e. Adjectives: nominative, singular and plural

		A.		B.			C.		D.			E.
		dumb	thick	clean	young	pretty	big	good	low	dear	deaf	bad
Sg	♀	głupi	gruby	czy**sty**	mło**dy**	ład**ny**	du**ży**	dob**ry**	ni**ski**	dro**gi**	głu**chy**	z**ły**
	△	głupia	gruba	czysta	młoda	ładna	duża	dobra	niska	droga	głucha	zła
	💡	głupie	grube	czyste	młode	ładne	duże	dobre	niskie	drogie	głuche	złe
Pl	✂	głupie	grube	czyste	młode	ładne	duże	dobre	niskie	drogie	głuche	złe
	👥	głupi	grubi	czy**ści**	mło**dzi**	ład**ni**	du**zi**	dob**rzy**	ni**scy**	dro**dzy**	głu**si**	**źli**

As we can see in **Table 6.1.e.** the basic nominative endings are *-y (-i)* for masculine singular, *-(i)a* for feminine singular, *-(i)e* for both neuter singular and for non-masculine personal plural, and *-i (-y)* for masculine personal plural.[3] The ending *-i* or *-(i)e* is typical for the soft stem adjectives. You cannot always tell on the basis of the consonant if the adjective is of the palatal type or the non-palatal type. For example *głupi* has a palatal stem, while *tępy* – 'dull' has a non-palatal stem. Palatal stem adjectives will need to be memorized, as most adjectives have hard stems.[4] Alternations can be found in the masculine personal forms. The columns **A. – E.** correspond to the place of articulation of the final consonant in the stem. Labial consonants (those articulated with the lips (bilabial: *p, b, m* or labiodental *w*) are the least often subject to alternations; although they are palatalized before *-i*, as a result there is no spelling change. Those consonants articulated with the tongue are subject to alternation (**B. – E.**): before *-i*, produced with a high and front tongue position, the consonants will move in that direction, see **Table 3.6.b.**

👁 Read the examples in **Table 6.1.f.** showing the case forms for plural adjectives. Are the alternations found in all of the cases? In which cases is it specified that there is at least one male person in the group?

Table 6.1.f. Examples: adjectives, plural

Nom	👓	głupi	grubi	ładni	du**zi**	dob**rzy**	nis**cy**	dro**dzy**	**źli**	lep**si**
◖	✂	głupie	grube	ładne	duże	dobre	niskie	drogie	złe	lepsze
Gen ☺		głupich	grubych	ładnych	dużych	dobrych	niskich	drogich	złych	lepszych
Dat ☞		głupim	grubym	ładnym	dużym	dobrym	niskim	drogim	złym	lepszym
Acc	✂					= Nom ◖				
♥	👓					= Gen ☺				
Inst ①		głupimi	grubymi	ładnymi	dużymi	dobrymi	niskimi	drogimi	złymi	lepszymi
Loc ◗						= Gen ☺				
Voc 📢						= Nom ◖				

Table 6.1.f. shows the plural endings for all cases. In the accusative case, notice the masculine personal forms are the same as the genitive, while the non-masculine personal forms are the same as the nominative. Also, genitive and locative endings in the plural are the same, as are the nominative and vocative. The instrumental is formed by adding an *-i* to the dative form.

Surnames ending in *-ski* (♀) and *-ska* (♂), *-cki* and *-cka*, *-dzki* and *-dzka* also decline like adjectives, similarly to adjectival names, as e.g., *Karol **Wielki**:* 'Charles the Great'.

6.2. Comparison of adjectives

In Polish, just as in English, for gradable adjectives (those whose meanings allow for comparison) there are three degrees of adjectival comparison with three distinct forms: positive ('X'), comparative ('X-er' or 'more X'), and superlative ('X-est' or 'the most X').

---

[3] There also exist several short masculine singular forms with no ending that are used as predicates, e.g. *gotów, ciekaw* 'ready, interested'.

[4] Adjectives referring to physical positions or points in time often have palatal stems ending in *-ni*, *przedni, ostatni, letni,* – 'front, last, summer'.

6.2.1. Formation of comparatives

 Look at the following table and see if you can spot any patterns.

Table 6.2.a. Adjectives: regular comparative formation, nominative masculine singular

Positive	Positive	Comparative	Positive	Positive	Comparative
young	młody	młod**szy**	pretty	ładny	ładn**iejszy**
thick	gruby	grub**szy**	beautiful	piękny	piękn**iejszy**
weak	słaby	słab**szy**	strong	silny	siln**iejszy**
new	nowy	now**szy**	tasty	smaczny	smaczn**iejszy**
old	stary	star**szy**	sad	smutny	smutn**iejszy**
rich	bogaty	bogat**szy**	difficult	trudny	trudn**iejszy**
interesting	ciekawy	ciekaw**szy**	important	ważny	ważn**iejszy**

The suffix *-sz-* builds comparative adjectives. When the consonant stem ends in two consonants, especially if the second of which is a sonorant (*r, n, ł*), the longer suffix *-ejsz-* is used.

 Look at the following table and see if you can spot any patterns.

Table 6.2.b. Adjectives: comparative forms with alternations, nominative masculine singular

Positive	Positive	Comparative	Positive	Positive	Comparative
ugly	brzyd**ki**	brzyd**szy**	wide	szer**oki**	szer**szy**
sweet	słod**ki**	słod**szy**	deep	głęb**oki**	głęb**szy**
fast	szyb**ki**	szyb**szy**	far	dal**eki**	dal**szy**
short	krót**ki**	krót**szy**	high	wys**oki**	wy**ższy**
heavy	cięż**ki**	cięż**szy**	low	nis**ki**	ni**ższy**
merry	wesoły	weselszy	white	biały	bielszy
nice	miły	milszy	warm	ciepły	cieplejszy
cheap	tani	tańszy	bright	jasny	jaśniejszy
expensive	drogi	droższy	wise	mądry	mądrzejszy

Notice that adjectives ending in the suffixes *-ki, -eki, -oki* lose these suffixes before the comparative is added (e.g. *słodki, słodszy*).

You may also notice several alternations in this table: before the comparative suffix *-sz-* or *-ejsz-* the consonants *-ł-, -n-, -g-* are softened to *-l-, -ń-, -ż-*. The consonant *-s-* before the comparative suffix is changed to *-ż-* and the combination *-ższ* is pronounced as a long *-sz-*.

Occasionally, one will also witness the *-e/-a* and *-e/-o* alternations in the formation of comparative adjectives, see *wesoły → weselszy, biały → bielszy*[5].

---

[5] 'merry → merrier, white → whiter'

Table 6.2.c. Adjective: irregular and compound comparative forms; nominative masculine singular

Irregular comparatives			Periphrastic comparatives		
Positive	Positive	Comparative	Positive	Positive	Comparative
good	dobry	lepszy	consistent	konsekwentny	bardziej / mniej konsekwentny
bad	zły	gorszy	interesting	interesujący	bardziej / mniej interesujący
small	mały	mniejszy	sick	chory	bardziej / mniej chory
light	lekki	lżejszy	womanly	kobiecy	bardziej / mniej kobiecy
big	duży, wielki	większy	manly	męski	bardziej / mniej męski

There are several irregularly formed comparative adjectives (the so-called suppletive forms). These are presented in the left side of the table above. Notice that these irregulars exist for very common words (as in English, *good – better – *gooder*).

In many cases a compound comparative is formed, and the adverbs **bardziej** 'more' or **mniej** 'less' must be used. It is not always easy to determine whether the simple (inflectional) or the compound (periphrastic) comparative should be used. However, there are a couple of patterns. In the case of adjectives derived from verbs, the compound comparative is obligatory (*bardziej interesujący, bardziej zadowolony*). Also borrowings and longer adjectives have a tendency to form compound comparatives.

Many comparative forms are traditionally formed with **bardziej** or **mniej**, especially when the simple comparative might sound 'strange', e.g. *bardzej chory* and not **chorszy*.[6]

6.2.2. Formation of superlatives

In **Table 6.2.d.** you find some examples of superlative forms of adjectives. Notice that they are formed directly from the comparative form with the prefix **naj-**. The same alternations and rules for the use of compound constructions that we see in the comparatives can be observed in the superlative forms.

Table 6.2.d. Adjectives: superlative forms, nominative masculine singular[7]

A.		B.		C.	
Prefix	Comparative	Prefix	Comparative	Prefix	Comparative
naj-	młodszy	naj-	weselszy	naj-	bardziej konsekwentny
	ładniejszy		bielszy		bardziej zajęty
	milszy		lepszy	naj-	mniej konsekwentny
	mądrzejszy		gorszy		mniej zajęty

---

[6] While this explanation is not exactly academic, there is not a more precise explanation available.

[7] 'A. youngest, prettiest, nicest, wisest; B. merriest, whitest, best, worst; C. most consistent, busiest, least consistent, least busy'

6.2.3. Common adverbial modifiers of adjectives

Adverbs are often used to modify both positive and comparative adjectives in Polish. See the table below.

Table 6.2.e. Adjectives with adverbial modifiers

My son {my daughter, my child} is ... My sons {my daughters} are ...	very	particularly	unusually	rather	wise.
♀ Mój syn jest					mądry.
♦ Moja córka jest					mądra.
♀ Moje dziecko jest	bardzo	szczególnie	niezwykle, wyjątkowo	dość, dosyć	mądre.
♔ Moi synowie są					mądrzy.
✂ Moje córki są					mądre.
My son {my daughter, my child} is ... My sons {my daughters} are ...	still, even	much	significantly		wiser.
♀ Mój syn jest					mądrzejszy.
♦ Moja córka jest					mądrzejsza.
♀ Moje dziecko jest	jeszcze	o wiele	znacznie		mądrzejsze.
♔ Moi synowie są					mądrzejsi.
✂ Moje córki są					mądrzejsze.

In **Table 6.2.e.** we see adverbs that qualify adjectives. As explained in § 6.1., you may notice that adjectives have endings for case and number, while adverbs do not change form.

A statement can be strengthened by using an adverb before a comparative form, e.g. *jeszcze* 'still', *o wiele* 'much', or *znacznie* 'significantly'.

The adverb *coraz* is used with comparatives to mean 'more and more'. *On jest coraz słabszy* 'He is getting weaker and weaker'.

6.2.4. Gradation of adjectives through word formation and idiomatic constructions

Look at **Table 6.2.f.** How can you intensify or modify the meaning of adjectives?

Table 6.2.f. Adjectives: idiomatic gradation

A.		C.	
superbogaty	super-rich	szybki jak błyskawica	fast as lightning
superszybki	super-quick	głupi jak but	\<dumb as a shoe\>
hiperaktywny	hyperactive	zdrowy jak ryba	\<healthy as a fish\>
ultrakonserwatywny	ultra-conservative	głodny jak wilk	\<hungry as a wolf\>
ekstramocny	extra strong	silny jak koń	\<strong as a horse\>
B.		**D.**	
przepiękny	very beautiful	miluchny	very nice
przeokropny	(very) terrible	cieplutki	nice and warm
przykrótki	rather short	słodziutki	nice and sweet
przygłupi	rather dumb	malusieńki	very small and adorable

There are many possibilities for intensifying or modifying adjectival meanings. Prefixes, both international (column **A.**) and typically Polish (column **B.**), can be used to intensify the meaning conveyed by an adjective. Colloquial similes (column **C.**), most frequent in spoken language and employed to make the conversation more vivid and expressive, belong to the pool of idiomatic expressions of a language. This means that they have to be learnt by heart, as analogies from one's own mother tongue can be misleading. And so, while in English you cannot be \<healthy as a fish\>, you apparently can in Polish (cf. *zdrowy jak ryba*, column **C.**). Conversely, while an English person can be 'ugly as sin', a Pole could only be \<ugly as the night\>, that is *brzydki jak noc.* column **D.** gives a handful of examples of diminutives, which in Polish are legion, and which are the focus of § 6.3.

6.3. Diminutive forms

Polish speakers have a rich inventory of suffixes they use to add a diminutive or endearing meaning to adjectives. Since English does not have such a rich system, it is difficult to translate directly these suffixes. Learners exposed to spoken Polish will start to gain an intuition of how these suffixes are used without too much difficulty. Beginners should be aware of several suffixes, including *-utki, -uchny, -uśki, -uteńki, -usieńki*, that may be used to denote endearment.

Table 6.3.a. Adjectives: diminutives

warm	ciepły	ciepl**utki**	ciepl**uchny**	ciepl**uśki**	ciepl**uteńki**	ciepl**usieńki**
short	krótki	króci**utki**	króci**uchny**	króci**uśki**	króci**uteńki**	króci**usieńki**
sweet	słodki	słodzi**utki**	słodzi**uchny**	słodzi**uśki**	słodzi**uteńki**	słodzi**usieńki**
small	mały	mal**utki**	mal**uchny**	mal**uśki**	mal**uteńki**	mal**usieńki**

One may hear comments like: *mój kochanieńki, słodziutki syneczek* 'my dearest sweetest son' (a mother to her son after the A-level exams); *jeszcze maleńką chwileczkę* 'just a short while more' (a professor in the last couple of minutes of a lecture).

This type of endearment is particularly common in family circles. However, it is very difficult to express in English.

6.4. Typical syntactic constructions with adjectives

6.4.1. Comparative constructions

In Polish there are several syntactic methods to form comparative constructions. Look at **Table 6.4.a.** Which of these methods do you find easiest to learn?

Table 6.4.a. Comparison by syntactic methods

Nom + niż/jak + Nom	Nom + od/z + Gen	Eng
Ewa jest tak ładna jak Anna (Ewa jest tak samo ładna jak Anna)	—	Ewa is as pretty as Anna
—	Ewa jest najładniejsza z nich (wszystkich)	Ewa is the prettiest of them all
Ewa jest starsza niż Adam	Ewa jest starsza od Adama	Ewa is older than Adam
to piwo jest lepsze niż tamto	to piwo jest lepsze od tamtego	this beer is better than that one
uczniowie są młodsi niż studenci	uczniowie są młodsi od studentów	pupils are younger than students
Ewa nie jest starsza niż Adam	Ewa nie jest starsza od Adama	Ewa is not older than Adam

In the left column, nominatives are used, with either *jak* 'as' or *niż* 'than'. In the column in the centre, comparative constructions are formed with the prepositions *od/z* and the genitive case. Notice that the prepositional constructions employ prepositions that would make the sentences sound odd if translated directly into English.

6.4.2. Position of the adjective relative to the noun it modifies

Since grammatical roles in Polish are expressed very precisely by the inflectional endings, word order is relatively free. Deviations from the standard word order may serve a pragmatic function. The meaning of nouns may also change, dependent on their position relative to adjectives.

Take a look at **Table 6.4.b.** below and try to figure out how the position change of the adjective relative to the noun can influence the adjective's meaning.

Table 6.4.b. Position of adjectives in a phrase

plum jam	dżem śliwkowy	plum dress	śliwkowa sukienka
Red Sea	Morze Czerwone	red car	czerwony samochód
orange juice	sok pomarańczowy	an orange shirt	pomarańczowa koszula
Yellow Birch	Brzoza Żółta	yellow birch	żółta brzoza

In Polish, adjectives may either precede or follow the nouns they modify. When the adjective precedes the noun (prenominal position), it may be thought of as being descriptive – it describes a property of the noun. In this case the adjectival phrase would answer the question 'What is X like?'. When the adjective follows the noun (postnominal position), it may be thought of as a categorization, in which case the phrase answers the question 'What type of X is X?'. For example, *żółta brzoza* (a yellow birch) is a birch which happens to be yellow in colour; *Brzoza Żółta* (Yellow Birch) is a deciduous tree of the genus betula, and it will belong to this genus even if you paint it red (then, it would be *czerwona Brzoza Żółta*). English maintains this distinction by means of stress, rather than word order, cf. 'the **White** House vs. a white **house**'.

6.4.3. The sentence type 'X is Y'

 In **Table 6.4.c.** the adjectives have been put either in nominative or in instrumental cases. What does it depend on?

Table 6.4.c. The sentence type 'X is Y'

	A. Nom ●	B. Inst ⓘ	C. Inst ⓘ[8]
♠	Ona jest sympatyczna.	Ona jest aktorką.	Ona jest sympatyczną aktorką.
♀	On jest zdolny.	On jest muzykiem.	On jest zdolnym muzykiem.
👥	Oni są młodzi.	Oni są malarzami.	Oni są młodymi malarzami.
✂	One są pracowite.	One są studentkami.	One są pracowitymi studentkami.

If in a sentence 'X is Y' the 'Y' contains a noun, then the whole 'Y' is in the instrumental, be it a noun on its own (see column **B.**) or a noun modified by an adjective (column **C.**). If, on the other hand, 'Y' is just an adjective, not followed by a noun, it is in the nominative, since the adjective is used predicatively in this case (see column **A.**).

---

[8] When actual names are used, a different construction is possible, without a verb and using the nominative case e.g. *Ewa to słynna aktorka* 'Ewa's a famous actress'. This construction has a meaning of introduction, whereas the instrumental construction serves more as a description.

7 Pronouns: *zaimki*

7.1. Introduction

Pronouns may substitute for nouns, noun phrases, or adjectives. They generally refer to already understood elements in the context of a conversation. As a result, pronouns are used extremely frequently and thus are crucial for foreign learners' success in achieving any level of proficiency in Polish.

Polish pronouns are often short, one-syllable words (or occasionally particles attached to words) that are generally not emphasized in speech. As a result, small differences in sound may make significant differences in meaning.

Observe the following examples:

- daj**my** spokój
  - daj **mi** spokój
    - daj **mu** spokój
      - dam **wam** spokój
        - daj **nam** spokój...[1]

The importance of pronouns can be seen in the possible misunderstandings that can occur if they are used incorrectly. The table below shows an example.

Table 7.1.a. Pronouns : dialogue

Ewa:	„Kocham **cię**, Janku..."	Ewa says:	I love you Jan ...
Jan odpowiada:	„Ja **się** też kocham."	Jan answers:	I love myself too.
Interpretacja Ewy:	„Ja **cię** też kocham."	Ewa's possible interpretation:	I love you too.

There are several different types of pronouns that will be discussed in this chapter. **Table 7.1.b.** provides examples of these different types. What do the pronouns in **A. – H.** represent?

---

[1] 'let's leave it in peace, leave me in peace, leave him in peace, I'll leave you (PL) in peace, leave us in peace ...'

Table 7.1.b. Nominative and genitive forms of various types of pronouns[2]

	Nom ●	Gen ☹
A.	**Ja** chcę kota, a **ty** psa.	Ewa nie lubi ani **mnie**, ani **ciebie**.
B.	**To** auto jest nowe, a **ten** motor – stary.	Daj mi trochę **tego** wina i **tej** sałatki.
C.	**Moja** siostra jest młodsza niż **twoja**.	Nie znam ani **twojego** brata, ani **twojej** siostry.
D.	**Kto** tu był? **Co** to jest?	**Kogo** jeszcze nie znasz? **Czego** nie rozumiesz?
E.	Powiedz mi, **kto** tu był. Powiedz mi, **co** to jest.	Powiedz mi, **kogo** jeszcze nie znasz. Powiedz mi, **czego** nie rozumiesz.
F.	**Ktoś** tu był. **Coś** tu ładnie pachnie.	Szukamy **kogoś**, kto zna japoński. Szukam **czegoś** do pisania.
G.	**Każdy** chce być szczęśliwy. **Nikt** nie chce mi pomóc.	Adam **każdego** się boi. Ewa **niczego** się nie boi.
H.	—	Nie widzisz **się** / **siebie** w lustrze?

The subclasses of pronouns are based on their function and meaning:

A. **Personal pronouns** replace nouns, e.g. *ja, ty, on* 'I, you, he'.

B. **Demonstrative pronouns** express the position of a noun in relation to the person who is speaking, e.g. *ten, tamten* 'this, that'.

C. **Possessive pronouns** express who the nouns they modify belong to, e.g. *mój, moja; twój, twoja*; 'my, your'. There is also a special reflexive possessive: *swój* 'one's own'.

D. **Interrogative pronouns** pose questions about a noun, e.g. *który? jaki? czyj?* 'which? what kind of? whose?'

E. **Relative pronouns** have two functions: they act as conjunctions to introduce a relative clause, and they play a grammatical role in the so-called *that clause*, e.g. *To jest ten człowiek, któremu wierzę / ta osoba, której wierzę*.[3]

F. **Indefinite pronouns** are used to refer to uncertain or non-existent entities, e.g. *ktoś, ktokolwiek, coś, cokolwiek* 'someone, whoever, something, whatever'.

G. **Determinate pronouns** stand before specific persons or things, e.g. *każdy, wszyscy, taki sam* 'each, everyone, the same'.

H. **Reflexive pronouns** refer back to the subject of the sentence. They are generally grouped with verbs, e.g. *Myję się / myję sobie ręce* 'I am washing myself/I am washing my hands'.

Since pronouns refer to nouns and noun phrases, they are also inflected for gender, number, and case. This means that there are many forms that the student must memorize. This chapter will try to point out as many patterns as possible in the Polish pronominal

---

[2] 'A. I want a cat, and you want a dog. Ewa likes neither me nor you. **B.** This car is new, and this motorcycle is old. Give me a little of this wine and that salad. **C.** My sister is younger than yours. I know neither your brother nor your sister. **D.** Who was here? What is this? Whom don't you know yet? What don't you understand? **E.** Tell me who was here. Tell me what this is. Tell me whom you don't know yet. Tell me what you don't understand. **F.** Someone was here. Something smells good here. We're looking for someone who knows Japanese. I'm looking for something to write with. **G.** Everyone wants to be happy. Nobody wants to help me. Adam's afraid of everyone. Ewa's not afraid of anything. **H.** Don't you see yourself in the mirror?'

[3] 'That is the person whom I believe'.

system. However, the student must be prepared to commit many forms to memory early in the learning process if he/she wants to communicate effectively in Polish.

7.2. Personal pronouns

Many of the personal pronouns have two or three different forms, the choice of which depends on whether the pronoun is emphasized or whether it follows a preposition. See **Table 7.2.a.**

Table 7.2.a. Personal pronouns: singular

	Case	Context 📷	1 Sg	2 Sg	3 Sg		
A.	Nom ●	a to...[4]	ja	ty	on	ono	ona
B.1.	Gen ⊗	nie widać	mnie	cię	go		jej
B.2.				**ciebie**	**jego**		
C.		prezent dla		**ciebie**	niego		niej
D.1.	Dat ➥	udało... się wygrać	mi	ci	mu		jej
D.2.		udało się wygrać...	**mnie**	**tobie**	**jemu**		
E.		dzięki	**mnie**	**tobie**	niemu		niej
F.1.	Acc ♥	można... lubić		cię	go	je	ją
F.2.		można lubić...	mnie	**ciebie**	**jego**		
G.		liczyć na		**ciebie**	niego	nie	nią
H.	Inst ⓘ	interesować się	mną	tobą	nim		nią
I.	Loc 👄	mówić o	mnie	tobie			niej
J.	Voc 📢	hej...	ja	ty	—		—

- In the case of many personal pronouns, we encounter both long and short forms (*ciebie* / *cię*; *tobie* / *ci*; *jemu* / *mu*; *jego* / *go*). The short forms are the basic forms, while the long forms are used to provide emphasis, *nie widzę cię / nie widzę* **ciebie**, *ale* **jego** *widzę* 'I don't see you / I don't see YOU, but I see HIM', or *lubię* **ciebie**, *ale nie* **jego** 'I like YOU, but not HIM'. The long forms can be thought of as answering specific questions of the type 'Who is it that you like?' See the examples in **B.1. / B.2., D.1. / D.2., F.1. / F.2.** The long forms are accented and can stand anywhere in the sentence. The short forms are not accented, and cannot be used to start a sentence. They have a tendency not to be used to end a sentence, except when it is unavoidable, as in very short sentences. The example in **D.1.** shows the neutral forms: *udało mi się wygrać / udało mu się wygrać*. In **D.2.** we see the long forms, specifying the specific pronouns and providing emphasis: *udało się wygrać* **mnie i tobie**, *ale* **jemu** *nie* 'YOU and I managed to win, but HE didn't[5].

- The third person long forms, when following a preposition, are formed by inserting an **ni-** at the beginning of the word in place of the **j-**. Thus, we can see the spelling changes in the following examples: *podziękuję* **jej** */ dzięki* **niej** *mam mieszkanie* 'I will thank her / thanks to her I have a flat', or in the genitive: *nie lubię* **go**, *ale mam dla* **niego** *prezent* 'I don't like him, but I have a present for him'.

---

[4] Often the verb *być* 'to be' is understood and not expressed overtly (e.g. when showing photographs one might say: *a to ja, a to ty...* 'and this is me, and that's you ...').

[5] Notice that in this sentence the logical subject is in the dative case.

- When addressing someone formally, the standard second person personal pronouns are not used. Instead, the appropriate form of **pan, pani** is used, e.g. *dziękuję* **panu / pani / państwu** 'I thank you'.
- When, in the same sentence, pronouns in both the dative and accusative are used, the dative form comes first, e.g. *Adam dał mi różę = On* **mi ją** *dał* 'Adam gave me a rose. He gave it to me'. This is different from the English word order.

Look at **Table 7.2.b.** What is important for the choice of personal pronouns in the plural?

Table 7.2.b. Personal pronouns: plural

Case	Context 🖳	1 PL	2 PL	3 PL +Mp 🐾	3 PL −Mp ✂
Nom ●	a to...	my	wy	oni	one
Gen ☹	nie widać	nas	was	ich	
Dat ➡	udało... się wygrać	nam	wam	im	
Acc♥	można... lubić	nas	was	ich	je
	/ można liczyć na...			**n**ich	**n**ie
Inst ①	interesować się	nami	wami	**n**imi	
Loc ◉	mówić o	nas	was	**n**ich	
Voc 🎙	hej...	my	wy	—	

In the nominative and accusative plural, one must pay attention to whether the group includes a male person. If so, the masculine personal form is used.

As in the singular, the 3rd person plural forms also insert an **n-** when they occur after prepositions, e.g. *liczę na* **nie** */ na* **nich** 'I am counting on them (non-masculine personal / masculine personal)'.

7.3. Possessive pronouns

7.3.1. Possessive pronouns: formation

What do the forms of the possessive pronouns resemble? This can be observed in **Table 7.3.a.**

Table 7.3.a. First and second person possessive pronouns

Subject form			Possessive pronoun forms			
				Examples	Gender	
SG	ja	m-	-ój	to **mój** rower	Masc ♀	SG
			-oje	to **moje** auto	Neut ♀	
			-oja	to **moja** komórka	Fem Δ	
	ty	tw-	-oi	to **moi** przyjaciele	+Mp 🐾	PL
			-oje	to **moje** książki	−Mp ✂	
PL	my	na-	-sz	to **nasz** rower	Masc ♀	SG
			-sze	to **nasze** auto	Neut ♀	
			-sza	to **nasza** komórka	Fem Δ	
	wy	wa-	-si	to **nasi** przyjaciele	+Mp 🐾	PL
			-sze	to **nasze** książki	−Mp ✂	

While the first and second person pronouns decline like soft-stem adjectives, the 3rd person pronouns *jego, jej, ich,* but also *pana, pani, państwa* do not decline, and remain the same in all cases.

Table 7.3.b. presents all of the nominative singular forms for Polish possessive pronouns. Which of these pronouns decline in order to agree in case, number, and gender with the nouns they modify?

Table 7.3.b. Possessive pronouns: nominative singular forms

Subject form (personal pronoun)		A. Context 🖳	B.		C.		D.	
			POSSESSIVE FORMS WITH SINGULAR NOUNS					
			PRON	ADJ+NOUN MASC ♀	PRON	ADJ+NOUN NEUT ♀	PRON	ADJ+NOUN FEM ♀
SG	ja	to jest 'this is'	mój	nowy lektor	moje (me)ˣ	nowe auto	moja (ma)ˣ	nowa lektorka
	ty		twój		twoje (twe)ˣ		twoja (twa)ˣ	
	on, ono		jego		jego		jego	
	pan		pana		pana		pana	
	ona		jej		jej		jej	
	pani		pani		pani		pani	
PL	my		nasz		nasze		nasza	
	wy		wasz		wasze		wasza	
	oni, one		ich		ich		ich	
	panowie, państwo, panie		panów, państwa, pań		panów, państwa, pań		panów, państwa, pań	

ˣ Short forms (*moje / me; moja / ma; twoje / twe; twoja / twa*) are outdated; nowadays they can be found in poetry. They are not considered in this chapter.

Table 7.3.c. Possessive pronouns: genitive singular forms

Subject form (personal pronoun)		A. Context 🖳	B.		C.	
			POSSESSIVE FORMS WITH SINGULAR NOUNS			
			PRON	ADJ+NOUN MASC ♀ and NEUT ♀	PRON	ADJ+NOUN FEM ♀
SG	ja	nie ma 'there is no'	mojego	starszego brata, nowego auta	mojej	nowej lektorki
	ty		twojego		twojej	
	on, ono		jego		jego	
	pan		pana		pana	
	ona		jej		jej	
	pani		pani		pani	
PL	my		naszego		naszej	
	wy		waszego		waszej	
	oni, one		ich		ich	
	panowie, państwo, panie		panów, państwa, pań		panów, państwa, pań	

Notice that the masculine and neuter forms are the same. This is true for all cases except the nominative in the singular.

Table 7.3.d. Possessive pronouns: dative singular

Subject form (personal pronoun)		A. CONTEXT 📷	B. POSSESSIVE FORMS WITH SINGULAR NOUNS		C.	
			PRON	ADJ+NOUN MASC ♀ and NEUT ♀	PRON	ADJ+NOUN FEM ♦
SG	ja	dzięki 'thanks to'	**mojemu**	starszemu bratu, nowemu autu	**mojej**	nowej lektorce
	ty		**twojemu**		**twojej**	
	on, ono		jego		jego	
	pan		pana		pana	
	ona		jej		jej	
	pani		pani		pani	
PL	my		**naszemu**		**naszej**	
	wy		**waszemu**		**waszej**	
	oni, one		ich		ich	
	panowie, państwo, panie		panów, państwa, pań		panów, państwa, pań	

As is the case with nouns and adjectives, the accusative singular forms of masculine possessive pronouns will depend upon whether the referent is an animate noun (compare columns **B.** and **C.** in **Table 7.3.e.**).

Table 7.3.e. Possessive pronouns: accusative singular

A. CONTEXT 📷	B. PRON	ADJ+NOUN MASC ♀ +AN 🐕	C. PRON	ADJ+NOUN MASK ♀ −AN 💀	D. PRON	ADJ+NOUN NEUT ♀	E. PRON	ADJ+NOUN FEM ♦
widać 'one can see'	**mojego**	nowego lektora	**mój**	nowy dom	**moje**	nowe auto	**moją**	nową lektorkę
	twojego		**twój**		**twoje**		**twoją**	
	jego		jego		jego		jego	
	pana		pana		pana		pana	
	jej		jej		jej		jej	
	pani		pani		pani		pani	
	naszego		**nasz**		**nasze**		**naszą**	
	waszego		**wasz**		**wasze**		**waszą**	
	ich		ich		ich		ich	
	panów, państwa, pań		panów, państwa, pań		panów, państwa, pań		panów, państwa, pań	

moje auto

jej auto

nasze auto

Table 7.3.f. Possessive pronouns: instrumental singular

Subject form (personal pronoun)		A. Context 📷	B. POSSESSIVE FORMS WITH SINGULAR NOUNS			C.
			PRON	ADJ+NOUN MASC ♀ and NEUT ♀	PRON	ADJ+NOUN FEM △
SG	ja		**moim**[6]		**moją**	
	ty		**twoim**		**twoją**	
	on, ono		jego		jego	
	pan	w porównaniu z 'compared to'	pana	starszym bratem, nowym autem	pana	nową lektorką
	ona		jej		jej	
	pani		pani		pani	
PL	my		**naszym**		**naszą**	
	wy		**waszym**		**waszą**	
	oni, one		ich		ich	
	panowie, państwo, panie		panów, państwa, pań		panów, państwa, pań	

Table 7.3.g. Possessive pronouns: locative singular

Subject form (personal pronoun)		A. Context 📷	B. POSSESSIVE FORMS WITH SINGULAR NOUNS			C.
			PRON	ADJ+NOUN MASC ♀ and NEUT ♀	PRON	ADJ+NOUN FEM △
SG	ja		**moim**		**mojej**	
	ty		**twoim**		**twojej**	
	on, ono		jego		jego	
	pan	dyskusja o 'a discussion about'	pana	nowym lektorze, aucie	pana	nowej lektorkce
	ona		jej		jej	
	pani		pani		pani	
PL	my		**naszym**		**naszej**	
	wy		**waszym**		**waszej**	
	oni, one		ich		ich	
	panowie, państwo, panie		panów, państwa, pań		panów, państwa, pań	

For masculine and neuter possessive pronouns, the instrumental and locative are identical. In the feminine, the genitive, dative, and locative forms are identical.

Whereas nouns have separate vocative forms, the vocative of adjectives and pronouns is always identical to the nominative. See **Table 7.3.h.**

---

[6] Some possessive pronouns have short forms in the instrumental and locative *moim / mym, twoim / twym, moją / mą, twoją / twą*; these are used very rarely (generally only in poetry due to metrical considerations) and are left out of the tables.

Table 7.3.h. Possessive pronouns: vocative singular and plural

Person		Masc ♀	Neut ♀	Fem ♦	+Mp 🐾	−Mp ✂
		WITH SINGULAR NOUNS			WITH PLURAL NOUNS	
Sg	ja	mój bracie!	moje dziecko!	moja siostro!	moi rodzice!	moje siostry!
Pl	my	nasz bracie!	nasze dziecko!	nasza siostro!	nasi rodzice!	nasze siostry!

Table 7.3.i. Possessive pronouns: nominative case plural forms

	Person	Context 📷	Pron	+Mp 🐾	Pron	−Mp ✂
Sg	ja		**moi**		**moje**	
	ty		**twoi**		**twoje**	
	on, ono		jego		jego	
	pan		pana		pana	
	ona		jej		jej	
	pani	to są	pani	nowi lektorzy	pani	nowe auta,
Pl	my	'there are'	**nasi**		**nasze**	lektorki
	wy		**wasi**		**wasze**	
	oni, one		ich		ich	
	panowie		panów		panów	
	państwo		państwa		państwa	
	panie		pań		pań	

- As we have seen, in Polish, negation is one of the primary functions of the genitive case, often expressing the absence of something or someone, e.g. *Nie było tam ani mnie, ani mojego nowego lektora* 'I was not there, and neither was my new teacher'.

- The short forms *cię, go* are neutral, e.g. *Nie widziałem* **cię** 'I did not see you'. The long forms *ciebie, jego* are used to provide emphasis or express contrast, e.g. **Ciebie** *tam widziałam, ale* **jego** *nie* 'I saw you there, but I didn't see him'.

Table 7.3.j. Possessive pronouns: genitive plural

	Person	Context 📷	Pronoun forms	Pl
Sg	ja		**moich**	
	ty		**twoich**	
	on, ono		jego	
	pan		pana	
	ona		jej	
	pani	nie ma	pani	nowych
Pl	my	'there are no'	**naszych**	lektorów, aut,
	wy		**waszych**	lektorek
	oni, one		ich	
	panowie		panów	
	panie		pań	
	państwo		państwa	

Table 7.3.k. Possessive pronouns: dative plural

	Person	Context 📷	Pronoun forms	Adj+Noun: Masc ♀, Neut ♀, Fem ♀
SG	ja	dzięki 'thanks to'	**moim**	nowym lektorom, autom, lektorkom
SG	ty		**twoim**	
SG	on, ono		jego	
SG	pan		pana	
SG	ona		jej	
SG	pani		pani	
PL	my		**naszym**	
PL	wy		**waszym**	
PL	oni, one		ich	
PL	panowie		panów	
PL	państwo		państwa	
PL	panie		pań	

Table 7.3.l. Possessive pronouns: accusative plural

	Person	Context 📷	Pron	Adj+Noun: +Mp 🐧	Pron	Adj+Noun: −Mp ✂
SG	ja	widać 'one can see'	**moich**	nowych lektorów	**moje**	nowe auta, lektorki
SG	ty		**twoich**		**twoje**	
SG	on, ono		jego		jego	
SG	pan		pana		pana	
SG	ona		jej		jej	
SG	pani		pani		pani	
PL	my		**naszych**		**nasze**	
PL	wy		**waszych**		**wasze**	
PL	oni, one		ich		ich	
PL	panowie		panów		panów	
PL	państwo		państwa		państwa	
PL	panie		pań		pań	

Table 7.3.m. Possessive pronouns: instrumental plural

	Person	Context 📷	Pronoun Forms	Adj+Noun: Masc ♀, Neut ♀, Fem ♀
SG	ja	w porównaniu z 'compared to'	**moimi**	nowymi lektorami, autami, lektorkami
SG	ty		**twoimi**	
SG	on, ono, pan		jego, pana	
SG	ona, pani		jej, pani	
PL	my		**naszymi**	
PL	wy		**waszymi**	
PL	oni, one		ich	
PL	panowie		panów	
PL	panie		pań	
PL	państwo		państwa	

Table 7.3.n. Possessive pronouns: locative plural

	Person	Context 🖿	Pronoun Forms	Adj+Noun: Masc ♀, Neut ♀, Fem ♀
Sg	ja	dyskusja o 'a discussion about'	**moich**	nowych lektorach, autach, lektorkach
	ty		**twoich**	
	on, ono		jego	
	pan		pana	
	ona		jej	
	pani		pani	
Pl	my		**naszych**	
	wy		**waszych**	
	oni, one		ich	
	panowie		panów	
	państwo		państwa	
	panie		pań	

7.3.2. Possessive pronouns: usage

As we can see from the preceding tables, the first- and second-person personal pronouns form the adjective-like possessives **mój, twój, nasz, wasz**.

The third-person possessive is essentially expressed by taking the genitive form of the personal pronoun, **jego, jej, ich, pana** etc. That is why these forms do not decline according to the case, number and gender of the noun phrase (although for different possessors they have different forms) – in essence the third person possessives are always genitive, the main function of which is to express possession (*To jest Jana / jego książka* – 'This is Jan's / his book').

7.3.3. Other pronouns with adjectival declension

There are many other pronouns that, like the possessives *mój, twój,* decline like adjectives. These include:

- Relative and interrogative pronouns[7]:
    - *który, które, która, którzy, które* 'which, who, that'
    - *jaki, jakie, jaka, jacy, jakie* 'what kind of'
    - *czyj, czyje, czyja, czyi, czyje* 'whose'
    - *taki, takie, taka, tacy, takie* 'such a'
- Demonstrative pronouns:
    - *ten, to, ta, ci, te* 'this, these'　　◆ *tamten, tamto, tamta, tamci, tamte* 'that, those'
- Indefinite and determinate pronouns:
    - *sam, samo, sama, sami, same* 'the same, by oneself'
    - *żaden, żadne, żadna, żadni, żadne* 'no kind of'
    - *niczyj, niczyje, niczyja, niczyi, niczyje* 'no one's'
    - *inny, inne, inna, inni, inne* 'other'
        - in singular: *każdy, każde, każda* 'each'　　* in singular: *wszystko* 'everything'
        - in plural: *wszyscy, wszystkie* 'everyone, all'

---

[7] 'How many / How much?' in Polish has two forms: *ile* (for –MP) and *ilu* (for +MP).

7.4. Reflexive pronouns

7.4.1. The reflexive possessive pronoun *swój*

When the possessor in a possessive phrase is the subject of the sentence, the reflexive possessive pronoun *swój* is used.

 Table 7.4.a. schematizes this notion

Table 7.4.a. Reflexive possessive pronoun *swój*

Possessor = Subject[8]	Possessor ≠ Subject[9]
Ja mam swój / (mój) klucz. Adam ma **swój** klucz.	Ja mam twój klucz. Adam ma jego klucz.
Ty masz swój / (twój) klucz. Ewa ma **swój** klucz.	Ty masz jej klucz. Ewa ma jej klucz.

Ja mam swój klucz.   Adam ma swój klucz.   Ewa ma swój klucz.   Ty masz swój klucz.

Ja mam twój klucz.   Adam ma jego klucz.   Ty masz jej klucz.   Ewa ma jej klucz.

A reflexive possessive pronoun does not exist in English, where the possibility for ambiguity exists. The English sentence *Adam has his keys* does not explicitly state whose keys Adam actually has. English speakers generally understand the intended meaning from context[10]. If we were to translate the above English sentence literally into Polish, we would get *Adam ma jego klucze*, which Poles would understand to mean that Adam has somebody else's keys.

Thus as we can see, *swój* would translate into English as 'one's own', where the referent of 'one' is dependent on the subject of the sentence.

---

[8] 'I have my (own) key.; Adam has his (own) key.; You have your (own) key.; Ewa has her (own) key.'

[9] 'I have your key.; Adam has his key (someone else's).; You have her key.; Ewa has her key (someone else's).'

[10] In everyday conversation, Polish speakers often leave out the possessive pronoun altogether, *Mam klucze* 'I have my keys'.

Tables 7.4.b. and **7.4.c.** show the declension of the reflexive possessive pronoun.

Table 7.4.b. Case forms for the reflexive possessive *swój*: singular

| Case | Context 🖿 | Masc ♀ | | Neut ♀ | Fem ♀ |
		+An 🐕 (Animate: Persons and animals)	−An 🕱 (Inanimate: Things)		
Gen ☺	X nie zna	swoj**ego** starszego brata, dziecka			swoj**ej** starszej siostry
Dat ➤	X wierzy	swoj**emu** starszemu bratu, dziecku			swoj**ej** starszej siostrze
Acc ♥	X lubi	swoj**ego** starszego brata	sw**ój** starszy dom	swoj**e** starsze dziecko	swoj**ą** starszą siostrę
Inst ①	X rozmawia z(e)	swo**im** starszym bratem, dzieckiem			swoj**ą** starszą siostrą
Loc ◒	X mówi o	swo**im** starszym bracie, dziecku			swoj**ej** starszej siostrze

Table 7.4.c. Case forms for the reflexive possessive *swój*: plural

Case	Context 🖿	+Mp 🏻	−Mp ✂
Gen ☺	X nie zna oni / one nie znają	swo**ich** now**ych** studentów ani studentek	
Dat ➤	X wierzy oni / one wierzą	swo**im** now**ym** studentom i studentkom	
Acc ♥	X lubi oni / one lubią	swo**ich** now**ych** studentów	swoj**e** now**e** studentki
Inst ①	X rozmawia oni / one rozmawiają z(e)	swo**imi** now**ymi** studentami i studentkami	
Loc ◒	X mówi o oni / one mówią o	swo**ich** now**ych** studentach i studentkach	

Notice again that the reflexive possessive **swój** declines like **mój**; and must agree in gender, number and case with the noun it modifies. It is also not used in the nominative case,[11] e.g. *jego żona zadzwoniła do niego* (and not **swoja żona zadzwoniła do niego*) 'his wife called him', which can be as ambiguous as it is in English.

7.4.2. The reflexive pronouns *się, siebie*

In addition to the reflexive possessive pronoun, Polish also has a reflexive personal pronoun, generally illustrated with the forms *się, siebie*, which resemble the forms for the accusative of the second person singular personal pronoun (cf. *cię, ciebie*). The short form *się*, however, has evolved to become a particle that often acts as part of the verb it accompanies. Many verbs cannot even exist without this particle: *cieszę się, boję się* 'I'm glad, I am frightened'.[12]

---

[11] There are cases where a nominative form of *swój* is used, essentially as an adjective with its own idiomatic meaning, e.g. *To jest swój człowiek* ('this fellow's all right; he's one of us').

[12] This notion can be difficult for English speakers to conceptualize.

Notice that such verbs are generally intransitive (they cannot have a direct object in the accusative case).[13] Generally *się* and *siebie*, like the reflexive possessive pronouns are used when they refer to the subject of the sentence, and in English could be thought of as 'Xself', where X refers to the subject (thus, depending on the subject, the English translation might be 'yourself, herself, ourselves', etc).[14] In some cases, the reflexive meaning of this pronoun is transparent, but not always. Also, these pronouns can be used in all of the cases except the nominative and the vocative, and the forms for each case resemble those of the second-person singular personal pronoun.

 Read the examples in **Table 7.4.d.** What determines the form of the pronoun? What are its equivalents in English?

Table 7.4.d. Reflexive pronouns *się*, *siebie*

	się	siebie	Eng
Gen ⊗	nie widzę się	nie widzę **siebie**, lecz ciebie	I don't see myself, but I see you
Dat ➡	—	kup coś **sobie**, a nie tylko mnie	buy something for yourself, not only for me
Acc ♥	umyj się	myj **siebie**, a nie lalkę	wash yourself, not the doll
Inst ⓘ	—	rozmawiali ze **sobą** długo	they talked to each other for a long time
Loc ⬯	—	Adam często mówi o **sobie**	Adam often talks about himself

Notice that, like the other personal pronouns, the reflexive may also have short and long forms, depending on whether it expresses contrast, provides emphasis, or is used with a preposition. When the subject is plural, the reflexive pronoun can carry a meaning of reciprocity: *Adam i Ewa patrzą na siebie* 'Adam and Eve are looking at each other'.

The dative form *sobie* is often used in informal speech to give a sentence a more personal character, e.g. *pośpij sobie dłużej i zjedz sobie śniadanko* sounds somewhat friendlier than *pośpij dłużej i zjedz śniadanie* 'sleep longer and eat breakfast'. The form can also give the sentence a somewhat indefinite meaning: *poszli sobie po północy* 'They left after midnight (but I don't really know where they went)'.

7.5. Demonstrative pronouns

 Table 7.5.a. illustrates the usage of *ten, to, ta*, demonstrative pronouns with the meaning of 'this'. The other demonstrative *tamten, tamto, tamta,* 'that' is formed identically.[15] With one exception, these pronouns decline in the same way as adjectives. See if you can spot the exception.

Table 7.5.a. Demonstrative pronouns: singular *ten, to, ta*

Case	Context 🖾	Masc ♀	Neut ♀	Fem △
Nom ◯	to jest	ten chłopak	to mieszkanie	ta kobieta
Gen ⊗	brakuje	tego chłopaka, mieszkania		tej kobiety
Dat ➡	dać szansę	temu chłopakowi, mieszkaniu		tej kobiecie
Acc ♥	lubić	tego chłopaka, ten samochód	to mieszkanie	**tę** kobietę
Inst ⓘ	interesować się	tym chłopakiem, mieszkaniem		tą kobietą
Loc ⬯	mówić o	tym chłopaku, mieszkaniu		tej kobiecie

---

[13] *Się* is often used to give sentences a passive or impersonal meaning: *robi się* 'one does, it is done'.

[14] The reflexive can also carry the meaning of 'each other' when the subject is plural: *kochają się* 'they love each other'.

[15] The difference between the two demonstratives, as in English, is based on the perspective of the person speaking. However, the scale seems somewhat different. Many times the Polish *to* is best translated as 'that': *nie wiem o tym* 'I don't know about that'.

Because these pronouns decline like adjectives, we might expect an accusative singular feminine form *tą*, instead of the actual form *tę*; indeed, this expected form is often heard in speech, although it is not seen in writing.

Table 7.5.b. Demonstrative pronouns: plural *ci, te*

Case	Context 🖵	+Mp 🏗	–Mp ✂
Nom ⬤	to są	ci chłopcy	te mieszkania, kobiety (te chłopaki)
Gen ⊗	brakuje	tych chłopców, mieszkań, kobiet	
Dat ➡	dać szansę	tym chłopcom, mieszkaniom, kobietom	
Acc ♥	lubić	tych chłopców	te mieszkania, kobiety
Inst ⓘ	interesować się	tymi chłopcami, mieszkaniami, kobietami	
Loc ☙	mówić o	tych chłopcach, mieszkaniach, kobietach	

In the plural as well, the endings for the demonstrative pronouns resemble those of adjectives. Notice in the masculine personal form the *-t* undergoes softening before the ending *-i* (as in the adjective *bogaty – bogaci*).

7.6. Interrogative, indefinite and relative pronouns

 Look at **Table 7.6.a.**, which shows the correspondences between interrogative, indefinite and relative pronouns in Polish. Column **1.** shows interrogative pronouns, columns **2.** and **3.** show the indefinites, and column **4.** shows the relative pronouns. Which pronouns are declined similarly? How are columns **2.** and **3.** similar?

Table 7.6.a. Interrogative, Indefinite and relative pronouns

	1.	2.	3.	4.
A.	**Kto** to jest? Who is this?	Kto**ś**. Someone.	Kto**kolwiek**... Whoever, anyone ...	**Ten, kto** cię lubi. The one who likes you.
	Co to jest? What is this?	Co**ś**. Something.	Co**kolwiek**... Whatever, anything ...	**To, co** chciałaś. What you wanted/the one you wanted.
B.	**Kogo** brakuje? Who's missing?	Kogo**ś**. Someone.	Kogo**kolwiek**... Whoever, anyone ...	**Tego, kogo** nie zaprosiłeś. The one you didn't invite.
	Czego brakuje? What's missing?	Czego**ś**. Something.	Czego**kolwiek**... Whatever, anything ...	**Tego, czego** nie kupiłeś. The one you didn't buy.
C.	**Komu** dałeś prezent? To whom did you give a present?	Komu**ś**. To someone.	Komu**kolwiek**... To whomever, anyone ...	**Temu, komu** chciałem dać prezent. The one I wanted to give a present to.
	Czemu się dziwisz? What are you surprised at?	Czemu**ś**. Something.	Czemu**kolwiek**... Whatever, anything ...	**Temu, czemu** ty też się dziwisz. The same thing you're surprised at.
D.	**Kogo** widzisz? Whom do you see?	Kogo**ś**. Someone.	Kogo**kolwiek**... Whomever, anyone ...	**Tego, kogo** wczoraj poznałem. The one I met yesterday.
	Co mi kupiłeś? What did you buy me?	Co**ś**. Something.	Co**kolwiek**... Whatever ...	**To, co** chciałaś. What you wanted/the one you wanted.

E.	**Z kim** rozmawiasz? Whom are you talking to?	Z kim**ś**. (to) Someone.	Z kim**kolwiek**... Whomever, anyone ...	**Z tym, z kim** będę pracować. The one I'll be working with.
	Z czym masz problem? What do you have a problem with?	Z czym**ś**. (with) Something.	Z czym**kolwiek**... Whatever, anything ...	**Z tym, z czym** ty też masz problem. The same thing that you have a problem with.
F.	**O kim** piszesz? Whom are you writing about?	O kim**ś**. (about) Someone.	O kim**kolwiek**... Whomever, anyone ...	**O tym, o kim** pisałem wczoraj. The one I was writing about yesterday.
	O czym piszesz? What are you writing about?	O czym**ś**. (about) Something.	O czym**kolwiek**... Whatever, anything ...	**O tym, o czym** pisałam wczoraj. The thing that I was writing about yesterday.

- Notice the different case forms for these pronouns, represented in the table by the labels **A.–F.**
- Interrogative and relative pronouns have another function (see § 7.1.), but they are declined similarly. They have a mixed, noun-adjective type declension (like the demonstrative pronouns).
- Notice in column **2.** that these indefinite pronouns are formed by adding -*ś* to the interrogative pronoun shown in column **1.** These indefinites can sometimes sound unfriendly or evasive when used to answer a question: *Z kim idziesz do kina? – Z kimś.* 'With whom are you going to the movies? – With someone'.
- The pronouns in column **3.** can indicate a shade of indifference or even desperation on the part of the speaker: *Z kim chciałabyś iść do kina? – Z kimkolwiek (byle nie sama!)* 'Who do you want to go the cinema with? – With whomever (but not alone!)', see **Table 7.6.b.**
- The interrogative pronouns may also be commonly used in combination with infinitive verbs to give an indefinite meaning of 'somewhere to, someone to, something to, etc.' *Mam gdzie spać, co robić, z kim rozmawiać* 'I have somewhere to sleep, something to do, someone to speak with'.

Table 7.6.b. Two types of indefinite pronouns

Possible meanings			
ktoś	coś	ktokolwiek	cokolwiek
someone	something	anyone, whoever	anything, whatever

How do you think the indefinite pronouns in **Table 7.6.c.** are declined?

Table 7.6.c. Nominative and genitive of several indefinite pronouns

Nom 😑			Gen 😣	
Masc ♂,	Neut ⚲,	Fem △	Masc ♂, Neut ⚲	Fem △
któr**y**ś,	któr**e**ś,	któr**a**ś	któr**ego**ś	któr**ej**ś
któr**y**kolwiek,	któr**e**kolwiek,	któr**a**kolwiek	któr**ego**kolwiek	któr**ej**kolwiek
jak**i**ś,	jak**ie**ś,	jak**a**ś	jak**iego**ś	jak**iej**ś

Column **4.** of **Table 7.6.a.** answers the questions posed in column **1.** of that same table. Thus, the relative pronouns are the same as the interrogative pronouns in the questions. Are there any other possibilities? Read the examples in **Table 7.6.d.** which show how two clauses in the same sentence might be combined in such a way that the relative pronoun is in a different case than its referent in the first clause.

Table 7.6.d. Relative pronouns in a sentence[16]

	Clause 1	Clause 2
A.	Daj prezent **temu**,	**kogo** lubisz.
B.	Spotkałam **tę**,	**której** dawno nie widziałam.
C.	Porozmawiaj **z tymi**,	**o których** ci wczoraj mówiłam.
D.	Nie lubię **tych**,	**którzy** mnie nie szanują.
E.	Zapytaj **te**,	**które** skończyły kurs.

Since in the subordinate clause the relative pronoun does not have to play the same grammatical role that it does in the main clause, we may encounter sentences such as those in the table above, where the pronoun and its antecedent are used in two different cases. **Table 7.6.e.** below summarizes the cases that are employed in the sentences in **Table 7.6.d.**

Table 7.6.e. Summary of cases used in the sentences from **Table 7.6.d.**

	Clause 1	Clause 2
A.	Dat 🐟	Acc ♥
B.	Acc ♥	Gen ☹
C.	Inst ⓘ	Loc 👄
D.	Gen ☹	Nom 🫑
E.	Acc ♥	Nom 🫑

Było ważne zadanie do zrobienia i **wszyscy** zostali poproszeni o jego wykonanie. **Każdy** przypuszczał, że **ktoś** inny to zrobi. **Każdy** mógł to zrobić, ale nie zabrał się za to **nikt**. **Ktoś** z tego powodu się zdenerwował, bo była to praca dla **każdego**. **Każdy** myślał, że **ktokolwiek** może to zrobić. **Nikt** nie zdawał sobie sprawy, że **nikt niczego** nie zrobi. Skończyło się na tym, że **każdy** winił **każdego**, podczas gdy **nikt** nie mógł winić **nikogo**. Winni byli **wszyscy**.

---

[16] 'A. Give the present to the one that you like. B. I met a person whom I hadn't seen in a long time. C. Speak to the ones I was telling you about yesterday. D. I don't like those who don't respect me. E. Ask those who have finished the course.'

7.7. The negative pronouns *nikt, nic, żaden*

 Take a look at the declension of the negative pronouns *nikt, nic, żaden*. What can you say about the way they inflect?

Table 7.7. The declension of the pronouns *nikt, nic, żaden*[17]

			nikt	nic
A.	Nom ●		**nikt** tu nie pracuje, **żaden** człowiek.	**nic** tu nie działa / tu **nic** nie funkcjonuje.
B.	Gen ☹		**nikogo** tu nie ma, **żadnego** człowieka.	**niczego** tu nie ma / tu **nic** nie ma.
C.	Dat ✍	Nie,...	**nikomu** nie wierzę, **żadnemu** człowiekowi.	**niczemu** się nie dziwię.
D.	Inst ⓘ		**z nikim** nie rozmawiam, z **żadnym** człowiekiem.	**niczym** się nie interesuję.
E.	Loc ◔		**o nikim** nie mówię, o **żadnym** człowieku.	**o niczym** nie myślę.

Żaden (żadna, żadne) declines like an adjective. The words *nic* and *nikt* display a similarity to the corresponding case questions, e.g. the genitive *kogo? czego? – nikogo, niczego*, etc. In the genitive, the form *nic* 'nothing NOM' is very often used in the spoken language instead of the correct *niczego* 'nothing GEN', the form characteristic of the written language.

If in an affirmative sentence the object is in the accusative, then in the negative the accusative automatically turns into the genitive: *mam samochód, willę i pieniądze / nie mam (żadnego) samochodu, (żadnej) willi, ani (żadnych) pieniędzy.*[18]

In Polish, unlike in English, double negative is not only allowed, but it is obligatory. The negative pronouns *nikt, nic, żaden* are not enough to negate a sentence; *nie* 'no' has to be used in front of the verb: *Nie znam tutaj nikogo. Nikomu niczego nie dałam*[19]. Consequently, the English 'Nobody knows her' translates into Polish as *Nikt jej nie zna* (Nobody does not know her), and English 'I didn't do anything' becomes Polish *Nic nie zrobiłem* (I didn't do nothing).

The correct negative answer to the question *Czy jest u ciebie Adam?* 'Is Adam at your place?' is not **Adam nie jest u mnie* (compare English 'Adam is not at my place'), but *Nie ma go u mnie*. In addition to that, in order to emphasise that it is Adam that we mean, we might say *Jego u mnie nie ma*. To conclude: in negative constructions of this sort the pronoun is in the genitive. Examples of negative sentences can also be found in **Table 12.a.**

---

[17] 'A. No, nobody works here, not a single person. / nothing works here, nothing is operational. B. No, nobody is here, not a single person. / nothing is here. C. No, I don't believe anybody, not a single person. / nothing surprises me. D. No, I don't talk to anyone, not a single person. / I'm not interested in anything. E. No, I am not talking about anyone, not a single person, I'm thinking about nothing.'

[18] 'I have a car, a villa and money / I don't have a car, a villa, or (any) money'.

[19] 'I don't know anyone here. I didn't give anything to anyone.'

8 Numerals: *liczebniki*

8.1. Cardinal numerals

Read the table of cardinal numerals below. See what patterns you can observe. Can you figure out how to say numbers that are not in the table?

Tabee 8.1.a. Cardinal numerals 0–20 000 000

0 – 10	11 – 19	20 – 90	22, 33, 44…	100 – 900
zero				
jeden[1]	jede**naście**			sto
dwa	dwa**naście**	dwadzieści**a**	dwadzieścia dwa	dwieś**cie**
trzy	trzy**naście**	trzy**dzieści**	trzydzieści trzy	trzy**sta**
cztery	czter**naście**	czter**dzieści**	czterdzieści cztery	cztery**sta**
pię**ć**	pię**tnaście**	pięćdziesiąt	pięćdziesiąt pięć	pięćset
sze**ść**	sze**snaście**	sześćdziesiąt	sześćdziesiąt sześć	sześćset
siedem	siedem**naście**	siedemdziesiąt	siedemdziesiąt siedem	siedemset
osiem	osiem**naście**	osiemdziesiąt	osiemdziesiąt osiem	osiemset
dziewię**ć**	dziewię**tnaście**	dziewięćdziesiąt	dziewięćdziesiąt dziewięć	dziewięćset
dziesięć	—	—	—	—

1 000 – 10 000	100 000 – 900 000	1 000 000 – 10 000 000[2]	11 000 000 – 20 000 000[3]
tysiąc	sto tysięcy	milion	jedenaście milion**ów**
dwa tysiąc**e**	dwieście tysięcy	dwa milion**y**	
trzy tysiąc**e**	trzysta tysięcy		
cztery tysiąc**e**	czterysta tysięcy		
pięć tysi**ęcy**	pięćset tysięcy	pięć milion**ów**	piętnaście milion**ów**
sześć tysi**ęcy**	sześćset tysięcy		
siedem tysi**ęcy**	siedemset tysięcy		
osiem tysi**ęcy**	osiemset tysięcy		
dziewięć tysi**ęcy**	dziewięćset tysięcy		
dziesięć tysi**ęcy**	—		

Once you have memorized the numbers from **1–10**, higher numerals become more or less predictable. Between **11–19**, the numerals are formed with the suffix *-naście*. Notice the slight changes to the final letter(s) of the base number in the following: *czte(r)naście, pię(t)naście, sze(s)naście, dziewię(t)naście*.

Multiples of ten (twenty, thirty, forty, etc.) are formed with a suffix that derives from the

---

[1] When counting, the form *raz*, which translates as 'once', is used instead of *jeden*.

[2] Subsequent numerals: *trzy, cztery miliony / pięć, sześć, siedem, osiem, dziewięć milionów*.

[3] Subsequent numerals: *dwanaście, trzynaście, czternaście, szesnaście, siedemnaście, osiemnaście, dziewiętnaście, dwadzieścia milionów*.

numeral *-dziesięć*. This suffix is subject to alternations (corresponding to case assignment rules to be discussed later in this chapter).[4] In the case of **20**, we have *dwadzieścia*, while for **30** and **40** we have the ending *-i* (*trzydzieści, czterdzieści*), while for numbers **50–90** the suffix surfaces as *-dziesiąt* (*pięćdziesiąt, sześćdziesiąt*, etc.). Polish combines tens and ones in a similar fashion to English: *22 – dwadzieścia dwa, 23 – dwadzieścia trzy, 45 – czterdzieści pięć*.

The numeral **100** is ***sto*** (resembling a neuter noun), which is subject to alternation in the numerals **200, 300,** etc. We see three variants: *-ście* (for **200** – *dwieście*, from the old dual form, see note 4), *-sta* (resembling the nominative plural, for **300, 400** – *trzysta, czterysta*), and *-set* (for **500, 600** and above – *pięćset, sześćset*; this suffix is in essence a genitive plural form). No additional words are necessary to form larger compound numerals: *333 – trzysta trzydzieści trzy*; *555 – pięćset pięćdziesiąt pięć*.

Important – The alternations that we see in the forms of the numerical suffixes reflect an important rule in Polish grammar regarding case usage with numerals. Case assignment with numerals (when the numerals themselves are in the nominative or accusative) depends on what the number ends in. Numerals ending in 2, 3, 4 generally group together[5] (and govern the nominative plural), as do those ending in 5–9 (governing the genitive plural). Numerals above 20 ending in 1 also take the genitive plural. This can be observed with the forms for 'thousand': **1000** – *jeden tysiąc* (nominative singular), **2000-3000-4000** – *dwa-trzy-cztery tysiące* (nominative plural), *5000 – pięć tysięcy* (genitive plural), *21000 – dwadzieścia jeden tysięcy* (genitive plural).

8.2. Arithmetic operations

Table 8.2.a. illustrates how to formulate arithmetic operations in Polish.

Table 8.2.a. Arithmetic operations in Polish

A.	B.	C.	D.	E.	F.	G.
Ile jest	X	dodać / plus	Y	?	jest / równa się / wynosi	Z
		odjąć / minus				
		razy				
		(podzielone) przez				

- The questions are formed using the order **A. + B. + C. + D. + E.**
- The answers can be formed in the following orders:
  - **B. + C. + D. + F. + G.**
  - **F. + G.**
  - **G.**

Examples: *Ile jest dwa razy trzy? Dwa razy trzy jest sześć.*
      Ile jest osiem (podzielone) przez dwa? Cztery.
      Ile jest pięć minus dziewięć? Jest minus cztery.[6]

- The forms on the right are more official.

[4] *-dzieścia* derives from an old dual (instead of the singular or plural) form, *-dzieści* from the nominitive plural, *-dziesiąt* from the genitive plural. Thus in essence, Poles say 'a pair of tens' for 20, 'three tens' for 30, 'four tens for 40, etc. A similar thing happens with hundreds, thousands, millions, etc.

[5] *Dwadzieścia* and *dwieście* are exceptions by which the numeral two produces a special form corresponding to the obsolete grammatical category of dual.

[6] What is …? 2 x 3 = 6; 8 : 2 = 4; 5 – 9 = –4

8.3. Introduction: numerals and quantifiers in syntactic constructions

 For English speakers, the variety of numerical forms in Polish, as well as the syntactic consequences of numerals and quantifiers, are extremely difficult. Indeed, even native speakers of Polish often have difficulty with these forms. Look at the examples in **Table 8.3.a.** What differences can you observe between column **A.** and column **B.**, as well as between row **1.** and row **2.**?

Table 8.3.a. Numerals and quantifiers in syntactic constructions

	A.	B.
1.	Tam byli aktorzy, ale też politycy i prezydent z dziećmi.	Tam byli **dwaj** aktorzy, ale by**ło** tam też pięc**iu** polityk**ów** i prezydent z **dwojgiem** dzie**ci**.[7]
2.	Na wsi były zwierz**ęta**: papugi, psy i koty.	Na wsi by**ło** dużo zwierz**ąt**: **dwie** papugi, **dwa** psy i pięć kot**ów**.[8]

The essential differences in this table that you need to keep in mind are as follows: first, in column **A.**, no specific quantities are given, the nouns are in the nominative case, and they agree with the verbs in number and gender. In column **B.**, however, all of the nouns are quantified, with serious consequences on the case assignment of the noun and the agreement of the verb. Between rows **1.** and **2.**, we may observe that in the first case, male persons are included among the nouns, while in the second case they are not. This distinction, which we have already seen in the case of noun and adjective formation, is an important factor in determining the correct forms of numerals to use, as well as the correct forms of nouns that may be quantified.

Numerals are not among the obligatory topics for passing **B1** (Threshold Level) of Polish as a Foreign Language Examination. As long as one has a passive knowledge of the numerals, for communication it is not so important to use the correct forms; if you said **mam dwa bracia i dwa siostry* for 'I have two brothers and two sisters' instead of the correct form *mam dwóch braci i dwie siostry*, Poles would probably understand you.

As we look in detail at numerals and quantifiers and how they behave in sentences in Polish, it is worth remembering the following categories of nouns, all of which will have some influence on the correct choice of forms to be used.

- Male persons
- Non-masculine personal masculine and neuter nouns
- Feminine nouns
- Collective nouns

Especially:
- Children and young animals
- Things that generally come in pairs (e.g. *oczy* – 'eyes')

---

[7] 'There were (two) actors, but also (five) politicians and the president with his (two) children.'

[8] 'In the village there were (a lot of) animals: (two) parrots, (two) dogs and (five) cats.'

8.4. Nouns formed from numerals

 While English occasionally uses numerical nouns (a pair, a threesome, a quartet), Polish quite liberally and productively uses numbers to form nouns, and these can refer to any number of different things, from television stations to numbers of buses and trams to marks received in school, to name just a few. Read the dialogues in **Table 8.4.a.** Notice that in each case, the numeral forms a feminine noun which declines.

Table 8.4.a. Numerical nouns in dialogues

– Trzeba jechać **piątką**. – **Piątką**? – Tramwajem numer pięć, a potem **dwójką**. – Tramwajem numer dwa? – Tak.	– You have to take the 5. – The 5? – Yes, tram number 5, and then the 2. – Tram number 2? – Yes.
– Proszę **dwójkę** z łazienką. – Z łazienką są tylko **trójki**, **dwójka** może być z prysznicem. – To proszę **trójkę**, na tydzień.	– I'd like a double room with a bathroom please. – Only triple rooms have a bathroom, the doubles have showers. – Then I'll take a triple for a week.
– Stuknęła mi **trzydziestka**, więc zapraszam was na urodziny. – **Trzydziestka**? Wyglądasz na **dwadzieścia**...	– I've just turned thirty, so let me invite you to my birthday party. – Thirty, you look like twenty ...
– Co dostałeś z historii? – **Szóstkę**, a ty? – **Piątkę**. – Też nieźle.	– What did you get in history? – A six,[9] and you? – A five. – That's not bad either.
– Ile Kowalscy mają dzieci? **Czworo**?[10] – Nie wiem dokładnie, **czwórkę** albo **piątkę**, a wy? – My mamy **dwójkę**, chłopca i dziewczynkę.	– How many kids have the Kowalskis got? Four? – I don't know exactly, four or five, and you? – We have got two, a boy and a girl.
– Hurra! Nasza **jedenastka** wygrywa. Stawiam wszystkim **setę** (COLL). Założę się o **stówę** (COLL), że wygramy trzy do dwóch. – Ale gdzie tam... Na razie jest jeden do zera, ale możecie jeszcze przegrać trzy do jednego...	– Hurrah! Our eleven (football side) is winning! The vodka's on me (in 100 ml glasses). I bet 100 zl that we'll win 3-2. – Wait a second ... Now it's 1-0, but you can still lose 1-3.
– Poproszę te sandały, rozmiar czterdzieści. – Czyli **siódemka**? – Tak, proszę.	– I would like these sandals, size 40. – You mean 7? – Yes, please.

---

[9] In the Polish school system, a six is the best mark, while a one is a fail.

[10] The form *czworo* is actually a collective numeral and not a numerical noun. In fact, Polish speakers will often use numerical nouns to avoid the difficulties of using collective numerals correctly.

The above table presents several examples of numerical nouns. We see them used for: ages (when a multiple of 10), sizes of clothes, number of people in a group, types of hotel rooms, banknote or coin denominations, and several other meanings not listed here. Notice that these are feminine nouns that decline like *matka* 'mother' (see **Table 5.5.h.**). These numerical nouns are extremely common and often replace collective numerals, which have much more complicated case forms (see § 8.11.).

Table 8.4.b. Numerical nouns

jedynka	jedenastka	
dwójka	dw**u**nastka	dwudziestka
trójka	trzynastka	trzydziestka
czwórka	cz**ter**nastka	czterdziestka
piątka	pię**t**nastka	pięćdziesiątka
szóstka	sze**s**nastka	sześćdziesiątka
siódemka	siedemnastka	siedemdziesiątka
ósemka	osiemnastka	osiemdziesiątka
dziewiątka	dziewię**t**nastka	dziewięćdziesiątka
dziesiątka		setka[11] / seta[12] / stówa[13]

The compound numbers above twenty tend not to form numerical nouns – in a clothes shop one might hear *proszę szesnastkę*, but *proszę rozmiar czterdziesty drugi* 'A size sixteen please' but 'A forty-two please'.[14]

8.5. The numeral one: *jeden*

 Read the examples in **Table 8.5.a.** How is the numeral *jeden* declined?

Table 8.5.a. Case forms of: *jeden,* singular[15]

Case	Context 🖿	Masc ♀		Neut ♀	Fem ⚲
		+An 🐎 (animate: persons and animals)	–An ☠ (inanimate: things)		
Nom ●	tu jest	**jeden** redaktor, pokój		**jedno** łóżko	**jedna** łazienka
Gen ⊗	brakuje	jedn**ego** redaktora, pokoju, łóżka			jedn**ej** łazienki
Dat ➡	dzięki	jedn**emu** redaktorowi, pokojowi, łóżku			jedn**ej** łazience
Acc ♥	lubię	jedn**ego** redaktora	jeden pokój	jedn**o** łóżko	jedn**ą** łazienkę
Inst ①	interesuję się	jedn**ym** redaktorem, pokojem, łóżkiem			jedn**ą** łazienką
Loc ●	mówię o	jedn**ym** redaktorze, pokoju, łóżku			jedn**ej** łazience

Jeden, jedno, jedna are declined like adjectives. The numeral *jeden* often translates into English as the indefinite article 'a'. Generally, you should be able to see from the context whether it

---

[11] A neutral form with many different meanings.

[12] A small glass (100 ml) for vodka, used in colloquial language.

[13] Used to denote a hundred zloty banknote, in colloquial language.

[14] These are the same sizes in two different systems.

[15] 'one editor; one room; one bed, one bathroom'; plural forms of *jeden: jedni ludzie* (+MP) or *jedne zwierzęta* (–MP), translate as 'some', 'some people/animals'

means 'a' or 'one'. Compare *Spotkałem wczoraj jednego redaktora, który opowiadał, że...*[16] vs. *Tam było trzech kelnerów, ale tylko jeden redaktor*[17].

 While when it is used by itself, the numeral *jeden* acts as an adjective that agrees in gender, number and case with the noun it refers to, when it is the final element of a compound numeral, *jeden* has a single form that does not change. Read the examples in **Table 8.5.b.**, which also show how the case usage depends on the numeral, as we saw in earlier examples.

Table 8.5.b. Compound numerals ending in *jeden*[18]

	2, 3, 4		Compound numerals ending in *jeden* „1"
	Verb: Pl → Noun: Nom ◓		Verb: Sg → Noun: Gen ☹
Masc ♀	tu są dwa dokumenty		tu jest dwadzieścia jeden dokumentów
Neut ♀	tu są trzy okna		tu jest trzydzieści jeden okien
Fem ⚱	tu są cztery bluzki		tu jest czterdzieści jeden bluzek

8.6. The numeral two: *dwa*

Table 8.6.a. The numeral two: *dwa*

Case	Context 🖼	+Mp 👥[19]	−Mp ✂		
Nom ◓	tu są	**dwaj** rolnicy	**dwa** psy, soki, ciastka		**dwie** herbaty
Gen ☹	brakuje	**dwóch**[20] rolników, psów, soków, ciastek, herbat			
Dat ➡	dzięki	**dwóm** rolnikom, psom, sokom, ciastkom, herbatom			
Acc ♥	widzę	**dwóch** rolników	**dwa** psy, soki, ciastka		**dwie** herbaty
Inst ⓘ	interesuję się	**dwoma** rolnikami, psami, sokami, ciastkami, (**dwiema**) herbatami			
Loc ◓	mówię o	**dwóch** rolnikach, psach, sokach, ciastkach, herbatach			

In the nominative and accusative cases we observe three gender categories for the numeral *dwa*. For male persons we have *dwaj* nominative and *dwóch* accusative, for masculine (non-masculine personal) and for neuter nouns the form is *dwa*, while for feminine nouns we get *dwie*. Section 8.10. will further discuss case usage of numerals with masculine personal nouns. For non personal masculine (and neuter) nouns, see § 8.9. The numerical pronoun *oba* 'both' uses the same declension pattern as *dwa*.

---

[16] 'Yesterday I met an editor, who told me ...'

[17] 'There were three waiters there, but only one editor'.

[18] 'There are two documents / three windows / four blouses here'.

[19] Unlike nouns and adjectives, where there only has to be one male person in a group to use the masculine personal form, with numerals the whole group must consist of male persons. When the group is mixed, the collective *dwoje* is used (see § 8.11.).

[20] There also exists a form *dwu*, which is rarely used (for exercises see Mędak 2004).

Look at the dialogue in **Table 8.6.b.** Notice how the numerical forms change according to what the customers in the coffee house are ordering.

Table 8.6.b. In a coffee house

Kelner	– Co państwo zamawiają?	What can I get for you?
Klienci	– Poprosimy **dwie** kawy, **jedną** z mlekiem, a **jedną** bez. I **dwa** soki pomarańczowe. Albo nie – poproszę **jeden** sok pomarańczowy i **jedną** wodę mineralną. I **dwa** ciastka z bitą śmietaną. A dla dzieci **cztery** cole.	Two coffees, one with milk and one without. And two orange juices. No, one orange juice and one mineral water please. And two pieces of cake with whipped cream. And four Coca Colas for the children.
Kelner	– Niestety, mamy tylko pepsi.	I'm sorry, we only have Pepsi.
Klienci	– Ale ja chcę sok jabłkowy! Ja też!	But I want an apple juice! Me too!
	– To proszę **dwa** soki jabłkowe i **dwie** pepsi.	Then two Pepsis and two apple juices, please.
	– I **cztery** porcje lodów pistacjowych: **dwie** porcje z bitą śmietaną, **jedną** z sosem czekoladowym i **jedną** z owocami.	And four portions of pistachio ice cream, two with whipped cream, one with chocolate sauce and one with fruit.
Kelner	– A dla państwa?	And for you?
Klienci	– **Dwie** duże wódki, **cztery** piwa, **dwa** kieliszki czerwonego wina i butelkę szampana. Aha, i lampkę koniaku dla szefa.	Two large vodkas, four beers, two glasses of red wine and a bottle of champagne. Oh, and a cognac for the boss.'

8.7. Nominative or genitive in sentence constructions

 Compare the constructions in **Table 8.7.a.** What differences do you notice between columns **A.** and **B.**?

Table 8.7.a. Numerals up to 4 and numerals 5 and up

A. 2, 3, 4	B. x ≥ 5	Eng
Tu są dwa kina.	Tu jest pięć kin.	There are 2 / 5 cinemas here.
Tu są sto dwa kina.	Tu jest sto dwadzieścia pięć kin.	There are 102 / 125 cinemas here.
Tu są trzy teatry.	Tu jest sześć teatrów.	There are 3 / 6 computers here.
Tu są cztery sale.	Tu jest czternaście sal.	There are 4 / 14 rooms here.
Tu są dwie restauracje.	Tu jest dwadzieścia restauracji.	There are 2 / 20 restaurants here.
Tu są owoce.[21]	Tu jest dużo owoców.	There is (lots of) fruit here.
Tu jest sok.	Tu jest mało soku.	There is (little) juice here.
Tu jest jabłko.	Tu jest ćwierć jabłka.	There is (a quarters of) an apple here.
Tu jest chleb.	Tu jest pół chleba.	There is (half a loaf of) bread here.

[21] The noun *owoce* 'fruit' may be used in the plural in Polish.

With the numerals 2[22], 3, 4, the numerals appear in the nominative plural and the verb is in the plural as well (verbs have to agree with a nominative subject if there is one, if there isn't a nominative subject, the verb is placed in the third-person (neuter) singular form). With the numerals 5–20, the noun is placed in the genitive plural. In these cases, there is no nominative subject for the verb to agree with, so the verb is used in the singular (neuter) form. The other quantifiers in these examples also take the genitive case.

Table 8.7.b. Nominative or genitive

	VERB: PL → NOUN: NOM	VERB: SG → NOUN: GEN
(...) 2 (...) 3 (...) 4	tu są dwa swetry[23] tu są trzy czapki tu są cztery płaszcze	—
(...) ≥ 5 (...) -naście (...) 0 dużo pół	—	tu jest pięć swetrów tu jest dwanaście czapek tu jest trzydzieści płaszczy tu jest dużo jabłek tu jest pół chleba

8.8. Accusative or genitive in sentence constructions

Compare the constructions in **Table 8.8.a.** What differences do you notice between columns **A.** and **B.**?

Table 8.8.a. Accusative or genitive in sentence constructions

A.	B.	ENG
Anna ma dwa **lata**.	Artur ma pięć **lat**.	X is 2 / 5 years old.
Barbara ma trzy **lata**.	Bogdan ma osiem **lat**.	X is 3 / 8 years old.
Ta książka ma tysiąc sto sześćdziesiąt cztery **lata**.	Ta książka ma tysiąc sto sześćdziesiąt siedem **lat**.	This book is 1164 / 1167 years old.
Beata ma cztery **koty**.	Krzysztof ma dziewięć **kotów**.	X has 4 / 9 cats.
Znam już dwadzieścia trzy **studentki**.	Znam już dwadzieścia jeden **studentek**.	I already know 23 / 21 students.
Zjedliśmy dwa **jabłka**.	Zjedliśmy jedenaście **jabłek**.	We ate 2 / 11 apples.
To kosztuje osiemdziesiąt dwa **złote**.	To kosztuje dwa miliony dwadzieścia **złotych**.	This costs 82 / 2,000,020 zloty.
Kupiłam **owoce**.	Kupiłam dużo **owoców**.	I bought (a lot of) fruit.
Daj mi **sól**.	Daj mi trochę **soli**.	Give me (a little) salt.
Poproszę **chleb**.	Poproszę pół **chleba**.	A loaf / half a loaf of bread, please.

---

[22] Do not forget the various forms of the numeral *dwa*.

[23] 'There are 2 / 5 jumpers here; 3 / 12 caps; 4 / 30 coats; a lot of apples; half a loaf of bread'.

In column **A.**, where the verbs combine in constructions with the numerals **2**, **3**, **4** or in constructions without a quantifier, the noun is used in the accusative case. In other words, in such constructions the numeral does not cause a change in the choice of case. *Beata ma (dwa) koty* 'Beata has (two) cats'. This situation is the same for compound numerals ending in **2**, **3**, **4** – *Znam już (dwadzieścia trzy) studentki* 'I already know (23) (female) students'.

In column **B.**, the verbs combine either with numerals greater than or equal to five, in which case the genitive plural is required, or with other quantifiers requiring the genitive case (either singular or plural depending on the specific noun/context).

Table 8.8.b. Compound numerals: accusative or genitive[24]

(...) 2 (...) 3 (...) 4	+ Acc ♥	(sto) dwa[25] soki trzy herbaty cztery kawy, wina, chleby
(...) ≥ 5 (...) -naście (...) 0 other quantifiers	+ Gen ☹	(sto) pięć soków dwanaście herbat dwadzieścia kaw trochę wina pół chleba

8.9. Numerals with non-masculine personal nouns

Read the examples in **Table 8.9.a.** and look for patterns. In particular notice how the form of *dwa* changes according to gender. Also, pay attention to the form of the verb that is used and what this choice may depend on.

Table 8.9.a. Cardinal numerals: non-masculine personal (–Mp ✄)

		Pres 👆 (and Fut 🖾)[26]			Past 🖾	
A.	tu **są** (tu **będą**)	**dwie**	kobiety	tu **były**	**dwie**	kobiety
B.		dwa	komputery, okna		dwa	komputery, okna
C.		trzy	komputery, okna,		trzy	komputery, okna,
		cztery	kobiety		cztery	kobiety
D.	tu **jest** (tu **będzie**)	pięć	komputerów, okien, kobiet	tu **było** 💡!	pięć	komputerów, okien, kobiet
		sześć			...	
		...			...	
		-naście			-naście	

---

[24] '(one hundred and two) juices; three teas; four coffees; bottles of wine, loaves of bread (a hundred and) five juices; 12 teas; 20 coffees; a little wine; half a loaf of bread'.

[25] Or: *(sto) dwie herbaty*; Do not forget the various forms of the numeral *dwa*.

[26] The future is formed as follows: *Tu będą dwa komputery / dwie kobiety; Tu będzie pięć komputerów / kobiet.*

Numbers ending in: 2, 3, 4

A. + B. + C. In these rows, the verbs are used in the PLURAL with **2, 3, 4** (*tu będą / tu są / tu były*). Notice again the forms of *dwa* depend on the gender – *dwa* komputery / *dwa* psy / *dwa* okna / *dwie* kobiety.

Numbers ending in 5 and higher ...

D. With numerals, unless they end in **2, 3, 4,** the verb goes into the singular. In these cases it is almost as if a default verb form is used because there is no nominative subject to the sentence. In the present tense that default is *jest* (third person singular), in the future it is *będzie* (third person singular), and in the past it is *było* (the singular neuter form).

8.10. Numerals with masculine personal nouns

Table 8.10.a. shows the forms of numerals referring to groups of male persons, as well as the case usage that is associated with these forms. Notice that in the case of numerals, unlike with nouns and adjectives, the ENTIRE group has to be made up of male persons in order for the masculine personal forms to be used (for groups of mixed gender, collective numerals are used, see § 8.11.).

Table 8.10.a. Numerical constructions with masculine personal and non-masculine personal nouns

	No male persons −Mp ✂	Exclusively male persons +Mp 🐴	
	A.	**B.**	**C.**
2 – 4	Tu są **dwie** ciocie, **dwa** auta / psy.	Tu jest **dwóch** wujków.	Tu są **dwaj** wujkowie.
	Tu są **trzy** auta.	Tu jest **trzech** policjantów.	Tu są **trzej** policjanci.
	Tu są **cztery** lalki.	Tu jest **czterech** chłopców.	Tu są **czterej** chłopcy.
x ≥ 5	Tu jest **pięć** sióstr.	Tu jest **pięciu** braci.	—
	Tu jest **sześć** kuzynek.	Tu jest **sześciu** kuzynów.	—
	Tu jest **tysiąc** studentek.	Tu jest **tysiąc** studentów.	—
	2 – 4: VERB: PL → NOUN: NOM ●	**2 – ∞:** VERB: SG → NOUN: GEN ☹ with special form of numeral, see Table 8.6.b.	**2 – 4:** VERB: PL → NOUN: NOM ●
	x ≥ 5: VERB: SG → NOUN: GEN ☹		**x ≥ 5:** —

In column **B.**, notice that everything goes into the genitive case, requiring that the verb be used in the singular. When deciding what form to use in numerical constructions with male persons, remember that the constructions in **B.** are always acceptable. Column **C.** shows special masculine personal forms for the numerals 2, 3, 4 [27]. These forms take the nominative plural and thus require a plural form of the verb. For numerals above 5, there are no nominative masculine personal forms, so the constructions in column **B.** must be used. For numbers **1000** and higher, the neutral forms of the cardinal numerals are used (see **Table 8.1.a.**).

---

[27] These forms are not heard very often in spoken Polish.

Can you fill in the rest of **Table 8.10.b.**?

Table 8.10.b. Cardinal numerals, masculine personal forms (+Mp 🐱)[28]

1 – 10	11 – 19	20 – 90	22, 33, 44…	100 – 999
jeden	jedenastu			stu
dwóch	dwunastu	dwudziestu	dwudziestu dwóch	dwustu
trzech	trzynastu	trzydziestu		trzystu
czterech	czternastu	czterdziestu		czterystu
pięciu	piętnastu	pięćdziesięciu		pięciuset
sześciu	szesnastu	sześćdziesięciu		sześciuset
siedmiu	siedemnastu	siedemdziesięciu		siedmiuset
ośmiu	osiemnastu	osiemdziesięciu		ośmiuset
dziewięciu	dziewiętnastu	dziewięćdziesięciu		dziewięciuset
dziesięciu				

 Table 8.10.c. presents some examples translated from English. Notice that sometimes you may use either column **B.** or **C.**, but the rest of the time you can only use column **B.**

Table 8.10.c. Numerical constructions with masculine personal nouns

	A.	B.	C.
PRES ✋	There are two doctors here.	tu jest dwóch lekarzy	tu są dwaj lekarze
	There are (one hundred and) three doctors here.	tu jest (stu) trzech lekarzy	tu są trzej lekarze
	There are (one hundred and) seven doctors here.	tu jest (stu) siedmiu lekarzy	—
	I see (three hundred and) three doctors.	widzę (trzystu) trzech lekarzy	—
	In the group there are thirty-eight students.	w grupie jest trzydziestu ośmiu studentów	—
	Twenty-eight students are missing from the group.	w grupie brakuje dwudziestu ośmiu studentów	—
PAST	There were two doctors here.	tu **było** dwóch lekarzy	tu **byli** dwaj lekarze
	There were five doctors here.	tu **było** pięciu lekarzy	—
FUT	Two doctors are coming here.	**przyjdzie** dwóch lekarzy	**przyjdą** dwaj lekarze
	Five doctors are coming here.	**przyjdzie** pięciu lekarzy	—

In spoken Polish, the constructions in column **B.** are much more common. Thus, it is a much more useful construction to learn than the one in column **C.**, since it is always usable for numbers up to **1000**, and must be used for all of these forms when the sentence is negated.

---

[28] Missing forms: „*trzydziestu trzech, czterdziestu czterech, pięćdziesięciu pięciu, sześćdziesięciu sześciu, siedemdziesięciu siedmiu, osiemdziesięciu ośmiu, dziewięćdziesięciu dziewięciu*".

8.11. Collective numerals

 Read the examples in **Table 8.11.a.** In the central columns *dwoje* (the collective form of *dwa*), is shown in all its case forms with the noun *dzieci* and its case forms. In the right-hand columns we see the numerical noun *dwójka* used with *dzieci*. Notice that with the numerical noun, the form of *dzieci* does not change – it is always the genitive plural. It is little wonder that native speakers often choose the construction in the right-hand column – it is much simpler.

Table 8.11.a. Declension of the collective numeral and numerical noun 2

Case	CONTEXT 📷	'Correct' form: collective numeral: **dwoje**		Everyday speech: numerical noun **dwójka**[29]	
NOM ⊜	tu jest	dwoje	dzieci	dwójka	
GEN ☹	nie ma	dwojga	dzieci	dwójki	
DAT ➡	wierzę	dwojgu	dzieciom	dwójce	
ACC ♥	lubię	dwoje	dzieci	dwójkę	dzieci
INST ⓘ	interesuję się	dwojgiem	dzieci	dwójką	
LOC ⬢	mówię o	dwojgu	dzieciach	dwójce	
VOC 🗣	o!	dwoje	dzieci	dwójko	

The collective numerals are referred to as such because they often are used with nouns that have some kind of collective meaning. Such nouns include the following categories with which the collective numeral forms are often encountered.

- Children and young animals, e.g. *jedno zwierzątko / troje zwierzątek.*[30]
- Groups of people that include both sexes, e.g. *dwoje rodziców.*[31]
- Nouns that often come in pairs, e.g. *jedno oko / dwoje oczu.*[32]
- Nouns that only exist in the plural, e.g. *dwoje drzwi.*[33]

Looking at **Table 8.11.a.**, we can see that the declension of the collective numeral is quite unusual, making the entire construction more complicated. This has led to a tendency to use the numerical noun. If we want to say 'to look for two children,' *szukać dwojga dzieci* is preferred by Polish grammarians. However, one is much more likely to hear *szukać dwójki dzieci*.

The norms of Polish grammar produce many forms with collective numerals that native speakers tend to avoid:

pięcioro nożyc / spodni 'five (pairs of) scissors, trousers', is typically replaced by *pięć par nożyc / spodni*, schematized in the construction:

*jedna **para**... +* genitive plural, e.g. *jedna **para** spodni*

*dwie, trzy, cztery **pary**... +* genitive plural, e.g. *dwie **pary** spodni*

x ≥ 5 ***par**... +* genitive plural, e.g. *siedem **par** spodni*

---

[29] Declined as a femine noun, like *matka*, see Table 5.5.h.

[30] 'one little animal, three little animals'

[31] 'two parents'

[32] 'one eye / two eyes'

[33] 'two doors'

The declension of the other collective numerals is similar to that of *dwoje* (so we see *trojga, czworga, pięciorga,* etc.). **Table 8.11.b.** shows just a couple of examples of nouns that in a prescriptive version of Polish grammar must be used with collective numerals.

Table 8.11.b. Nouns with collective numerals[34]

troje aktorów[x]	czworo studentów[x]	pięcioro polityków[x]	sześcioro dziewcząt
siedmioro kociąt	ośmioro skrzypiec	dziewięcioro drzwi	dziesięcioro uszu

[x] the groups contain both men and women

8.12. Summary

To close this chapter on numerals, it is worth taking a final look at this difficult aspect of Polish grammar as a whole. When dealing with numerals, there are two basic issues to consider.

- What is the nature of the number itself? What does it end in? Remember an important category is those numbers higher than (or ending in a digit higher than) 5. Thus for the numeral itself we are looking at two categories that affect the behaviour of the forms in a sentence.

  a) 2 – 4

  b) 5 – 21, 25 – 31, …

- What is the nature of the noun that is to be used with the numeral? Remember that in these cases we were dealing with three categories of nouns:

  a) masculine personal,

  b) non-masculine personal,

  c) collectives.

Table 8.12.a. shows examples of each of these three categories embedded in small texts in which all of the grammatical cases are represented.

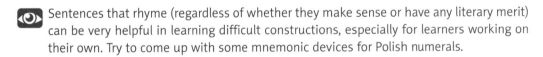 Sentences that rhyme (regardless of whether they make sense or have any literary merit) can be very helpful in learning difficult constructions, especially for learners working on their own. Try to come up with some mnemonic devices for Polish numerals.

- Column **A.**: the prescriptive norms
- Column **B.**: everyday speech
- The italicised portions in column **A.** can be replaced with those from column **B.**

---

[34] 'three actors, four students, five politicians; six girls, seven kittens; eight violins, nine doors (pluralia tantum); ten ears (paired objects)'

Table 8.12.a. Verses with numerical constructions

Cases	A. Standard prescriptive forms	B. Everyday speech
NOM	Przed lustrem są trzej bracia, trzy siostry, no i **troje dzieci** tam stoi; Jest niby sześciu braci, sześć sióstr i **sześcioro dzieci**, bo się wszystko dwoi.[35]	*trójka dzieci* *szóstka dzieci*
GEN	Brakuje dwóch braci i dwóch sióstr, czyli **dzieci czworga**. Będziemy wytrwali. Rymujemy dalej: Brakuje pięciu braci i pięciu sióstr, czyli **dzieci dziesięciorga**...[36]	*czwórki dzieci* *dziesiątki dzieci*
DAT	Początek testamentu: Gratuluję dwom braciom, dwom siostrom i **pięciorgu** ich **dzieciom**: trzem wnukom, dwom wnuczkom i innym spadkobiercom...[37]	*piątce dzieci*
ACC	Mam dwóch braci, dwie siostry, **dwoje dzieci** i dwie żony, ale ten wierszyk nie jest skończony. Masz pięciu braci, pięć sióstr, pięć żon i **pięcioro dzieci**, a tu już następny bocian leci...[38]	*dwójkę dzieci* *piątkę dzieci*
INST	Z dwoma braćmi, z dwoma siostrami i z **dwojgiem** kochanych **dzieci** – miło czas leci.[39]	*dwójką dzieci*
LOC	Bajkę pisałam o dwóch siostrach i o pięciu braciach, czyli o **siedmiorgu dzieciach** i bardzo szybko czas mi zleciał.[40]	*siódemce dzieci*

 Try using the examples in the table as a model to form similar texts about your friends. Try not to think about the theory. Make a note of the construction you use most often.

8.13. Battleships

Pairs such as 13 : 30; 14 : 40 sound very similar and thus give beginners many problems. Those having problems might try playing Battleships in Polish (for those who don't know this game from their childhood, it is simple and can be learned quickly).[41] You need two sheets of paper with numbers as in the model below, and a few expressions that are summed up in **Table 8.13.a.**

Since numerals feature many difficult groups of consonants, the game also provides a useful exercise for pronunciation and listening comprehension.

---

[35] 'NOM 3 brothers, 3 sisters, and 3 children are standing in front of the mirror. It looks like there are 6 brothers, 6 sisters, and 6 children, because everything looks double.'

[36] 'GEN Two brothers and two sisters are missing; that's four children. We'll be persistent , we'll carry on rhyming. Five brothers and five sisters are missing; that's ten children.'

[37] 'DAT The beginning of a will: I congratulate my two brothers, my two sisters, and their five children: three grandsons, two granddaughters, and my other heirs.'

[38] 'ACC I have two brothers, two sisters, two children and two wives, but this poem is not yet finished. You have five brothers, five sisters, five wives, and five children, and the next stork is on the way ...'

[39] 'INST Time passes nicely with two brothers, two sisters, and two lovely children.'

[40] 'LOC I wrote a fable about two sisters and five brothers, that is, about seven children, and the time just flew.'

[41] See for instance http://www.activity village.co.uk/battleships.htm

Table 8.13.a. Expressions for playing Battleships

Ships	Comments	Komentarz
1 Ship with 5 points	'miss'	nietrafiony/pudło
2 Ships with 4 points	'hit'	trafiony
3 Ships with 3 points	'sunk'	znaleziony/zatopiony
4 Ships with 2 points	'What do you say?'	Co mówisz?
5 Ships with 1 point	'Repeat, please'	Powtórz, proszę.

With this game one can communicate for hours in Polish. Have fun!

Examples of ship arrangements:

Gra w okręty

A. Ewa

B. Adam

9 Adverbs: *przysłówki*

 The examples in **Table 9.a.** let us compare adjectives and adverbs. The adjectives are printed in bold and the adverbs in italics. What differences do you notice in form between the two parts of speech? What functions do they have?

Table 9.a. Adjectives vs. adverbs

Szybki samochód *szybko* jedzie.	A fast car drives fast.
Szybkim samochodem można *szybko* jechać.	In a fast car you can drive fast.
Dobre wino *dobrze* smakuje.	A good wine tastes good.
Dobra pralka *dobrze* pierze.	A good washing machine washes clothes well.
Inteligentni politycy mówią *inteligentnie*.	Intelligent politicians speak intelligently.
Dobre ciastka *dobrze* smakują.	Good cakes taste good.
Ewa *bardzo szybko* mówi, ale *bardzo wolno* pisze.	Ewa speaks very quickly, but she writes very slowly.
Twoja córka jest **bardzo sympatyczna**.	Your daughter is very nice.
Masz **bardzo sympatyczną** córkę.	You have a very nice daughter.

Since adjectives refer to nouns; in Polish they are inflected for case, number, and gender just as nouns are. Adverbs, on the other hand, modify either a verb or an adjective, and in Polish do not change forms. We can see this in the examples in the table. In English, a common way of forming adverbs is by adding the suffix *-ly* to an adjective ('comfortable' – 'comfortably'). Notice that while in some cases in English (e.g. 'fast') you can only tell from the context whether a word is an adjective or an adverb, in Polish it is clear from the ending which part of speech we are dealing with. Also, notice in the table that the English translations do not always use the same parts of speech as the Polish. For example, verbs like 'taste' in English are used with adjectives (as is the verb 'to be'), while in Polish the equivalent *smakować* is modified by an adverb.

Adverbs and adverbial expressions can come in many varieties in Polish. While the most basic variety includes those formed from adjectives, we may also observe adverbials formed from nouns and prepositional expressions (e.g. *po polsku, na złość*). In **Table 9.b.** adverbials are presented (printed in bold letters) according to what types of questions they might answer.[1]

Table 9.b. Adverbs and adverbial phrases in sentence constructions

| jak? | how? | **Całkiem dobrze** wyglądasz. **Lepiej** niż wczoraj? On mówi **naprawdę dość dobrze (wyraźnie, bezbłędnie) po polsku**, ale gorzej **po niemiecku**. Powiedz mu **po prostu** prawdę. **Nawet nieźle** mi poszło. | You look quite good.[2] Better than yesterday? He speaks Polish really quite well (clearly, correctly), but he speaks worse in German. Just tell him the truth. I didn't do badly at all. |
| kiedy? | when? | Myślę o tobie **często**: **rano**, **w południe, wieczorem** i **w nocy**. **Właśnie teraz** o tobie myślę. | I often think about you: in the morning, in the afternoon, in the evening, and at night. Right now I am thinking about you. |

[1] Using question words can be a useful way of remembering when to use given grammatical forms in Polish.

[2] This is another case where English will use an adjective while Polish uses an adverb. Other examples include the verbs *czuć się, brzmieć* ('feel, sound').

gdzie?	where?	Byłam **tu** i **tam**, **blisko** i **daleko**, **wszędzie** go szukałam, **nigdzie** go nie znalazłam.	I was here and there, near and far. I looked everywhere for him. I didn't find him anywhere.
ile?	how many?	Miałem **bardzo dużo** pieniędzy, a teraz mam **bardzo mało**.	I had a lot of money, but now I have very little.
dlaczego?	why?	Uciekłam z domu **na złość** rodzicom. Nie szukali mnie **ze złości**.	I ran away from home to spite my parents. They didn't look for me out of spite.

Adverbs are most often formed from adjectives with the help of either the suffix *-(i)e* or *-o*, *ładn/y* : *ładnie, wysok/i* : *wysoko*.

Many adverbs also have comparative forms, generally formed with the suffix *-ej*. Some of the more common adjectives form irregular comparatives: *dobrze* → *lepiej*.

Look at the examples in **Table 9.c.** What do the adverbs end in? What stem alternations can you observe?

Table 9.c. Adverbs and their comparative forms

Positive	Positive	Comparative	Positive	Positive	Comparative
A.			**C.**		
warm-heartedly	serdecznie	serdeczn**iej**	very	bar**dzo**	bar**dziej**
nicely, well	ładnie	ładn**iej**	often	czę**sto**	czę**ściej**
exactly	dokładnie	dokładn**iej**	difficult	trud**no**	trud**niej**
interestingly	ciekawie	ciekaw**iej**	easily	ła**two**	ła**twiej**
early	wcześnie	wcześn**iej**	late	póź**no**	póź**niej**
beautifully	pięknie	piękn**iej**	quietly	ci**cho**	ci**szej**
clearly	wyraźnie	wyraźn**iej**	loudly	gło**sno**	głoś**niej**
cool, super[3]	fajnie	fajn**iej**	long	dłu**go**	dłu**żej**
B.			**D.**		
a lot/many	dużo, wiele	więcej	fast	szyb**ko**	szyb**ciej**
little	mało	mniej	close	bli**sko**	bli**żej**
well	dobrze	lepiej	far	dal**eko**	dal**ej**
badly	źle	gorzej	high	wy**soko**	wy**żej**
lightly	lekko	lżej	deep	głę**boko**	głę**biej**

Observe the endings that are used to form adverbs from adjectives. Also notice that in some of these cases, the Polish usage will not always match up with the English meaning (e.g. *ładny* 'pretty' vs. *ładnie* 'well, nicely'). In addition, in some instances (e.g. *fajnie*), English would not use an adverb.

A. In the forms in column **A.**, we find adverbs ending in *-(i)e* that derive from adjectives in *-ny*, e.g. ***serdeczny* : *serdecznie*, *ładny* : *ładnie*** (though unfortunately not all such adjectives form this kind of adverb, see column **C.**). To form the comparative of these adverbs, simply add *-j*.

---

[3] These cannot be used as adverbs in English.

B. A few adverbs, referred to as suppletive, form comparatives from completely different words (consider 'good' vs. 'well' in English). Such forms must unfortunately be memorised, but since they are so commonly used, learners should acquire them quickly: *dobrze : lepiej, mało : mniej, dużo : więcej, źle : gorzej.*

C. A number of adjectives form adverbs ending in *-o*: *długi → długo, tygodniowy → tygodniowo, duży → dużo, stary → staro.* Some adjectives in *-ny* also have adverbs in *-o*: *trudny → trudno, brudny → brudno.*

C. + D. Adverbs ending in *-o* undergo alternations in the comparative form (see § 3.6.). The ending *-ej* palatalises the consonant at the end of the stem: *-sto → -ściej (często → częściej), -cho → -szej (cicho → ciszej).* Adverbs containing the suffix *-ko, -eko,* or *-oko* will lose this suffix in the comparative form – the *-ej* ending is added directly to the stem, causing alternations: *blis(ko) → bliżej.*

As with adjectival comparison, there are two main possible ways of forming comparative adverbial constructions. Read the examples in **Table 9.d.** Are there any parallels with the adjectival constructions in Chapter 6?

Table 9.d. Comparative constructions

niż + Nom	od + Gen	ENG
Zacząłem czytać wcześniej **niż** ty.	Zacząłem czytać wcześniej **od** ciebie.	I started reading earlier than you.
Jeżdżę na nartach szybciej **niż** wy.	Jeżdżę na nartach szybciej **od** was.	I ski faster than you.
Śpiewam lepiej **niż** Beata.	Śpiewam lepiej **od** Beaty.	I sing better than Beata.

The construction *niż + nominative* is somewhat easier to learn and generally used more frequently than *od + genitive*.

Table 9.e. shows some examples of these superlative adverbial constructions. Can you spot any patterns?

Table 9.e. Comparative and superlative adverbial constructions

Który z tych obrazów **najbardziej** ci się podoba?	Which of these pictures do you like best?
Kto z was **najlepiej** mówi po polsku?	Who among you speaks Polish best?
Ewa najczęściej odwiedza rodziców, bo **najbliżej** mieszka.	Ewa visits her parents most often because she lives the closest.
Z kim **najchętniej** rozmawiasz o swoich problemach?	With whom are you most willing to talk about your problems?
Kto **najszybciej** pisze SMS-y?	Who writes text messages the fastest?
Chciałabym △ **jak najwięcej** zarabiać i **jak najmniej** pracować.	I would like to earn as much as I can and work as little as I can.
Chcę, żebyś **jak najszybciej** przyjechał ⚲ i **jak najdłużej** tu został ⚲.	I want you to come as quickly as possible and stay as long as possible.

Dowiedziałam się Δ o tym **najpóźniej** ze wszystkich.	I was the last to find out about this.
Wyglądała Δ **najpiękniej** ze wszystkich.	She looked the best of them all.
Nasze dzieci zachowują się **coraz bardziej tajemniczo**.	Our children are behaving more and more secretively.
Adam przychodzi do biura **coraz mniej punktualnie**.	Adam comes to the office less and less punctually.

As with adjectives, superlative adverbial constructions are also formed with the help of the prefix *naj-*. Note that with adverbs we also see simple and compound comparatives and superlatives. Notice two useful constructions with the superlative in the above table. The first, with *jak*, gives the meaning 'as X as possible', *skończę jak najwcześniej* – 'I will finish as soon as possible'. The other with *coraz* expresses the notion of 'more and more' (or 'less and less', i.e. the adverb in increasing or decreasing magnitude), *Mówisz coraz lepiej po polsku* – 'You speak Polish better and better'. Diminutive adverbs are used to express some sort of affection on the part of the speaker toward what is being said. They are exceedingly difficult to translate into English. Advanced learners of Polish will start to develop an intuition for their use. **Table 9.f.** shows some examples. Note that there are two grades of diminutive.

Table 9.f. Adverbs: Diminutive

Positive	Dim 1. Grade	Dim 2. Grade	ENG
mało	ma**lutko**, ma**leńko**	ma**ciupeńko**	very little
szybko	szyb**ciutko**	szyb**ciuteńko**	very quickly
krótko	kró**ciutko**	kró**ciuteńko**	very short
trochę	tro**szkę**	tro**szeczkę**[4]	very little, just a little bit

Table 9.g. shows a dialogue with some examples of diminutives in action. Try to translate the dialogues yourself before reading the translation.

Table 9.g. Diminutive adverbs in context

Context	Examples	
At the table:	– Może jeszcze troszkę sałatki? – No dobrze, ale tylko troszeczkę. – A winka? – Chętnie, ale tylko maciupeńko, jestem zmęczony.	– Maybe a bit more salad? – OK, but just a little bit. – And a bit of wine? – OK, but just a little bit, I am tired.
Mother and son:	– Mamuniu, mogę iść do kolegi? – No dobrze, ale wróć szybciuteńko, bo zaraz będzie obiadek.	– Mummy, can I go to my friend's house? – Ok, but come back quickly because we're having dinner soon.
Father and daughter:	– Tatuś, mogę wziąć samochód? – Nie. – Tatulku... – Daj spokój. – Tatuleńku, proszę, na króciutko. – Hmmm...	– Dad, can I take the car? – No. – Daddy ... – Give it a rest. – But Daddy, please, just for a short time. – Hmmm ...

[4] In everyday speech, the most common diminutive form is *troszeczkę* 'a little bit'.

10 Prepositions: *przyimki*

10.1. Prepositions with cases

A preposition is a non-inflected word that expresses some kind of relationship between the main element of a sentence and the noun phrase that the preposition modifies. Prepositions may govern a single case or many cases (with different meanings). As far as meaning is concerned prepositions can be divided into the following categories:

- prepositions expressing location, position, or spatial relationships (*obok* 'next to'; *naprzeciwko* 'across from'),
- prepositions expressing temporal relationships (*podczas* 'during'; *o* 'at (a certain hour')),
- causal prepositions expressing reason (*dzięki* 'thanks to; *z powodu* 'because of').

Of course, as in English, in Polish prepositions can have many other figurative meanings. Also, very often we will notice that when a preposition has a different function it will use a different case: *idę na wystawę*: accusative; *jestem na wystawie*: locative.[1] The first sentence answers the question: 'where to?', and the second one answers the question 'where?'. Notice that while in English the distinction is made by using a different preposition – '**to** the exhibition vs. **at** the exhibition', Polish employs the same preposition in both situations, but a different case of the following noun is required depending on whether a location ('where?') or a destination ('where to?') is meant. In the above example, in the first sentence, the *na* with the accusative expresses that the noun is a destination, while the locative after *na* expresses a location.

Polish prepositions for each case are presented in **Tables 10.1.a.** to **10.1.f.** which include examples. The most common prepositions are printed in bold.

Many prepositions ending in a consonant will show alternations, with an *-e* appearing at the the end, e.g. **z(e), w(e).** It is worth remembering the following: the vowel will often appear before consonant clusters, see **bez** *ciebie i* **beze** *mnie* 'without you and without me'.

The English equivalents of the prepositions are not given in the table, since there are many possible discrepancies in translation due to the many meanings prepositions can have (e.g. *od* literally means 'away from', but can also mean 'since, from, than', etc.)

[x] = The upper case x symbol (PxP)marks what might be called compound prepositions, essentially made by combining two prepositions into one word, e.g. *z* 'from'+ *pod* 'under' = *spod* 'from under'. These often express the direction and source of physical movement.

Table 10.1.a. Prepositions with the Genitive (*kogo? czego?*)

Preposition	Examples	ENG
bez	zadanie domowe **bez** błędów	homework without mistakes
	idź do kina **beze** mnie	go to the cinema without me
	bez problemu	no problem
	niebo **bez** gwiazd	sky without stars
	wyszła **bez** słowa	she went out without a word
dla	to (nie) **dla** ciebie	this is (not) for you
	piszę wiersze d**la** przyjemności, a nie **dla** pieniędzy	I write poems for pleasure, not for money
	przedział **dla** niepalących	a compartment for non-smokers
	jesteś **dla** niego niesprawiedliwy	you are not fair to him

[1] 'I'm going to the exhibition, I am at the exhibition'.

Preposition	Examples	Eng
do	nie idę ani **do** koleżanki, ani **do** teatru, lecz **do** domu	I am not going to my friend's, nor am I going to the theatre. I am going home. (destination)
	Czy chcesz coś **do** picia?	Do you want something to drink?
	piszę list **do** przyjaciółki	I'm writing a letter to my friend
	będę czekać **do** czwartej	I will wait until four
	pasta **do** zębów	toothpaste
dookoła ≈ dokoła, wokół, naokoło	pies biega **d(o)okoła / wokół / naokoło** stołu	the dog is running around the table
	podróż **dookoła** świata	a trip around the world
koło[2] ≈ obok	znalazłam tego kota **koło** dworca	I found this cat by the station
	usiądź **koło / obok** mnie	sit next to me
	basen jest **koło / obok** hotelu	the swimming pool is by the hotel
mimo	pracuję **mimo** choroby	I am working despite my illness
naprzeciw ≈ naprzeciwko	szpital jest **naprzeciw(ko)** ratusza	the hospital is across from the townhall
od(e)	to prezent **od** taty i **ode** mnie	this is a present from me and from dad
	Od czego boli cię głowa?	Why (from what) do you have a headache?
	pracuję **od** ósmej **do** dwunastej	I work from 8 until 12
	od dzisiaj będę więcej pracować	as of today I will work more
	jesteś starszy **od** Ewy i **ode** mnie	you are older than Ewa and me
	syrop **od** kaszlu	cough mixture/syrup
około ≈ koło	wrócił **(o)koło** północy	he came back at about / around midnight
	to wino ma **(o)koło** pięciu lat	this wine is about 5 years old
oprócz	wszyscy **oprócz** mnie tam byli	everyone was there except for me
	ten hotel jest zaniedbany, a **oprócz** tego za drogi	this hotel is run down, and aside from that it is too expensive
podczas	**podczas** lekcji nie należy spać	during class you shouldn't sleep
	podczas koncertu zadzwonił telefon	the phone rang during the concert
	przytyłam **podczas** wakacji	I gained weight during the summer holiday
poniżej	część Holandii leży **poniżej** poziomu morza	part of the Netherlands lies below sea level
	sprzedał dom **poniżej** jego wartości	he sold his house for less than it was worth
powyżej	mieszkają **powyżej** wsi	they live above the village
spod[x]	wyjmij walizkę **spod** łóżka	take the suitcase out from under the bed
	pochodzę **spod** Wiednia	I come from outside of Vienna
spomiędzy[x]	wyciągnij mój zeszyt **spomiędzy** książek	take out my notebook from in between/ among the books

---

[2] *koło* and *obok*: position (e.g. *koło / obok stołu* 'by the table'); *koło* and *około*: time (e.g. *koło / około północy* 'about midnight')

Preposition	Examples	Eng
spośród	**spośród** twoich znajomych najbardziej lubię Jana	of all your friends I like Jan the best
spoza ≈ zza[x]	księżyc wyszedł **spoza** chmury	the moon came out from behind the cloud
	kot nie mógł wyjść **zza** szafy	the cat couldn't get out from behind the wardrobe
	on pochodzi **spoza** Polski	he comes from outside of Poland
sprzed[x]	pociąg uciekł mi **sprzed** nosa	the train escaped from in front of my nose
	to zdjęcia / fotografie **sprzed** wojny	these are photos from before the war
u	mieszkamy **u** rodziców	we live at our parents'
	podpisz się tu **u** góry	sign here at the top
w czasie ≈ w ciągu	poznaliśmy się **w czasie** urlopu	we met during our leave from work
	w ciągu trzech lat nakręciła osiem filmów	she made 8 films in 3 years
według	**według** prawa	in accordance with the law
	według mnie	in my opinion
wśród	dobrze się czuję **wśród** młodych ludzi	I feel good among young people
wzdłuż	szliśmy **wzdłuż** rzeki	we walked along the river
z(e)	jestem **z** Polski, a on **ze** Szwecji	I am from Poland and he's from Sweden
	mam zegarek **ze** złota	I have a watch made of gold
	moje mieszkanie składa się **z** trzech pokoi	my apartment consists of three rooms
	nie lubię zdjęć **z** bliska	I don't like close-up shots
zamiast	Nie masz soku? Daj mi **zamiast** tego herbatę.	Don't you have juice? Give me tea instead.
	zamiast ryżu poproszę ziemniaki	instead of rice I'd like potatoes
znad[x]	jutro wracamy **znad** morza	we're returning from the seaside tomorrow
z powodu	odwołał referat **z powodu** choroby	he cancelled his talk because of illness

Table 10.1.b. Prepositions with the dative (*komu? czemu?*)

Preposition	Examples	Eng
dzięki	nauczyłam się pływać **dzięki** twojej pomocy	thanks to your help I learnt/learned to swim
naprzeciw ≈ naprzeciwko	Ala wyszła **naprzeciw** matce	Ala went forward to meet her mother
na przekór ≈ na złość	nie chciał studiować **na przekór** rodzicom	he didn't want to go to University to spite his parents
przeciw ≈ przeciwko	wszyscy są **przeciwko** mnie	everyone is against me

Table 10.1.c. Prepositions with the Accusative (*kogo? co?*)

Preposition	Examples	ENG
między ≈ pomiędzy[x]	schowaj pieniądze (**po**)**między** dwie książki	put the money between two books
na	połóż gazetę **na** stół	put the newspaper on the table
	on jest chory **na** grypę	he is sick with the flu/he has flu
	idź **na** górę, nie schodź **na** dół	go upstairs, not downstairs
	idę **na** uniwersytet, a potem **na** pocztę i **na** koncert	I am going to the university, then to the post office, then to a concert
	sto kilometrów **na** godzinę	100 kilometers per hour
	idziemy **na** zebranie	we are going to the meeting
	chcę wyjechać tylko **na** tydzień, a nie **na** zawsze	I only want to leave for a week and not forever
	ptaki lecą **na** południe	the birds are flying south
nad	idę **nad** rzekę	I am going to the river
	jadę **nad** morze, a ty **nad** jezioro	I am going to the seaside, and you to the lake
o	kłócimy się **o** drobiazgi	we quarrel about little things
	znów pytał **o** ciebie	he asked about you again
	oprzyj się **o** mnie	lean on me
	proszę **o** sok pomarańczowy	an orange juice, please
po	proszę dwa lody **po** trzy euro	two ice creams at/for 3 euro apiece
	przyjedź **po** mnie na lotnisko	come get me at the airport
pod	kot wszedł **pod** szafę	the cat went under the wardrobe
	przyjdę **pod** wieczór	I will come towards the evening
	zdrowe ryby płyną **pod** prąd	healthy fish swim against the current
	podjedź **pod** garaż	drive up to the garage
ponad	czekam już **ponad** godzinę	I've been waiting for more than an hour
	to drzewo wyrosło **ponad** inne	this tree grew higher than the others
poza[x]	**poza** pracą nic go nie interesuje	aside from work, nothing interests him
przed(e)	wyjdź **przed** dom	go out in front of the house
przez(e)	nie przechodź sama **przez** ulicę	don't cross the street alone
	trzeba przejechać **przez** centrum	you have to drive across the city centre
	przeze mnie masz teraz kłopoty	because of me you have problems now
	kłócili się (**przez**) trzy lata	they quarreled for three years
w(e)	jedź **w** lewo, a potem **w** prawo	go left and then right
	przyjadę **we** wtorek albo **w** piątek	I will come on Tuesday or on Friday
	biegaliśmy **w** dół i **w** górę	we ran up and down
	zrobimy to **w** trójkę	the three of us will do it
	ma sukienkę **w** kratkę, a bluzkę **w** paski	she has a checked dress and a striped blouse
za	schowaj się **za** dom	hide behind the house
	za bilet zapłaciłam osiem euro	I paid 8 euros for the ticket
	przyjdę **za** godzinę	I will come in an hour

Table 10.1.d. Prepositions with the Instrumental (*z kim? z czym?*)

Preposition	Examples	Eng
między ≈ **pomiędzy**[x]	chcę siedzieć (**po**)**między** córką i synem	I want to sit between my daughter and my son
nad	lecimy **nad** Warszawą	we are flying above Warsaw
	jestem **nad** rzeką	I am on the riverbanks
	jestem **nad** morzem, a ty **nad** jeziorem	I am at the seaside and you are by the lake
	zasnęłam dopiero **nad** ranem	I fell asleep before dawn
pod	kot śpi **pod** szafą	the cat's sleeping under the wardrobe
	pracuję **pod** Krakowem	I work in the suburbs of Krakow
	pod warunkiem, że tego więcej nie zrobisz	on the condition that you don't do that anymore
ponad[x]	lecimy **ponad** chmurami	we are flying above the clouds
poza[x]	mieszkamy **poza** Warszawą	we live outside of Warsaw
	a **poza** tym wszystko w porządku	aside from that, everything's OK
	poza pracą nic go nie interesuje	besides work he's not interested in anything
przed(e)	czekam **przed** domem	I'm waiting in front of the house
	przyjdź do nas **przed** dziewiątą	come before nine
	przede wszystkim przestań płakać	first of all, stop crying
w związku z	dostałem list **w związku z** wypadkiem	I got a letter in connection with the accident
zgodnie z	Nie umiesz jeździć **zgodnie z** przepisami?	Can't you drive in accordance with the Highway Code?
z(e)	sąsiadka **ze** starym psem kłóci się **z** sąsiadką **z** kotem	the neighbour with the old dog is quarreling with the neighbour with the cat
za	schował się **za** drzewem	he hid behind the tree
	detektyw szedł **za** podejrzanym	the detective trailed the suspect

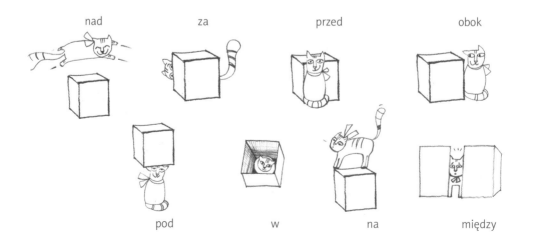

nad   za   przed   obok

pod   w   na   między

Table 10.1.e. Prepositions with the Locative (*o kim? o czym?*)

Preposition	Examples	Eng
na	gazeta jest **na** stole	the newspaper is on the table
	Jesteś **na** uniwersytecie czy **na** poczcie?	Are you at the university or at the post office?
	chcę mieszkać **na** górze, a nie **na** dole	I want to live upstairs, not downstairs
	mieszkał **na** wsi, **na** Ukrainie	he lived in the country, in Ukraine
o	mówię **o** synu i (**o**) córce	I am speaking about my son and daughter
	wróć **o** dziesiątej	come back at ten
	opowiedz mi **o** swoim przyjacielu	tell me about your friend
	myślę **o** was	I'm thinking about you
po	**po** pracy przyjdę **po** ciebie	after work I will come and get you
	nie skacz **po** kanapie	don't jump around on the sofa
	mam czas **po** południu	I have time in the afternoon
przy	usiądź **przy** mnie	sit down by me
	Chce pani siedzieć **przy** drzwiach czy **przy** oknie?	Do you want to sit by the door or by the window?
	Mógłbyś to **przy** okazji załatwić?	Could you take care of this at the same time?
	przy tej okazji chcę ci pogratulować	(on this occasion) I would like to congratulate you
w(e)	**w** nocy pracuję **w** barze	at night I work in a bar
	byliśmy w górach, **w** Tyrolu, **w** Austrii i **we** Włoszech	we were in the mountains, in Tyrol, in Austria and in Italy
	pomóż mi **w** pracy	help me at work
	jestem **w** delegacji	I am on a business trip
	urodził się **w** sierpniu albo **we** wrześniu, **w** roku 1979	he was born in August or September, in 1979

Summary:

It can be difficult to determine which preposition and which case to use. It is often useful to think of the possible questions they might answer, in particular the words ***dokąd, gdzie, skąd*** ('where to? (destination)[3], where?, (location), where from? (origin)). For example, if the noun is in the accusative, the phrase most likely expresses a destination (*idziemy **na** zebranie* – 'we're going to the meeting'). The question words *dokąd, gdzie, skąd* are answered with nouns denoting places. These types of places can be divided into three categories:

1. a person
2. an enclosed space, town or country
3. an open space or event.

With these categories of places we may find some patterns in connection with the question words. While there are many exceptions, learning these tendencies (summed up in **Table 10.1.f.**) will help one to know which preposition and which case should be used in a given situation:

---

[3] See § 4.7. on verbs of motion; these verbs may explicitly express the notion of a destination as opposed to a location.

Try to figure out what is the grammatical structure of the examples given in **Table 10.1.f.**

Table 10.1.f. Some tendencies in the choice of preposition and case

	dokąd?	gdzie?	skąd?
a person	Idziemy do babci.	Jesteśmy u babci.	Wracamy od babci.
	Idę do fryzjera.	Jestem u fryzjera.	Wracam od fryzjera.
a town, country or enclosed space	Idę do biura.	Jestem w biurze.	Wracam z biura.
	Jan idzie do swojego pokoju.	Jan jest w swoim pokoju.	Jan wyszedł z pokoju.
	Jedziemy do parku czy do lasu?	Gdzie wczoraj byłeś, w parku czy w lesie?	Skąd wracacie, z parku czy z lasu?
	Pojechałem do Warszawy.	Byłem w Warszawie.	Skąd wracacie, z parku czy z lasu?
	On przyjedzie do Polski.	On będzie w Polsce.	On wrócił z Polski.
an open space or event	Idziemy na boisko.	Jesteśmy na boisku.	Wracamy z boiska.
	Idziemy na mecz Polska-Niemcy.	Jesteśmy na meczu Polska-Niemcy.	Wracamy z meczu Polska-Niemcy.
a person	We're going to grandma's.	We're at grandma's.	We're returning from grandma's.
	I'm going to the hair-dresser's.	I'm at the hairdresser's.	I'm returning from the hairdresser's.
a town, country or enclosed space	I'm going to the office.	I'm at the office.	I'm returning from the office.
	Jan is going to his room.	Jan is in his room.	Jan left the room.
	Are we going to the park or to the forest?	Where were you yesterday, at the park or in the forest?	Where are you (plural) coming from, the park or the forest?
	I went to Warsaw.	I was in Warsaw.	I got back from Warsaw.
	He will come to Poland.	He will be in Poland.	He got back from Poland.
an open space or event	We're going to the pitch / court.	We are on the pitch / court.	We're returning from the pitch / court.
	We're going to the Poland – Germany match.	We're at the Poland – Germany match.	We're returning from the Poland – Germany match.

Table 10.1.g. helps to make a summary of the grammatical structures shown in **Table 10.1.f.**

Table 10.1.g. Dynamic and static syntactic structures

	Where are you going? (dynamic structure) dokąd?	Where are you? (static structure) gdzie?	Where are you coming back from?(dynamic structure) skąd?
a person	do + genitive	u + genitive	od + genitive
a town, country or enclosed space	do + genitive	w + locative	z + genitive
an open space or event / abstract / goal	na + accusative	na + locative	z + genitive

Notice that these prepositions take the accusative with destinations, the locative with locations, and the genitive for origins.

Overall, prepositions are a very difficult area of Polish for English speakers. The learner must overcome the natural urge to try to translate literally from his or her native language, since often there is simply no direct equivalent. A preposition such as *na* can have multiple equivalents in English: *idę na pocztę, jestem na poczcie, idziemy na kawę, ksiażka jest na stole* 'I'm going *to* the post office, I am *at* the post office, we're going *for* coffee, the book is *on* the table'. These different meanings will often have to be memorized. At the same time Polish may use prepositions where English does not, and vice versa.

10.2. Prepositions and verbal prefixes

 Compare **Table 10.2.a.** with **Table 4.8.d.** (modification of verb meaning using prepositions). Can you see the connections between the prefixes and the prepositions?

Table 10.2.a. Prepositions and Verbal prefixes

naklej znaczek **na** kopertę	glue the stamp on the envelope
odejdź **od** mojego auta	get away from my car
zejdź **z** drzewa	get down from the tree
podłóż serwetkę **pod** talerz	put the napkin under the plate
przechodź ostrożnie **przez** ulicę	cross the street carefully

Although prepositions like *podczas* 'during' and *wzdłuż* 'along' translate perfectly well into English as they may be listed in the dictionary, in general it is a good idea to learn prepositions using entire prepositional phrases. Since a single preposition can have so many meanings, phrases will be much more helpful. For example, *o* can translate as '*about*' (*myślę o pracy* – 'I am thinking about work'), '*for*' (*prosiłem o miejsce przy oknie* – 'I asked for a window seat'), or '*at*' (*wstałem o ósmej* – 'I got up at eight').

It is imperative for learners to master prepositions in context, especially through conscious reading exercises. One can, for example, underline all the prepositions in an interesting text, and then go back and analyse the constructions. This way, one can learn an entire expression including the case form.

11 Conjunctions: *spójniki*

11.1. Conjunctions in sentences

Conjunctions are used to combine words, groups of words, phrases, or clauses. One unusual feature of Polish conjunctions is that they may have personal endings attached to them (see § 11.3.). Also, one of the most frequently encountered Polish conjunctions, namely *a*, does not quite have a direct English equivalent (see § 11.2.), translatable by 'and' or 'but' depending on the situation. Thus, although one may find equivalents in a dictionary, it takes time and practice to use them correctly in sentences.

 Table 11.1.a. shows examples of common Polish conjunctions in use. The doubletilde ≈ indicates that the two conjunctions have essentially the same meaning. In such cases the example on the left is typical of the spoken language, while the one on the right is more likely to be found in written Polish or in more formal spoken language.[1] What is the difference between the conjunctions in **A.** and **B.**?

Table 11.1.a. Polish Conjunctions and their English equivalents

A.			
a	Ja mam pięćdziesiąt lat, **a** mój mąż czterdzieści.	I am 50 years old, and/but my husband is 40.	and (with contrast), but
albo ≈ lub	Kup bułki **albo** / **lub** chleb.	Buy rolls or bread.	or
albo..., albo	Mogę ci pomóc **albo** w niedzielę, **albo** we wtorek.	I can help you either on Sunday or on Tuesday.	either ... or
ale ≈ lecz	Chciałabym ci pomóc, **ale** / **lecz** nie mam czasu.	I would like to help you, but I don't have time.	but
ani..., ani	**Ani** siostra, **ani** brat nie pomogli mi przy przeprowadzce.	Neither my sister nor my brother helped me when I was moving.	neither ... nor
czyli	Nie przyszedł, **czyli** muszę wszystko zrobić sama.	He did not come, so I have to do everything myself.	so; that means
dlatego ≈ toteż	Pomogliście mi, **dlatego** / **toteż** mam dla was niespodziankę.	You helped me, so I have a surprise for you.	therefore, so
i ≈ oraz	Chciałbym mieć małe mieszkanie w mieście **i** / **oraz** domek nad jeziorem.	I would like to have a small flat/apartment in the city and a cottage by a lake.	and
i... i	Widziałam **i** Ewę, **i** Adama.	I saw both Ewa and Adam.	both ... and

---

[1] The longer version is often more official, e.g. *bo*: common in the spoken language for 'because'; it has other variants: *ponieważ / gdyż / (al)bowiem*, which are typical for the written language.

jednak(że)	Chciałam być ratownikiem, **jednakże** ojciec mi na to nie pozwolił.	I wanted to be a lifeguard, but my father did not let me.	but, however
tak..., jak i ≈ zarówno..., jak i	**Zarówno** Niemcy, **jak i** Związek Radziecki napadły na Polskę we wrześniu 1939 roku.	Both Germany and the Soviet Union attacked Poland in 1939.	both ... and
też ≈ także / również	Siostra mi pomogła, brat **też** / **także** / **również**. Pomagałam ci w środę i w czwartek, a **także** w sobotę.	My sister helped me, and my brother helped me too. I helped you on Wednesday and on Thursday, and also on Saturday.	too, also
natomiast	Siostra mi pomogła, **natomiast** brat nawet nie zadzwonił.	My sister helped me, while my brother didn't even call.	while, whereas (on the other hand)
nie tylko... lecz także / ale także / ale i	**Nie tylko** brat i siostra, **ale także** wszyscy sąsiedzi nam pomagali.	Not only my brother and sister, but also all our neighbours helped us.	not only ... but also
to znaczy (tzn.) / to jest (tj.)	Przymiotniki można odmieniać, **to znaczy**, (**że**) należą one do deklinabiliów.	Adjectives can change form, which means they are declinable.	which (that) means
więc ≈ zatem	Bardzo mi pomogliście, **więc** chciałabym was zaprosić na kolację.	You really helped me a lot, so I would like to invite you for dinner.	so, thus
B.			
aż	Pił i pił, **aż** wszystko wypił.	He drank and drank until he had drunk everything.	until
bo ≈ ponieważ / gdyż / bowiem	Zamknij okno, **bo** mi zimno. Powstanie Warszawskie upadło, **gdyż** / **bowiem** / **ponieważ** alianci nie udzielili Polakom obiecanej pomocy.	Close the window because I am cold. The Warsaw Uprising failed because the Allies failed to give the Poles the assistance they had promised.	because
czy	Nie wiem, **czy** on mi pomoże.	I don't know if he will help me.	if, whether
chociaż / choć	**Chociaż** / **choć** wzięła taksówkę, nie zdążyła na pociąg.	Even though she took a taxi she still missed her train.	though, although, even though
chociaż**by**, choć**by**	**Chociażbyś** / **choćbyś** wzięła taksówkę, nie zdążysz już na ten pociąg.	Even if you take a taxi you still won't catch your train.	even if
dopóki..., dopóty	Będę ci pomagać finansowo (**dopóty**), **dopóki** nie znajdziesz dobrej pracy.	I will help you financially for as long as it takes for you to find a good job.	so long as, as long as it takes

gdyby... (to)	Zadzwoniłby, **gdyby** potrzebował pomocy. **Gdyby** potrzebował pomocy, **toby** zadzwonił.	He would call if he needed help.	if (with conditional clauses)
jakby	Wygląda, **jakby** był pijany.	He looks as if he were drunk.	as if
jeżeli = jeśli	**Jeśli** chcesz, mogę ci pomóc. Mogę ci pomóc, **jeżeli** chcesz.	If you want I can help you. I can help you if you want.	if
kiedy ≈ gdy, (to)	Pomogę ci, **kiedy / gdy** będę miał czas. **Kiedy / gdy** będę miał czas, **to** ci pomogę.	I will help you when I have time. When I have time, I will help you.[2]	when
chociaż ≈ mimo że	**Mimo że / chociaż** był chory, pomógł mi w przeprowadzce.	Despite the fact that he was sick, he helped me move.	despite (the fact that), although nevertheless
mimo to	Był chory; **mimo to** pomógł mi w przeprowadzce.	He was sick. Nevertheless he helped me move.	
pomimo[3]	Pomógł mi w przeprowadzce **pomimo** choroby (**pomimo**, że był chory).	He helped me move despite his sickness.	despite
niż	Wolę pomagać tobie **niż** jemu.	I prefer to help you than him.	than
odkąd	**Odkąd** mi pomagasz, zdaję wszystkie egzaminy.	Ever since you have been helping me, I have been passing all my exams.[4]	ever since
tak..., że	Mówił **tak** niewyraźnie, **że** nikt go nie rozumiał.	His speech was so unclear that no one understood him	so ... that
zanim	**Zanim** ci pomogę, muszę coś zjeść.	Before I help you I have to eat something.	before
że ≈ iż	Miałam nadzieję, **że / iż** mi pomożesz.	I was hoping that you would help me.	that
żeby ≈ (a)**by**	Wstałem o szóstej, **żeby** zdążyć na pociąg. Chciałam, **żebyś / abyś / byś** mi pomógł.	I got up at six in order to catch the train. I wanted you to help me.	in order to (with infinitives) not easily translatable with 'conditional' 'subjunctive' clauses: (orders, wishes, requests, etc)

[2] Notice that in English the present tense is used here in the subordinate clause, while in Polish the future is used.

[3] *Chociaż, mimo że, mimo to* and *pomimo* have a similar function, but they appear in different constructions; *pomimo* takes the genitive (*pomimo deszczu, zimna i mgły*: 'despite the rain, cold, and fog'), while *mimo to* cannot appear at the beginning of a sentence.

[4] Notice here that the present tense in Polish is used in the meaning 'have been helping', indicating that the action started in the past, has continued to the present time, and is still going on.

- **Section A.** of the table contains what are called coordinate conjunctions, i.e. conjuctions that join words, groups of words, or independent clauses (that could stand on their own as sentences). In most cases these conjunctions are preceded by a comma in Polish. However, conjunctions such as *i, oraz, lub, albo* are preceded by a comma only when their function is repeated, e.g. *kup i bułki, i chleb*.[5] In English, the use of commas with coordinate conjunctions is often unnecessary.

- **Section B.** contains subordinate conjunctions, which combine two clauses in a dependent relationship, i.e. one clause is dependent on the other. Dependent clauses in Polish are always separated by commas, while in English they often are not (*Chcę, żebyś przyszedł*, 'I want you to come'). Many of these constructions (e.g. *aż, bo, gdyż, niż, że, iż*) cannot be used to start a sentence. Others, like *chociaż, gdyby, kiedy, jeżeli* can be used either at the beginning of a sentence or to start the second clause, e.g. *Jeżeli chcesz, pójdziemy do kina. / Pójdziemy do kina, jeżeli chcesz*.[6] When the subordinate construction begins the sentence, the main clause may be introduced by *to*, e.g. *Jeżeli chcesz, (**to**) pójdziemy do kina*.

11.2. The conjunction *a*

 Table 11.2.a. contrasts the usage of the conjunctions *i, a* and *ale*. The sentences marked with an asterisk * are not possible. Can you figure out the functions of the conjunction *a* in Polish? How is the usage of *a* limited?

Table 11.2.a. The conjunction *a*

A.	Lubię kawę **i** herbatę. Lubię kawę ***a** herbatę. To mój brat **i** moja siostra.	I like coffee and tea. — This is my brother and my sister.
B.	Ja lubię kawę, **a** mój mąż herbatę. Ja lubię kawę, ***i** mój mąż herbatę.	I like coffee and / but my husband likes tea. —
C.	Ja lubię pływać, **a** / **ale** ty lubisz tańczyć. Ja lubię pływać, ***i** ty lubisz tańczyć. To (jest) mój brat, **a** to (jest) moja siostra.	I like to swim and/but you like to dance. — This is my brother, and this is my sister.
D.	teoria **a** praktyka	theory versus practice

The conjunction *i* 'and' in Polish is used to combine similar ideas and meanings, or ideas and meanings that go together (see **A.**). The conjunction *a* can also translate as 'and', but carries a meaning of contrast, often being translated as 'but' (see **B.**). The conjunction *ale* presents a stronger contrast or even a contradiction, and always translates as 'but'. When combining two verbs with different meanings, *i* is impossible, *a* or *ale* is used depending on the level of contrast (see **C.**).

The conjunction *a* can also carry the meaning 'versus' as in **D.**, *faszyzm a komunizm* 'fascism vs. communism'.

---

[5] 'Buy rolls as well as bread.'

[6] 'If you want, we'll go to the cinema/movies.'

11.3. Conjunctions with personal endings

 Read the examples in **Table 11.3.a.** How do they differ from English?

Table 11.3.a. Conjunctions with personal endings

Ojciec chciał,	że**bym** mu pomógł / pomogła.	Father wanted	me to help him.
	że**byś** mu pomógł / pomogła.		you to help him.
	że**by** syn mu pomógł. że**by** córka mu pomogła.		his son to help him. his daughter to help him.
	że**byśmy** mu pomogli / pomogły.		us to help him.
	że**byście** mu pomogli / pomogły.		you to help him.
	że**by** oni mu pomogli. że**by** one mu pomogły.		them to help him.
Chciałabym, żebyś / abyś nie palił(a).		I would like you not to smoke.	
Życzę wam, żebyście / abyście byli zdrowi / były zdrowe.		I wish you health.	
Wątpię, żebyś / abyś jeszcze zdążył na ten pociąg.		I doubt that you will catch that train.	
Kupiłam wam nowe łóżko, żebyście / abyście mogli lepiej spać.		I bought you a new bed so you can sleep better.	

The conjunction *żeby* has two functions. The first, with infinitives, is relatively straightforward, translating into English as 'in order to'. In the examples in **Table 11.3.a.** however, *żeby* is used with finite (conditional) verb forms. In these cases, the subject of the subordinate verb is marked by a personal ending (see § 4.10.) attached to the end of *żeby*. Such constructions are used to express orders, wishes, possibilities, or requests. However, they are only used when the subject of the main clause differs from that of the subordinate, *Chcę, żebyś miał dobre stopnie.*[7] When the subject is the same, the infinitive is used without *żeby*. Instead of saying **Chcę, żebym miała lepsze stopnie*, which is impossible; one says: *Chcę mieć lepsze stopnie.*[8]

These constructions are closely related to the conditionals presented in Chapter 4, and can be schematically presented as follows:

Table 11.3.b. Conjunctions with *żeby*: Sentence structure

Chcę, ('I want you to have a house')	że**byś** miała dom.	że**byście** mieli dom.	że**byście** miały dom.
	↗ ↖	↗ ↖	↗ ↖
Conditional forms ('you would have a house')	miała**byś** ◬	mieli**byście** 🔭	miały**byście** ✂

Essentially, such constructions are formed by adding the conditional ending *-by*, marked for person, to the conjunction *że*. Then comes the past form of the verb, marked for gender and number.

---

[7] 'I want you to get good grades.'

[8] 'I want to get better grades.'

Several other conjunctions can carry personal endings (see § 4.10.). **Table 11.3.c.** shows a few such conjunctions and their forms.[9]

Table 11.3.c. Conjunctions with personal endings

	Sg		Pl
ja	(a)**bym**, gdy**bym**, chociaż**bym**	my	(a)**byśmy**, gdy**byśmy**, chociaż**byśmy**
ty	(a)**byś**, gdy**byś**, chociaż**byś**	wy	(a)**byście**, gdy**byście**, chociaż**byście**
on, ona ono	(a)**by**, gdy**by**, chociaż**by**	oni, one	(a)**by**, gdy**by**, chociaż**by**

The conjunctions *chociaż / choć* and *chociażby / choćby* are quite similar. The first pair translates as 'although' and expresses some kind of asymmetrical connection, *Nie zdał egzaminu, chociaż dużo się uczył.*[10] Adding *-by-* with personal endings gives a meaning of supposition or doubt, translatable by '*even if*', *Chociażbym się dużo uczył, i tak nie zdam tego egzaminu.*[11]

Constructions with the conjunctions *chociażby*, *choćby* can be schematically presented as follows:

Table 11.3.d. Examples with *chociażby*[12]

		Main clause	Subordinate clause chociaż**by** + personal ending Verb in Past ➙
A.	Verb: Future	Nie **przeczytamy** całej tej książki,	chociaż**byśmy** czytali cały dzień.
B.	Verb: Conditional form	Nie **przeczytalibyśmy** całej tej książki,	

- **A.** Contrary-to-fact condition in future: these constructions address a doubt or an assumption.
- **B.** Contrary-to-fact condition in the past or future: expressing an impossible state of affairs.

---

[9] It is also possible to delete the conjunction, using only the conditional particle with a personal ending, e.g. *Chciałam, byś nie palił.* 'I wanted you not to smoke.'); such forms are more often found in the literary language.

[10] 'He did not pass the examination, although he had studied a lot.'

[11] 'Even if I study a lot, I still won't pass this examination.'

[12] '**A.** We won't read this whole book, even if we read all day. **B.** We wouldn't have read this whole book, even if we had read all day'.

12 Particles: *partykuły*

A particle is a suffix, an enclitic form, independent word or a group of words that affects the meaning of another word, phrase, or an entire sentence. They can play a variety of roles, including intensification, expression of the speaker's attitude, question formation, and many others. Particles do not change in form, and often do not have an independent meaning that may be found in a dictionary. In Polish, particles can take many of the forms mentioned above. As a result, it can be difficult to think of them as an independent part of speech – very often the same word that in one context is a particle in another can be a verb, adverb, etc. For example, *może* may translate as 'perhaps, supposedly, maybe, how about? (particles), or as 'he/she can' (3rd person singular of the verb *móc*).

 Read the examples in **Table 12.a.** Do you notice how the placement of *nie* changes the meaning of the sentence?

Table 12.a. The function of *nie*

Nie,	**nie** Jan poszedł do teatru, lecz Paweł.	No, it wasn't Jan that went to the theatre, but Paweł.
	Jan **nie** poszedł do teatru, lecz pojechał.	No, Jan didn't walk to the theatre, he drove.
	Jan poszedł **nie** do teatru, lecz do kina.	No, Jan didn't go to the theatre, he went to the cinema.

In Polish the negative pronoun **nie** stands just before the word it negates. In addition it can begin a sentence.

 Read the examples in **Table 12.b.** Can you see how the placement of *nie* changes the structure of the sentence?

Table 12.b. The particle *nie* and direct objects

Affirmative construction/question	Negative construction	Eng
Lubię mleko i herbatę.	Nie lubię ani mleka, ani herbaty.	I like milk and tea / I like neither milk nor tea.
Tu zawsze wszyscy byli.	Tu nigdy nikogo nie było.	Everybody was always here / No one was ever here.
Czy ona tu jest?	Nie, jej tu nie ma.	Is she here? No, she is not here.

Negated direct objects take the genitive case (see also § 7.7.).

Table 12.c. shows a collection of phrases in which various particles (printed in bold) appear. Notice the different forms in which particles can appear. How would deleting the particle change the meanings of the sentences in **Table 12.c.**? What function do they really play?

Table 12.c. Particles in context

A.	– **Czy** wiesz, czy on przyjdzie? – **Tak, na pewno**.	– Do you know if he's coming? – Yes, for sure.
B.	– A **właściwie** to gdzie ty mieszkasz? – Chciałabyś wiedzieć, **nie**?	– And where do you actually live? – You'd like to know, wouldn't you?
C.	– Jesteś **może** głodny? – **Oczywiście**, skąd wiesz? – **No** bo cię znam.	– Maybe you're hungry? – Of course, how'd you know? – Well, because I know you.
D.	– On się **pewnie** z nią ożeni. – **Ależ skąd**!	– He'll marry her, I suppose. – No way!
E.	– Czy ty **czasem** nie masz gorączki? – **Chyba nie**.	– You don't by any chance have a fever? – I suppose not.
F.	– Idź**że** wreszcie do lekarza! – **Przecież** ci mówię, że nie mam czasu!	– Get going to the doctor's! – But I'm telling you I don't have time!
G.	– Daj **no** piwko. – **Rzekomo** przestałaś pić. – Ależ piwo to nie **żaden** alkohol! – **Właśnie** tak się zaczyna...	– Give me a beer. – I thought you'd stopped drinking. – But beer isn't alcohol! – That's just how it starts ...
H.	– **Podobno** ma znowu padać... – **A niech sobie spokojnie** pada, **po prostu** zostaniemy w domu.	– I guess it's supposed to rain again ... – Let it rain, we'll just stay at home.
I.	– **Dopiero co** schudłeś, a **już znowu** przytyłeś, **czyż nie**? – **Owszem**, **niestety** tak **już** jest.	– You had just lost weight, and now you've put it back on again, haven't you? – Indeed, unfortunately that's the way it is.
J.	– Kupimy **sobie** domek, i będziemy **sobie** śpiewać, i posadzimy **sobie** kwiatki w ogródku, i kupimy **sobie** pieska, a **może nawet** dwa... – **A przede wszystkim** wyślemy dzieci na wakacje...	– We'll buy ourselves a little house, and we'll sing, and plant flowers in the garden, and buy ourselves a dog, or maybe two ... – But first of all we'll send the kids on holiday ...
K.	– **Dopiero co** cię poznałam, a kocham cię **nawet**, kiedy śpisz. A ty? Czy ty mnie **w ogóle** kochasz? – **Mhm**.	– I've just met you, and I love you even when you're asleep. And you? Do you love me at all? – Mmm.
L.	– **Co za** pech! Nie zabrałem **ani** pieniędzy, **ani** kluczy, **ani** karty kredytowej, **ani** komórki... **Aż** mi słabo... – **Tylko** się nie denerwuj!	– What bad luck! I haven't taken any money, keys, a credit card, or my mobile phone ... I'm feeling faint ... – Just don't get upset!

- **Question formation**

In some languages you form questions by changing the word order, as in English, 'You are sleeping / Are you sleeping?' In Polish the word order is relatively unrestricted, and cannot be used to form yes/no questions. Rather Polish may use the particle ***czy*** to form questions (like in **A.**), e.g. *Czy śpisz?* The particle *czy* can also act as a subordinate conjunction, see *Czy wiesz, czy on przyjdzie?* In the first clause, it plays the role of an interrogative particle (*Czy wiesz...*), in the second it is a conjunction (*czy on przyjdzie*).

One can also form questions by changing the intonation, e.g. *On przyjdzie...* (statement) versus *Czy on przyjdzie?* (question)[1].

- **Functions of *nie***

In example **B.** the particle *nie* (*Chciałabyś wiedzieć, nie?*) has a completely different meaning than the negative *nie*; it functions as an invitation to a response, just as English questions tagged onto the ends of sentences, e.g. 'didn't I?, wouldn't you?, don't you?'. This is typical of particles: many of them can act as other parts of speech as well, and one needs to 'get the feel' of them with the help of context, rather than translating them with the help of a dictionary. In addition, there are no general positional restrictions affecting particles.

- **Modal particles**

Unchangeable words and phrases that can act as answers to yes/no questions can be thought of as modal particles. In additions to ***tak*** and ***nie***, one can answer such questions with ***na pewno, oczywiście, naturalnie, prawdopodobnie, częściowo, niestety nie, bynajmniej.***[2]

- **Particles of degree, attitude**

Particles such as ***dopiero*** (*dopiero co*), ***nawet, zwłaszcza***[3] have a degree specifying, identifying, or intensifying function. Particles such as ***ależ, chyba, może, niby, podobno, po prostu, przecież, rzekomo, właśnie*** express the attitude of the speaker to the situation. There are not clear boundaries between the various subtypes of particles. In addition it is generally not possible to find a one-to-one translation for them.

In order to master particles, one needs a lot of practice with the spoken language, since generally dictionaries are not so helpful in this area, e.g. **H.** *a niech sobie spokojnie pada...*; *spokojnie* means 'calmly'. Here, however, the sentence does not mean that the rain will fall calmly, but rather that the weather is not an important consideration for the speaker, i.e. the speaker doesn't care whether it rains or not.

---

[1] 'He will come. / Will he come?'

[2] 'for sure; of course; naturally; probably; partially; unfortunately not; not at all'

[3] 'only (just); even; especially'

The particle **by**, as well as many other particles, can carry personal endings, see **Table 12.d.**

Table 12.d. Particles with personal endings

neutral	somewhat old-fashioned	ENG
A. **Czy** znowu nie zdaliście egzaminu?	**Czyżbyście** znowu nie zdali egzaminu?	Have you failed the exam again?
B. **Czy** się znowu spóźniłaś?	**Czyś** ty się znowu spóźniła?	Are you late again?
C. A **to** mi zrobiłeś niespodziankę!	A **toś** mi zrobił niespodziankę!	You really surprised me!

- **Particles and pragmatic function**

Particles of attitude, together with intonation, have an influence on the mood of a conversation: they can express intimacy, trust, or distance. Particles may help to shape the feeling of a verbal exchange, be it friendly or cool, pleasant or stiff, informal or official.

Since particles generally have rather imprecise meanings, many of them can be left out of a conversation. Whether they are used can be an individual, stylistic, or cultural question. In any case, they are typical of the spoken language. Many speakers have their favourite particles that they use most often, e.g. *po prostu* or *właśnie*. When scientific texts are translated from English into Polish, the translator must often insert a few particles to make the text stylistically appropriate. Otherwise it may sound dry or arrogant. On the other hand, a literal translation of Polish academic texts can appear immature and unprofessional in English if one does not delete at least some of the particles.

13 Interjections: *wykrzykniki*

Interjections (expressing excitement or emotion on the part of the speaker) often have no concrete (lexical) meaning, and may not be considered independent parts of speech. They are often sounds, rather than 'proper' words, and many are difficult to express in orthography. A few interjections are similar in Polish and in English; however, false usage or incorrect interpretation of interjections can easily lead to misunderstandings. Also, certain 'content' words may abandon their literal meaning and function as interjections.[1]

Read the dialogue in **Table 13.a.** and try to find English equivalents of the Polish interjections (printed in bold). In the dialogue, Anna is telling her friend about her last evening with her (now) ex-boyfriend Hugo, who understands Polish pretty well, but still misses a few things. How could this dialogue be described?

Table 13.a. Interjections in a dialogue

Anna	– No to ci opowiem, jak Hugo się na mnie pogniewał. **Oj**, jakie to było straszne! **Hej**, słuchasz mnie?	– Well, then, let me tell you how angry Hugo was with me. Oh, it was terrible! Hey, are you listening?
Rozmówca	– **Mhm**...	– Mhm ...
Anna	– **Ach**, nie mówiłam ci, byliśmy wtedy na... na tej wyspie, **aha**, na Rodos, no i ja stałam na takiej desce nad wodą i tak sobie skaczę, **hopsasa**, a tu nagle **trach**, deska się złamała, a ja **bęc** do wody. **Ej**, ty, a ty mnie słuchasz?	– *Oh yeah*, I forgot to tell you, we were on ... on that island, *uh*, Rhodos, and I was standing on this board above the water, jumping, *hop*, and suddenly *crack*, the board breaks and *plonk*, into the water I go. *Hey*, are you listening to me?
Rozmówca	– **Mhm**...	– Mhm ...
Anna	– No to Hugo **hop**, wskoczył do tej wody i ciągnie mnie za nogi, no to ja krzyczę „**aua**, nie wygłupiaj się", no i **hops**, wstaję na nogi, a on nagle, **o Jezu**, tak mnie przytulił i nic nie mówi... Słuchasz?	– And then *up*, Hugo jumps into the water and pulls me out by the legs and I am screaming *ow*, don't fool around, and *up*, I'm on my feet, and he, suddenly, *oh Jesus*, he started holding me so tight, not saying anything ... Are you listening?
Rozmówca	– **Mhm**...	– Mhm ...

---

[1] E.g. *To cię, cholera, nic nie obchodzi* 'that doesn't concern you': The word *cholera* (whose literal meaning is a disease), is used in a similar fashion to English 'Damn it'.

Anna	– No to ja też się przytuliłam i tak fajnie było, no i mówię „**ojejku**" ze szczęścia tego, a ty wiesz, co on na to, **hmm**? Wiesz, co on na to? To on się pyta: „Kto to jest ten Jejku?". I już więcej nie zadzwonił.	– Well, I held him too and it was so great, so I say *ojejku*, since I was so happy, and do you know what he said to that? Do you know, **hmm**? He asks me: so who is this Jejku? And after that he stopped calling me.
Rozmówca	– Jak mogłaś zamiast „Hugo" nazwać go „Jejku"?!	– How could you call Hugo "*Jejku*"?
Anna	– **Ojejku**, przecież „**jejku**" to nie żaden Jejku, tylko tak się mówi, nie rozumiesz?	– *Oh*, "*jejku*" is not a guy's name, it's just that's what you say, don't you understand?'

Spontaneous speech is characterised by emotionally marked linguistic items (interjections and particles) and repetitions, as well as loosely connected phrases. Interjections can be used to convey strong feelings, excitement, and emotions.

 Read the examples in **Table 13.b.** In column **A.**, try to match the interjections with the emotions that they express. In column **B.**, match the animals with the sounds that they make.

Table 13.b. Emotion words, commands and animal sounds[2]

A. words of emotion, requests or commands			B. Animal sounds	
1. Disgust	obrzydzenie	**a.** pst, cśś, sza	1. pies[3]	**a.** beee
2. Calling	zawołanie	**b.** mhm, aha, no	2. kot	**b.** muuu
3. Surprise	zaskoczenie	**c.** ała, aj, oj	3. kogut	**c.** ku ku
4. Pain	ból	**d.** oh, och, ach, oj, ojoj, ojej, jejku	4. kukułka	**d.** kukuryku
5. Assent, Agreement	potakiwanie	**e.** halo	5. krowa	**e.** miau
6. Request, order for silence	uciszenie	**f.** brr, fuj	6. owca	**f.** hau hau

The choice of interjections, and the frequency of their use will depend on individual preferences and on the situations. A learner may easily acquire strong words from native speakers without realising how vulgar they are. It can also happen that certain 'decent' interjections may be based on vulgar words, e.g. *kurcze / kurczę* or *kurde*, are milder forms of *kurwa* (!).[4], which is an extremely rude (and frequently used in certain circles) vulgarism. Vulgarisms produced with a foreign accent tend to sound more ridiculous and laughable than they do aggressive, so we advise against using them.

---

[2] Solution: 1-f, 2-e, 3-d, 4-c, 5-b, 6-a.

[3] '1. dog; 2. cat; 3. rooster; 4. cuckoo; 5. cow; 6. sheep'

[4] The dictionary meaning of *kurczę* is 'chick', *kurwa* literally means 'whore'. This set of words is used in a similar fashion to English 'fudge!' (*kurczę*) and 'fuck!' (*kurwa*). Again, the literal meaning of the word is lost, so *daj mi, kurwa, spokój* would not mean 'leave me alone, you whore' but rather 'leave me the fuck alone'.

14 Participles: *imiesłowy*

14.1. The functions of participles

What is the difference between the sentences in the first and second columns of **Table 14.1.a.**? What functions do the participles perform (printed in bold in the second column)?

Table 14.1.a. Functions of participles: examples

	1.	2.[1]
A.	Osoby, **które studiują** za granicą, są bardziej niezależne.	Osoby **studiujące** za granicą są bardziej niezależne.
B.1.	Nie znoszę, gdy ktoś rusza książki, **które czytam**.	Nie znoszę, gdy ktoś rusza **czytane** przeze mnie książki.
B.2.	Książki, **które się przeczytało**, można komuś oddać.	**Przeczytane** książki można komuś oddać.
C.	Lubię się kąpać, a jednocześnie **słuchać** muzyki lub **śpiewać**.	Lubię się kąpać, **słuchając** muzyki lub **śpiewając**.
D.	**Zakochał się** w niej **po tym**, jak zobaczył ją w bikini.	Zakochał się w niej, **zobaczywszy** ją w bikini.

Participles count as verb forms that do not conjugate. They often serve a stylistic purpose and shorten subordinate clauses. In Polish there are four different types of participle; two of them are adjectival in nature (and thus take adjectival endings), while the other two are adverbial.

Adjectival participles are, of course, declined like adjectives:

• **A.** The present active adjectival participle generally carries the meaning of 'who is X-ing': thus *czytająca kobieta* 'the woman who is reading', *piszący człowiek* 'the person who is writing', *śpiewające dziecko* 'the child who is singing', *nieobawiający się aresztowania złodzieje* 'the thieves who do not fear arrest'; these participles may only be formed from imperfective verbs.

• **B.** Passive adjectival participles: *czytana gazeta, przeczytany artykuł, wypite piwo*[2]; these participles may be formed either from imperfective verbs, in which case they carry the meaning 'that is/was being X-ed', or from perfectives with the meaning 'that was X-ed'.

Adverbial participles are indeclinable[3]:

• **C.** Participles of simultaneity generally carry the meaning of 'while X-ing': *śpiewając, tańcząc, pisząc, czytając, widząc*[4], e.g. *śpiewał i tańczył*: (a) *śpiewając tańczył* (b) *śpiewał tańcząc*. These participles may only be formed from imperfective verbs.

---

[1] 'A. People who study abroad are more independent.; B1. I can't stand it when someone moves the book I'm reading.; B2. Books that have already been read can be given to someone else.; C. I like to bathe while singing or listening to music.; D. He fell in love with her after he saw her in a bikini'.

[2] 'the newspaper being read (imperfective), the article that was read (perfective), the beer that was drunk (perfective)'

[3] Their forms do not change.

[4] 'singing, dancing, writing, reading, seeing'

- **D.** Past adverbial participles carry the meaning of 'having X-ed': *napisawszy, przeczytawszy, zobaczywszy* [5], e.g. **Napisawszy** *referat, poszedł spać* [6]. These participles refer to some action that has been completed before another action takes place, and thus are only formed from perfective verbs.

Adjectival participles are in many ways similar to adjectives. If one only wants to learn Polish passively, it is not necessary to study them in detail: the meaning can be guessed from the verb; they are declined just like adjectives [7] (but cannot form comparatives). In some cases, forms that were originally adjectival participles have come into common usage as adjectives, e.g. *śpiący, otwarty, zadowolony* 'sleepy, open, content'.

Adverbial participles (particularly the past adverbials) are less common and more typical of the written language, since they are used to combine two separate sentences with a specific temporal relation.

Participles are, on the whole, relatively straightforward – it is not difficult to form them if you know the verb conjugations.

14.2. Imperfective adverbial participles and present active adjectival participles

The examples in **Table 14.2.a.** show how imperfective adverbial participles and present active adjectival participles are formed.

Table 14.2.a. Formation of imperfective adverbial participles and present 👆 active adjectival participles

A.	B. Adverbial participles of simultaneity [8]	C. Adjectival participles PRES 👆 Active [9]	NOM 👄	
czytają	czytają**c**	czytają**ca** dziewczyna	SG	FEM △
jedzą	jedzą**c**	jedzą**ce** dziecko		NEUT 👁
piszą	piszą**c**	piszą**cy** student		MASC 👁
wiedzą	wiedzą**c**	wszystkowiedzą**ce** szefowe	PL	–MP ✂
kochają	kochają**c**	kochają**cy** rodzice		+MP 👥
(będą)	będą**c**	osoby będą**ce** w niebezpieczeństwie		–MP ✂

- **A.** Both the adjectival and adverbial participles are formed from the 3rd person plural form of the present tense. (The only exception is the verb *być* which uses the future stem: *będą* (future) / *będąc* / *będący* 'being').

- **B.** To form the adverbial participle, simply add -*c* to the 3rd person plural form.

---

[5] 'having written, having read, having seen'

[6] 'Having written the article, he went to bed'

[7] In many grammar textbooks they are introduced together with adjectives.

[8] 'reading, eating, writing, knowing, loving, being'

[9] 'a girl who is reading, a child who is eating, a student who is writing, bosses (FEM) who know everything, loving parents, people in danger'

- **C.** In the case of the adjectival participles, you add the same suffix *-c*, followed by the adjectival ending: e.g. feminine singular *-ca*, masculine *-cy*, neuter *-ce*, masculine personal *-cy* and non-masculine personal *-ce* in the nominative case.

Some examples of the above-mentioned constructions:

Kochający *rodzice,* **wiedząc,** *że dzieci mają prawo do samodzielności,*

nie zachowują się, jakby byli **wszystkowiedzącymi** *bogami.*

Są dziewczyny **czytające** *i* **piszące** *tylko wiersze.*

Nie znoszę osób **jedzących** *i* **mówiących** *jednocześnie.*

Jedząc, *nie należy mówić, a* **mówiąc,** *nie należy jeść.*

Będąc *skromnym nie zostaniesz ani bogaty, ani sławny.*[10]

Important: Constructions with adverbial participles have the same subject in both the main clause of the sentence and in the participial clause. One can of course say:

Idąc do szkoły, zostałam ochlapana przez samochód.[11]

What is wrong with the following example?:

*Idąc do szkoły, ochlapał mnie samochód.
'While going to school, a car splashed me.'

As in English, this sentence would be a grammatical mistake, unless the speaker means to say that it was the car that was going to school, since *samochód* would then be the subject of both clauses.

Opalając się, rozmawiały i piły lemoniadę.

---

[10] 'Loving parents, knowing that children have a right to be independent, do not behave as if they were all-knowing gods.; There are girls who only read and write poems.; I can't stand people who eat and talk at the same time.; While eating you should not speak, and while speaking you should not eat.; Being humble, you will become neither rich nor famous.'

[11] 'While going to school I was splashed by a car.'

14.3. Passive adjectival participles

Formation of the past passive participle is based on the infinitive stem of the verb.[12] The examples in **Table 14.3.a.** show some basic patterns of their formation.

Table 14.3.a. Formation of passive adjectival participles

	A.	B.1.	B.2.	C.[13]
A.1. **-ny**	prze-czyta-ł	przeczyta**ny**	czyta**ny**	przeczytany artykuł
	z-rozumia-ł	zrozumia**ny**	rozumia**ny**	niezrozumiana teza
	u-gotowa-ł	ugotowa**ny**	gotowa**ny**	rozgotowany makaron
	da-ł / dawa-ł	da**ny**	dawa**ny**	dane przykłady
A.2. **-ony**[14]	z-robi-ł	**z**robi**ony**	robi**ony**	zrobione ćwiczenie
	na-uczy-ł	naucz**ony**	ucz**ony**	nauczeni porządku
	z-męczy-ł	zmęcz**ony**	męcz**ony**	zmęczeni ludzie
	po-chwali-ł	pochwal**ony**	chwal**ony**	chwaleni chłopcy
	kupi-ł / kupowa-ł	kupi**ony**	kupowa**ny**	dziś kupione auto
A.3. **-ty**	po-bi-ł	pobi**ty**	bi**ty**	bita śmietana
	wy-pi-ł	wypi**ty**	pi**ty**	chętnie pite piwo
	u-my-ł	umy**ty**	my**ty**	nieumyci sportowcy
Mixed	bra-ł / wzią-ł	zabra**ny**	wzię**ty**	niezabrane rzeczy
	mówi-ł / powiedzia-ł	powiedzia**ny**	mówi**ony**	niewypowiedziane słowa
	zaczą-ł / zaczyna-ł	zaczę**ty**	zaczyna**ny**	zaczęta praca

- **A.** The third-person singular past tense generally forms the basis for passive adjectival participles. However, sometimes one must also consider the infinitive form.
- **A.1.** The ending *-ny* is found in past stems ending in *-a-*.
- **A.2.** The ending *-ony* is found in multi-syllable verbs ending in *-i-* or *-y-* as well as past stems ending in a consonant, such as *nieść: niósł / niesiony* 'carry' (with hard-soft alternations § 14.6.).
- **A.3.** The ending *-ty* is used in one-syllable past stems ending in *-i-, -y-, -u-* as well as verbs ending in *-(i)ąć*.
- **Mixed forms**: the tendencies described in **A.1. – A.3.** also hold for irregular verbs.

---

[12] The formation of the past passive participle is unfortunately not so easy to learn: there are often differences between the infinitive and the past stem, and you must know both in order to form the correct past passive participle (here the most common tendencies will be discussed). The adverbial past participle, however, is formed fairly simply from the past stem of perfective verbs.

[13] 'the article that was read; misunderstood thesis; overcooked pasta; the given examples; a finished exercise; those who were taught tidiness; tired people; boys who were praised; a car bought today; whipped cream; willingly drunk beer; unwashed athletes; things that were not taken along; unsaid words; a job that was started'

[14] These forms have a vowel alternation, −MP: *z/robione, z/męczone*; +MP: *zrobieni, zmęczeni*.

14

Participles: *imiesłowy*

- **B.** The passive adjectival participle may be formed from both perfective (**B.1.**) and imperfective (**B.2.**) verbs. Formation from perfective verbs is more common.
- **C.** The endings, just like for adjectives, denote gender, number, and case, and are subject to the typical alternations found in adjectives.
- **Nominative:** feminine *-na, -ta,* masculine *-ny, -ty,* neuter *-ne, -te,* masculine personal (plural) *-ni, -ci* and non-masculine personal (plural) *-ne, -te*.
- **Note:** Another type of past participle (neither adjectival nor adverbial) ending in *-no, -to* can be used in impersonal constructions, either with an infinitive (*zaczęto jeść* 'they started to eat') or with an **accusative** object[15] (*zorganizowano wystawę* 'an exhibition was organised'). These constructions are quite unusual, and in English may be translated either with a passive construction, e.g. 'an exhibition was organized', or with an impersonal 'they' construction, e.g. 'they showed this play for the first time' – *sztukę pokazano po raz pierwszy*.

14.4. Past adverbial participles

On the basis of the examples in **Table 14.4.a.**, try to say what the rule for forming past adverbial participles is.

Table 14.4.a. Formation of past adverbial participles

A.	B.	C.	D.
przeczyta-ł	przeczyta-**wszy**	wyszed-ł	wyszed-**łszy**
zrozumia-ł	zrozumia-**wszy**	znalaz-ł	znalaz-**łszy**
zrobi-ł	zrobi-**wszy**	schud-ł	schud-**łszy**
kupi-ł	kupi-**wszy**	zjad-ł	zjad-**łszy**

- **A. + C.** The 3rd person singular past form (minus the *-ł-*) serves as the basis for the participle formation.
- **B.** After a vowel, the suffix *-wszy* is added.
- **D.** After a consonant, you add *-łszy* to the stem.

The past adverbial participles express the completion of one action before another one takes place (i.e. a sequence of actions), and thus may only be formed from perfective verbs (completed actions). They carry the basic meaning of 'having X-ed'. Like the present adverbials, constructions with participles must have the same subject for both clauses:

Schudłszy, kupiła sobie szorty.
Znalazłszy na ulicy pieniądze, szybko je schował do kieszeni.
Zrobiwszy zakupy, pojechały na wakacje.
Nauczywszy się imiesłowów, poszli spać.[16]

---

[15] Since the object of these *-no, -to* participles is in the accusative, one can not really call them passive, even though they are formed with the same suffix as the regular passive participles.

[16] 'Having lost weight, she bought herself shorts.; Having found money on the street, he quickly put it in his pocket.; Having done the shopping, they (–MP) left on holiday.; Having learned participles, they (+MP) went to sleep.'

Zrobiwszy zakupy, pojechały na wakacje.

14.5. Participles: summary

In **Tables 14.5.a.** and **14.5.b.** the endings for participles are shown together with appropriate examples.

Table 14.5.a. Adjectival participles: declensional endings

Adjectival participles						
Pres 👆 Active pisać 'to write'			Past 🖐 Passive kochać 'to love' u / myć 'to wash'			
Sg	Sg / Pl		Sg		Sg / Pl	Pl
Fem △	Neut Sg 💡 and −Mp Pl ✂	Masc Sg 💡 and +Mp Pl 👥	Fem △	Masc 💡	Neut Sg 💡 and −Mp Pl ✂	+Mp 👥
-ąca	-ące	-ący	-na -ta	-ny -ty	-ne -te	-ni -ci
pisząca	piszące	piszący	kochana u/myta	kochany u/myty	kochane u/my**te**	kochani u/my**ci**

Table 14.5.b. Adverbial participles

Adverbial participles		
Present (simultaneous) pisać 'to write'	Past napisać 'to write', wyjść 'to go out'	
-ąc	vowel + ***-wszy***	consonant + ***-łszy***
pisząc	napis**a**wszy	wysze**d**łszy

14.6. Declension of adjectival participles

 For the singular, let us consider the examples *u/myty pies; zepsuty komputer; śpiące dziecko* and *znudzona wnuczka*, see **Table 14.6.a.**[17] Try to decline these examples yourself (for the adjectival model, see § 6. Adjectives).

Note: Notice that in the case of *śpiący*, the English equivalent can either be 'sleepy' or 'sleeping'.

on jest śpiący	'he is sleepy'
my jesteśmy śpiący	'we are sleepy'
to jest śpiący mężczyzna	'that is a sleeping / sleepy man'
to są śpiący ludzie	'these are sleeping / sleepy people'
nie wolno łaskotać śpiącego męża	'you can't tickle a sleeping / sleepy husband'

Table 14.6.a. Declension of adjectival participles: singular

Case	Masc ♀ +An 🐕	Masc ♀ −An 💀	Neut 💡	Fem △
Nom ⬤	umyty pies,	zepsuty komputer	śpiące dziecko	znudzona wnuczka
Gen ☹	umytego psa,	zepsutego komputera,	śpiącego dziecka	znudzonej wnuczki
Dat 🐾	umytemu psu, zepsutemu komputerowi, śpiącemu dziecku			znudzonej wnuczce
Acc ♥	umytego psa	zepsuty komputer	śpiące dziecko	znudzoną wnuczkę
Inst ①	umytym psem,	zepsutym komputerem,	śpiącym dzieckiem	znudzoną wnuczką
Loc ⬤	umytym psie,	zepsutym komputerze,	śpiącym dziecku	= Dat 🐾
Voc 🗯	umyty psie,	zepsuty komputerze,	śpiące dziecko	znudzona wnuczko!

Adjectival participles have regular declensions (just like adjectives).

Nie wolno budzić śpiącego psa.

---

[17] *umyty pies* '{washed dog}: the dog that has been washed'; *myty pies* '{washed dog}: the dog that is being washed'; *zepsuty komputer* 'the broken computer'; *śpiące dziecko* 'sleeping / sleepy child'; *znudzona wnuczka* 'bored granddaughter'

For adjectival passive participles ending in *-ony*, one must remember the following alternations, but only in the nominative and vocative plural:

+Mp 🗒 : *pracujący, zmęczeni / męczeni, męczący się ludzie*
−Mp ✂ : *pracujące, zmęczone / męczone, męczące się zwierzęta*[18]

 See the examples in **Table 14.6.b.**: *męczący się z/męczeni ludzie* and *pracujące, z/męczone zwierzęta*. Try to decline these examples yourself (for the adjectival model, see § 6. Adjectives).

Table 14.6.b. Declension of adjectival participles: plural

Case	+Mp 🗒	−Mp ✂
Nom ●	męczący się, z/męcz**eni** ludzie	pracujące, z/męcz**one** zwierzęta
Gen ⊗	męczących się, z/męczonych ludzi / zwierząt	
Dat ➥	męczącym się, z/męczonym ludziom / zwierzętom	
Acc ♥	z/męczonych, męczących się ludzi	pracujące, z/męczone zwierzęta
Inst ①	męczącymi się, z/męczonymi ludźmi / zwierzętami	
Loc ☁	męczących się, z/męczonych ludziach / zwierzętach	
Voc 🎤	męczący się, zmęcz**eni** ludzie!	pracujące, zmęcz**one** zwierzęta!

The dialogue below shows how participles may be used in sentences (notice how in the English translation they can be expressed with different parts of speech):

Table 14.6.c. Participles in a dialogue

Ewa	– Jesteś **zmęczony**?		– Are you tired?
Adam	– Tak, miałem bardzo **męczący** dzień. W końcu jestem **pracującym** człowiekiem. A co u ciebie?		– Yes, I have had such a tiring day. After all I am a working man. What's new with you?
Ewa	– Kiedy wróciłam do domu, wszystko było **posprzątane**: naczynia **pozmywane**, ubrania **wyprasowane**. Nawet okna były **wymyte**! Prawdę **mówiąc**, przestraszyłam się, **zobaczywszy** ten porządek.		– When I got home, everything had been tidied up. The dishes washed, the clothes ironed. Even the windows had been cleaned! To tell you the truth, I got scared seeing such order.
Adam	– Kto to mógł zrobić?!		– Who could have done it?
Ewa	– Tylko nasze **kochane** dzieci.		– Only our dear children.

Adjectival participles, as the name suggests, decline like adjectives. Adverbial participles, however, remain uninflected.

---

[18] 'working, tired, getting tired people/animals'

In **Table 14.6.d.** so-called *-no*, *-to* forms are presented in context. How do they function?

Table 14.6.d. The *-no*, *-to* forms in a dialogue.

Ewa	– No i jak było na weselu?	– Well, how was the wedding?
Adam	– Panna młoda była piękna. Jej suknię **uszyto** w Paryżu, kwiaty **zamówiono** w Holandii. Najpierw **przeczytano** życzenia od tych, którzy nie mogli przyjechać. Potem **podano** egzotyczne przystawki. Specjalnie na tę okazję **ugotowano** upieczono trzy dziki. **Wypito** też to i owo. Wyobraź sobie, że Anny nie **zaproszono**.	– The bride was beautiful. Her gown was sewn in Paris. The flowers were brought in from Holland. First, wishes were read from all those who could not come. Then they served exotic appetizers. Three wild boars were roasted especially for the occasion. A little bit of this and that was drunk. Imagine that Anna was never invited.
Ewa	– Dlaczego?	– Why?
Adam	– Chyba o niej **zapomniano**.	– I guess they forgot about her.

Forms ending in "*-no*" and "*-to*" (outdated neuter participles) are in the same grammar group as the non-inflected verb forms. The "*-no/-to*" forms are structured similarly to adjectival participles, see **Table 14.3.a.** These forms are frequently used in Polish writing and have a slight distancing effect.

15 Table of verbs: *tabela czasownikowa*

A schematic representation of the structure of Polish verbs

Prefix (optional)	Stem	Ending (Suffix)
Aspect (*modification of meaning*)	Meaning	Tense Person Number Gender Mode

Table 15 shows more than two hundred of the most common Polish verbs with suppletive forms and prefixes, formation of aspectual pairs, and any corresponding meaning changes. Short examples illustrate the structures with which these verbs are used. Remember that it is useless to learn a verb without a context, see § 4.2. You will need to learn two stems in Polish verb formation: the present stem and the infinitive stem. The present stem of irregular verbs undergoes alternations that you will also have to learn. In the first (*-ę, -esz*) and second (*-ę, -isz*) conjugation types you can observe alternations in the 2nd and 3rd person singular and in the 1st and 2nd person plural forms (the middle of the paradigm), while in the third type (*-m, -sz*) the stem can only alternate in the 3rd person plural form.

On this basis, in addition to the infinitive, only two forms of the present will be presented, representing the minimum required for predicting the entire conjugation: the 1st and 2nd person singular for Conjugation Types 1 and 2, and the 1st person singular and 3rd person plural for the Conjugation Type 3.

As past tense and future forms in Polish are formed regularly (see § 4.4. – 4.5.), in **Table 15** only one 3rd person singular form of the past is presented (except in the case of a vowel alternation in the stem, e.g. *niósł* 'he carried' versus *niosła* 'she carried'. In other cases the feminine is marked with a superscript [a]. The neuter form is predictable from the feminine and is not indicated in the table.

Each prefix that may be used to form aspectual pairs is listed on the left. Those prefixes which significantly change the meaning are italicised, e.g. *pod*-pisać 'to sign'.

Guide to the verb table

6. Meaning: verbs.

5. Translation of Polish examples of short phrases/sentences using the given verb.

4. Examples of short phrases/sentences using the given verb in Polish.

3. For each verb the following present tense forms are given:
- 1st and 2nd person singular (for verbs in *-ę, -esz* and *-ę, -isz/-ysz*); *boję się, boisz się*
- 1st person singular and 3rd person plural (for verbs in *-m, -sz*); *badam, badają*

In the past tense of imperfective verbs, only the 3rd person masculine and feminine in singular are given: *bała się*.

In the case of suppletion (perfective forms based on different stems, e.g. *brać : wziąć*), the appropriate forms of both the perfective future (*wezmę, weźmiesz*) and past (*wziął, wzięła*) are given.

2. The infinitives of imperfective verbs are given in alphabetical order.

The reflexive pronoun *się*, when it is not obligatory, is given in parentheses: compare *opiekować się* and *czesać (się)* For verbs of motion, the infinitive forms of the habitual or iterative verbs are also given: (*biegać : biec*).

1. Prefixes that form perfective verbs without a significant change in meaning

are given in plain text (non-italicized), e.g. **prze-** *czytać*. Prefixes that involve significant changes in the meaning of a given verb are italicized: see the sample excerpt from the table below. The short examples illustrate the basic (but of course not all) structures or idiomatic expressions in which a given verb may be used. A superscript after a word shows its case: *oblałam sobie kawą nową sukienkę*. This example shows that after the verb *oblałam* we may see the dative (*sobie*), instrumental (*kawą*), and the accusative (*nową sukienkę*). It must be remembered that studying verbs without context is not particularly helpful.

1	2
1. za- 2. *po-* 3. *w-* 4. *wy-* 5. *od-* 6. *prze-*	prowadzić (się)

Infinitive perfective ↓ (by means of prefix or suppletion)	Infinitive imperfective ↕ or infinitive iterative (non destinational) ⇄ (by means of suffix)	⤵ present imperfective: ↕ 1 Sg + 2 Sg (TYPES 1+2) 1 Sg + 3 Pl (TYPE 3) ⇶ past imperfective: ↕ 3 Sg Masc ♀ / Fem ⚥ With irregular aspectual pairs: ⬒ ↓ future perfective: 1 Sg + 2 Sg (TYPES 1+2) 1 Sg + 3 Pl (TYPE 3) ⤷ ↓ past perfective: 3 Sg Masc ♀ / Fem ⚥	Examples: Polish phrases	Examples: English phrases	Definition: verbs
1	2	3	4	5	6
	bać się	⤵ boję się, boisz się ⇶ bał[a] się	1. boisz się Anny GEN? 2. nie bój się jej GEN 3. boję się o Annę ACC	1. are you afraid of Anna? 2. do not be afraid of her 3. I am worried about Anna	be afraid, fear
z-	badać	⤵ badam, badają ⇶ badał[a]	1. lekarz zbadał pacjenta ACC 2. on bada polską kulturę ACC	1. the doctor examined the patient 2. he investigates Polish culture	examine, study, research, investigate
po-	bawić (się)	⤵ bawię się, bawisz się ⇶ bawił[a] się	1. bawię się z dziećmi INST w chowanego ACC 2. bawimy się z bratem INST (z: *with a partner*) 3. pobaw się lalką INST (without preposition: *with a toy*) 4. dobrze się bawiliśmy	1. I play hide-and-seek with the children 2. we play with my brother 3. play with a doll 4. we had a good time / we enjoyed ourselves	play, enjoy, have a good time
po-	bić (się)	⤵ biję, bijesz ⇶ bił[a]	1. złodziej pobit policjanta ACC kijem INST 2. nie bijcie się	1. the thief beat the policeman with a stick 2. do not fight	beat, fight, bang

Table of verbs: *tabela czasownikowa*

15

1	2	3	4	5	6
po-	biec	☞ biegnę, biegniesz 🗣 biegł^a	pobiegnij do sklepu ᴳᴱᴺ po jajka ᴬᶜᶜ	run to the shop for eggs	run
po-	biegać ⇅ biec	☞ biegam, biegają 🗣 biegał^a	często biegam po parku ᴸᴼᶜ	I often jog in the park	run, jog
za-	boleć	☞ 3 LP boli, 3 LMN bolą 🗣 bolał^a	1. boli mnie ᴬᶜᶜ głowa 2. boli mnie ᴬᶜᶜ twoja niesprawiedliwość	1. my head hurts / aches 2. I am pained / hurt by your unfairness	hurt, ache, pain
wziąć za-	brać (się)	☞ biorę, bierzesz 🗣 brał^a ☷ wezmę, weźmiesz 🗣 wziął ϙ, wzięła ⚠	1. wziął ode mnie ᴳᴱᴺ pieniądze ᴬᶜᶜ na komputer ᴬᶜᶜ 2. weź moje auto ᴬᶜᶜ 3. zabierz mnie na obiad ᴬᶜᶜ 4. bierze go strach 5. wziął ślub ᴬᶜᶜ 6. zabierz / weź się do pracy ᴳᴱᴺ	1. he took money from me for a computer 2. take my car 3. take me out for dinner 4. he is getting scared 5. he got married 6. get to work	take, get
z-	budować	☞ buduję, budujesz 🗣 budował^a	buduję dom ᴬᶜᶜ	I am building a house	build
o-	budzić (się)	☞ budzę, budzisz 🗣 budził^a	1. obudź mnie ᴬᶜᶜ o piątej ᴸᴼᶜ 2. często budzę się za późno	1. wake me up at five 2. I often wake up too late	wake up
	być *see § 4.1., § 4.9.*	☞ jestem, jesteś 🗣 był^a	1. pan Nowak jest lekarzem ᴵᴺˢᵀ 2. on jest dobry 3. on jest dobrym lekarzem ᴵᴺˢᵀ 5. ilu tam jest studentów / ile tam jest studentek? 6. co jest / będzie na kolację? 7. jej tu nie ma (*see § 7.7.*)	1. Mr Nowak is a doctor 2. he is good 3. he is a good doctor 5. how many students are there? 6. what is for supper today? 7. she is not here	be, exist
	chcieć	☞ chcę, chcesz 🗣 chciał^a	1. chcę spać 2. chcę ten samochód ᴬᶜᶜ / to auto ᴬᶜᶜ 3. czego ᴳᴱᴺ (ᶜᴼᴸᴸ) / co ᴬᶜᶜ chcesz?	1. I want to sleep 2. I want this car 3. what do you want?	want

1	2	3	4	5	6
1. — 2. po- 3. po-	chodzić ⇄ iść *see § 4.7.*	👉 chodzę, chodzisz 🔁 chodził[a]	1. już dwa lata chodzę do szkoły GEN 2. chcę (po)chodzić po parku LOC 3. pochodzę z Polski GEN 4. chodź tu	1. I've been going to school for two years now 2. I want to walk a bit in the park 3. I am from Poland 4. come here	go, walk, come
za-	chorować	👉 choruję, chorujesz 🔁 chorował[a]	1. chorował na grypę ACC 2. zachorował wczoraj	1. he was sick with the flu 2. he got sick yesterday	be sick, get sick
s-	chować (się)	👉 chowam, chowają 🔁 chował[a]	1. schowaj lekarstwa ACC przed dziećmi INST 2. nie chowaj się 3. wy-chowałem się u dziadków GEN	1. put the medicine away (from the kids) 2. do not hide 3. I was brought up by my grandparents	put away, hide, conceal, be brought up
u-	cieszyć (się)	👉 cieszę, cieszysz 🔁 cieszył[a]	1. cieszę się z twojego sukcesu GEN 2. cieszę się, że wygrałeś 3. cieszy mnie ACC (to), że wygrałeś 4. zawsze się cieszę ACC na spotkanie ACC z tobą GEN	1. I am glad about your success 2+3. I am glad you won 4. I always look forward to meeting you	be glad, be pleased, look forward
po- = za-	czekać	👉 czekam, czekają 🔁 czekał[a]	1. (po)czekaj na mnie ACC / zaczekaj na mnie ACC 2. nie wiedział, co go ACC czeka	1. wait for me 2. he did not know what awaited him	wait, await
u-	czesać (się)	👉 czeszę, czeszesz 🔁 czesał[a]	1. czesała długie włosy ACC drewnianym grzebieniem INST 2. on się czesze tylko raz w tygodniu LOC	1. she combed her long hair with a wooden comb 2. he combs his hair just once a week	comb

Table of verbs: *tabela czasownikowa*

1	2	3	4	5	6
po-	częstować (się)	⮑ częstuję, częstujesz ▤ częstował[a]	1. poczęstuj gości [Acc] bigosem [INST] 2. proszę się poczęstować 3. poczęstował nas polskimi potrawami [INST]	1. let your guests have some bigos 2. please help yourself 3. he treated us to some Polish dishes	offer, treat, take / give food or drink
po-	czuć	⮑ czuję, czujesz ▤ czuł[a]	1. czuję zapach[Acc]kawy 2. czuję, że będzie burza 3. czuję się, że będzie deszcz	1. I smell the aroma of coffee 2. I feel there will be a storm 3. It feels like it is going to rain	smell, sense feel
po-	czuć się	⮑ czuję, czujesz się czuł[a] się	1. jak się pan / pani czuje?	1. how do you feel!? / how are you?	feel
wy-	czyścić	⮑ czyszczę, czyścisz czyścił[a]	moja babcia czyściła zamszowe buty [Acc] skórką [INST] od chleba [GEN]	my grandmother cleaned her suede shoes with a bread crust	clean, cleanse
prze-	czytać	⮑ czytam, czytają ▤ czytał[a]	1. często czytam dzieciom [DAT] wiersze [Acc] 2. przeczytałam już wszystkie dramaty [Acc] Szekspira [GEN]	1. I often read poetry to children 2. I have already read all Shakespeare's plays	read
dać	dawać	⮑ daję, dajesz ▤ dawał[a] ⮜ dam, dadzą ▤ dał[a]	1. dałam ojcu [DAT] gazetę [Acc] 2. daj mi [DAT] pić 3. nie dajesz mi [DAT] wyboru [GEN] 4. daj, ja to [Acc] zrobię 5. dałem auto [Acc] do naprawy [GEN]	1. I gave my father the newspaper 2. give me something to drink 3. you do not offer / give me a choice 4. let me do it 5. I gave my care to be fixed / serviced	give, offer
z-	denerwować	⮑ denerwuję, denerwujesz ▤ denerwował[a]	1. denerwujesz mnie [Acc] tym swoim gadaniem [INST] (COLL) 2. on mnie [Acc] denerwuje	1. you are annoying me with your chatter 2. he gets on my nerves	make nervous, annoy, irritate
z-	denerwować się	⮑ denerwuję, denerwujesz	1. denerwuję się (tym [INST]), że dzieci nie wróciły do domu [GEN] 2. on mnie [Acc] denerwuje	1. I am worried that the kids are not back yet 2. he annoys me	be nervous, worry, annoy

1	2	3	4	5	6
dostać	dostawać	👉 dostaję, dostajesz 👉 dostawał[a] 👉 dostanę, dostaniesz 👉 dostał[a]	1. dostałem prezent ACC od żony GEN 2. dostała awans ACC 3. dostał się na studia ACC	1. I got a present from my wife 2. she was promoted 3. he was admitted to university	get
dowiedzieć się	dowiadywać się	👉 dowiaduję się, dowiadujesz się 👉 dowiadywał[a] się 👉 dowiem się, dowiedzą się 👉 dowiedział[a] się	1. dowiedział się od niej GEN czegoś nowego GEN o wypadku LOC 2. dowiedziałam się, że palisz papierosy ACC	1. he found out something new about the accident from her 2. I found out that you smoke cigarettes	find out
	dziać się	👉 3 LP dzieje się 👉 3 LP działo się	1. co się dzieje? 2. co się tu działo? 3. co się z tobą INST dzieje?	1. what's going on? 2. what happened? 3. what is the matter with you?	happen
	działać	👉 działam, działają 👉 działał[a]	1. alkohol źle działa na Ewę ACC 2. to nie działa 3. on działa w naszej partii LOC od dwóch lat GEN 4. ten adwokat działa w moim imieniu LOC	1. alcohol has a bad effect on Ewa 2. this doesn't work 3. he's been active in our party for two years 4. this lawyer acts on my behalf	have an effect, work (of a machine, mechanism), act
po-	dzielić (się)	👉 dzielę, dzielisz 👉 dzielił[a]	1. on dzieli ludzi na kulturalnych ACC i barbarzyńców ACC 2. 6 podzielone przez 2 ACC jest 3 3. podziel się czekoladą INST z koleżanką INST 4. podzielmy się kosztami INST	1. he divides people into cultured people and barbarians 2. 6 / 2 = 3 3. share the chocolate with your friend 4. let us split the costs	share, divide, split, separate, distribute
po-	dziękować	👉 dziękuję, dziękujesz 👉 dziękował[a]	1. dziękuję ci DAT za pomoc ACC 2. nie ma za co ACC dziękować	1. thank you for your help 2. do not mention it / not at all	thank

Table of verbs: *tabela czasownikowa*

1	2	3	4	5	6
za-	dzwonić	⮑ dzwonię, dzwonisz ⮐ dzwonił[a]	1. telefon dzwoni 2. zadzwoń do mnie GEN	1. the phone is ringing 2. give me a call	phone, ring, call, clink, jangle
po-	gadać	⮑ gadam, gadają ⮐ gadał[a]	1. pogadałam trochę z przyjaciółką INST o znajomych LOC (COLL) 2. szkoda gadać (COLL)	1. I talked a bit with my friend about the people we know. 2. there is nothing to say	talk (informal), speak (informal) chat, chatter, babble
po-	gniewać się	⮑ gniewam się, gniewają się ⮐ gniewał[a] się	dlaczego / o co ACC się na mnie ACC gniewasz?	what are you angry with me about?	get/be angry
u-	gotować	⮑ gotuję, gotujesz ⮐ gotował[a]	na obiad ACC (u)gotuję ryż ACC z jabłkami INST	I'm cooking rice with apples for dinner	cook, boil, get ready, prepare
za-	grać	⮑ gram, grają ⮐ grał[a]	1. lubię grać na gitarze LOC 2. zagram z Anną INST w tenisa ACC 3. grasz na wyścigach LOC ?	1. I like to play the guitar 2. I will play tennis with Anna 3. do you gamble on the horses?	play, gamble
po-	informować (się)	⮑ informuję, informujesz ⮐ informował[a]	1. muszę poinformować studentów ACC o terminie LOC egzaminu GEN 2. proszę się poinformować w kasie LOC, czy są jeszcze bilety	1. I must inform the students about the date of the exam. 2. please inquire in the box office if there are still any tickets left	inform, inquire, instruct, notify
za-	interesować (się)	⮑ interesuję, interesujesz ⮐ interesował[a] się	1. interesuję się literaturą INST i sportem INST 2. interesuje mnie ACC literatura i sport	1+2. I am interested in literature and sport	be interested
za-	istnieć	⮑ istnieję, istniejesz ⮐ istniał[a]	UFO (nie) istnieje	UFOs (do not) exist	exist (come into being)

1	2	3	4	5	6
pójść	iść (chodzić ‡) see § 4.7.	👋 idę, idziesz / ⬛ szedłem ◊, szłam ◊ / € pójdę, pójdziesz / ⬛ poszedł ◊, poszła ◊	1. idę z bratem INST do restauracji GEN na obiad ACC / 2. idziemy do mojego brata GEN / 3. idź za mną INST	1. I'm going with my brother to a restaurant for dinner / 2. we're going to my brother / 3. follow me	go (on foot), walk, stride (*do* + GEN: location / concrete; *na* + Acc: abstract)
po-	jechać (jeździć ‡) see § 4.7.	👋 jadę, jedziesz / ⬛ jechał[a]	1. jadę do Polski GEN na wakacje ACC / 2. pojadę do rodziców GEN na urodziny ACC / 3. piłeś? nie jedź!	1. I'm going to Poland on holiday / 2. I am going to my parents for a birthday party / 3. don't drink and drive	go (by vehicle) (*do* + GEN: location / concrete; *na* + Acc: abstract)
z-	jeść	👋 jem, jedzą / ⬛ jadł[a]	na śniadanie ACC jem chleb ACC z serem INST	I eat bread and cheese for breakfast	eat
po-	jeździć jechać, see § 4.7.	👋 jeżdżę, jeździsz / ⬛ jeździł[a]	1. lubię jeździć samochodem INST / 2. jeżdżę na nartach LOC całkiem dobrze / 3. często jeżdżę za granicę ACC	1. I like to go by car / 2. I ski quite well / 3. I often travel abroad	ride (a vehicle, horse, on skis, etc.) drive, travel
wy-	kąpać (się)	👋 kąpię, kąpiesz / ⬛ kąpał[a]	1. kąpiemy dziecko ACC w wannie LOC / 2. lubię się kąpać w morzu LOC	1. we are bathing the child in the bathtub / 2. I like to bathe in the sea.	bathe, wash
położyć	kłaść (się)	👋 kładę, kładziesz / ⬛ kładł[a] / € położę, położysz / ⬛ położył[a]	1. połóż się / 2. połóż się spać / 3. połóż swoje książki ACC na półkę ACC	1. lie down / 2. go to bed / 3. put your books on the shelf	lie down, place in a lying position, put
po-	kłócić się	👋 kłócę się, kłócisz się / ⬛ kłócił się	1. czemu tak często kłócisz się z kolegami INST o drobiazgi ACC? / 2. nie kłóć się ze mną INST	1. why do you quarrel so often with your friends about little things? / 2. do not argue with me	quarrel, argue, disagree

Table of verbs: *tabela czasownikowa*

1	2	3	4	5	6
1. — 2. się 3. za- 4. po- 5. się	kochać (się)	kocham, kochają kochał[a]	1. kocham swojego syna [ACC] i swoją córkę [ACC] 2. kocham się w twoim bracie [LOC] 3. zakochałam się w nim [LOC] dwa dni temu 4. pokochałam go [ACC] dwa dni temu 5. sąsiedzi kochają się co wieczór 6. oni bardzo się kochają	1. I love my son and my daughter 2. I am in love with your brother 3. I fell in love with him two days ago 4. I started loving him two days ago 5. our neighbours make love every night 6. they love one another a lot	love, be in love with, fall in love with, start loving, make love, love one another
s-	kończyć	kończę, kończysz kończył[a]	1. często kończę pracę o godzinie [LOC] trzeciej / piętnastej [ACC] 2. już skończyłam list [ACC] 3. skończ!	1. I often finish work at 3 pm. 2. I've already finished the letter 3. stop it!	finish, end, conclude
s- (za-)	kończyć się	kończę się, kończysz się kończył[a] się	w Polsce [LOC] komnizm skończył się w tysiąc dziewięćset osiemdziesiątym dziewiątym roku [LOC]	in Poland communism ended in 1989	end
(s-)	kosztować	3 LP kosztuje, 3 LMN kosztują kosztował[a]	1. ile to kosztuje? 2. skosztuj (= spróbuj) trochę wina [GEN] 3. skosztuj (= spróbuj) to wino [ACC]	1. how much does this cost? 2. try some wine 3. try this wine	cost, to try (taste)
po-	kroić	kroję, kroisz kroił[a]	1. dlaczego kroisz chleb [ACC] brudnym nożem [INST]? 2. nie krój tego!	1. why are you slicing the bread with a dirty knife? 2. do not cut that!	slice, cut
krzyknąć	krzyczeć	krzyczę, krzyczysz krzyczał[a] krzykne, krzykniesz krzyknął, krzyknęła	1. nie krzycz tak 2. dlaczego krzyczysz na dziecko [ACC]?	1. don't scream like that 2. why are you shouting at the child?	shout, scream

1	2	3	4	5	6
kupić	kupować	⮩ kupuję, kupujesz / ⏚ kupowała / ⮬ kupię, kupisz / ⏚ kupiła	1. kup prezent [ACC] przyjaciółce [DAT] 2. kup prezent [ACC] dla przyjaciółki [GEN]	1. buy your friend a present 2. buy a present for your friend	buy
ob- *na-*	lać oblewać ⇄	⮩ leję, lejesz / ⏚ lała / ⮩ oblewam, oblewają / ⏚ oblewała	1. oblałam sobie [DAT] kawą [INST] nową sukienkę [ACC] 2. nalej mi [DAT] wody [GEN] 3. nie oblejesz tego egzaminu [GEN] (Coʟʟ)	1. I spilt coffee on my new dress 2. pour me some water 3. you will not fail this exam	spill, fail, pour
	latać ⇄ (*see* lecieć)	⮩ latam, latają / ⏚ latała	lubię latać helikopterem [INST]	I like to fly in a helicopter	fly
po-	lecieć	⮩ lecę, lecisz / ⏚ leciała	1. lecisz jutro (samolotem [INST]) do Krakowa [GEN]? 2. leć po wino [ACC] (Coʟʟ)	1. are you flying to Krakow tomorrow? 2. run and get some wine	fly, run
wy-	leczyć (się)	⮩ leczę, leczysz / ⏚ leczyła	1. on leczy chorych [ACC] na raka [ACC] 2. czy hipnoza może wyleczyć depresję [ACC]? 3. leczę się z ran [GEN] 4. leczy się na serce [ACC]	1. he treats those with cancer 2. can hypnosis cure depression? 3. I'm recovering from my wounds 4. he's receiving treatment for a heart condition	treat, heal, cure
po-	leżeć	⮩ leżę, leżysz / ⏚ leżała	1. lubię leżeć z książką [INST] na kanapie [LOC] 2. książki leżały na stole [LOC]	1. I like to lie on the sofa with a book 2. the books lay on the table	lie
po-	liczyć	⮩ liczę, liczysz / ⏚ liczyła	1. policz pieniądze [ACC] 2. na Annę [ACC] / na pomoc [ACC] Anny [GEN] zawsze mogę liczyć 3. licz się ze słowami [INST]	1. count the money 2. I can always count on Anna / Anna's help 3. mind what you say	count, count on, mind, calculate

15

Table of verbs: *tabela czasownikowa*

1	2	3	4	5	6
po-	lubić	⇨ lubię, lubisz ⇒ lubił[a]	1. lubię Grzegorza Acc za jego optymizm Acc 2. lubię dobrą muzykę Acc	1. I like Grzegorz for his sense of humour 2. I enjoy good music	like, enjoy
1. po- 2. w-	łączyć (się)	⇨ łączę, łączysz ⇒ łączył[a]	1. włącz radio Acc 2. proszę mnie Acc połączyć z dyrektorem Inst 3. na wiosnę Acc ptaki łączą się w pary Acc 4. lubię łączyć przyjemne Acc z pożytecznym Inst	1. turn on the radio 2. please put me through to the (managing) director / CEO 3. in the spring, birds form couples 4. I like to combine business with pleasure	turn on (a device), connect, join, unite, combine, associate, merge
1. na- 2. po- 3. u-	malować (się)	⇨ maluję, malujesz ⇒ malował[a]	1. namalował ten obraz Acc grubym pędzlem Inst 2. pomaluj pokój Acc na biało 3. umalowałaś się za mocno (= masz za mocny makijaż Acc)	1. he painted this picture with a thick brush 2. paint the room white 3. you have put on too much make-up.	paint, make up
z-	martwić (się)	⇨ martwię, martwisz ⇒ martwił[a]	1. nie martw się o mnie Acc 2. nie martw się drobiazgami Inst	1. don't worry about me 2. don't worry yourself with little things	worry, sadden, upset, trouble
po-	marzyć	⇨ marzę, marzysz ⇒ marzył[a]	zawsze marzyła o karierze Loc w filmie Loc	she always dreamed about a career in film	dream, daydream, fantasize
	mieć	⇨ mam, mają ⇒ miał[a]	1. mam kawę Acc, herbatę Acc, piwo Acc i sok Acc 2. mam na imię Anna (*not used with family names, see 'nazywam się'*) 3. masz szczęście Acc 4. mam metr siedemdziesiąt 5. pociąg ma godzinę Acc spóźnienia Gen 6. jej Gen tu nie ma (*see § 7.7.*)	1. I have coffee, tea, beer and juice 2. my name is Anna 3. you are lucky 4. I am 170 cm tall 5. the train is one hour late 6. she is not here	have

1	2	3	4	5	6
	mieszkać	☞ mieszkam, mieszkają ☷ mieszkał^a	mieszkam w akademiku ᴸᴼᶜ	I live in a dormitory / hall of residence	live (reside)
	można	—	1. czy tu można palić? 2. czy tu można płacić kartą ᴵᴺˢᵀ ?	1. can you smoke here? / may I smoke here? 2. is it possible to pay with a credit card?	can one? is it permitted? is it possible?
	móc	☞ mogę, możesz ☷ mógł ǫ, mogła ∆	1. czy mogę państwu ᴰᴬᵀ w czymś ᴸᴼᶜ pomóc? 2. nie mogę nic ᴬᶜᶜ zrobić 3. staram się jak mogę 4. umiem nurkować, ale teraz nie mogę, bo jest za zimno	1. can I help you with something? 2. I am unable to do anything 3. I am doing the best I can 4. I can dive, but now I can't because it is too cold	be able (can), be capable
powiedzieć	mówić	☞ mówię, mówisz ☷ mówił^a ☵ powiem, powiedzą ☷ powiedział^a	1. mówisz o niej ᴸᴼᶜ głupstwa ᴬᶜᶜ (COLL) 2. powiedz prawdę ᴬᶜᶜ 3. Adam mówi świetnie po polsku 4. mów dalej 5. mówiłem mu ᴰᴬᵀ żeby przyszedł później 6. proszę mi mówić po imieniu ᴸᴼᶜ	1. you are talking nonsense about her 2. tell the truth 3. Adam speaks Polish very well 4. keep talking 5. I told him to come later 6. please call me by my first name	speak, say, tell, talk
	musieć	☞ muszę, musisz ☷ musiał^a	1. musisz sobie ᴰᴬᵀ kupić nowy płaszcz ᴬᶜᶜ 2. muszę to ᴬᶜᶜ zrobić	1. you have to buy yourself a new coat 2. I must do it / I have to do it / I need to do it	have to, must, need
u-	myć (się)	☞ myję, myjesz ☷ mył^a	1. rano myję ręce ᴬᶜᶜ pachnącym mydłem ᴵᴺˢᵀ 2. umyj okna ᴬᶜᶜ 3. umyj zęby ᴬᶜᶜ	1. in the morning I wash my hands with scented soap 2. clean the windows 3. brush your teeth	wash, clean, brush
po-	myśleć	☞ myślę, myślisz ☷ myślał^a	1. myślę o nim ᴸᴼᶜ 2. myślę, że masz rację ᴬᶜᶜ	1. I am thinking about him 2. I think you're right	think, reason

1	2	3	4	5	6
	należeć	należę, należysz / należał[a]	1. to należy do mnie GEN 2. ona należy do naszej grupy GEN 3. należy często chwalić dzieci ACC 4. należy ci DAT się nagroda NOM	1. this belongs to me 2. she belongs to our group 3. one should praise children often 4. you deserve a prize	belong, one should
nazwać	nazywać (się)	nazywam, nazywają / nazywał[a] // nazwę, nazwiesz / nazwał[a]	1. nazywam się (Anna) Nowak *(used with family names)* 2. chcę nazwać mojego psa ACC Dudi 3. jak to się nazywa?	1. my name is (Anna) Nowak 2. I want to name my dog Dudi 3. what is it called / what do you call it?	be called, name
1. za- 2. przy-	nieść	niosę, niesiesz / niósł ǫ, niosła Δ	1. zanieś paczkę ACC do hotelu GEN 2. przynieś potwierdzenie ACC odbioru GEN	1. take the package to the hotel 2. bring (me) the receipt confirmation	carry, take, bring
	nosić ⇄ nieść	noszę, nosisz / nosił[a]	1. chętnie noszę dżinsy ACC 2. nosił ją ACC na rękach LOC	1. I like to wear jeans 2. he carried her in his arms	carry, wear
odejść	odchodzić *(see § 4.7.)*	odchodzę, odchodzisz / odszedłem ǫ, odeszłam Δ // odejdę, odejdziesz	1. nie odchodź ode mnie GEN 2. pociąg odchodzi o godzinie piętnastej LOC 3. nie odchodź od tematu GEN	1. don't leave me 2. the train leaves at 3.00 pm 3. do not stray from the subject / topic	leave, go away, walk away, depart, stray
oddać	oddawać	oddaję, oddajesz / oddawał[a] // oddam, oddadzą / oddał[a]	1. oddaj mi DAT moje skarpetki ACC 2. zawsze oddaję długi ACC	1. give me my socks back 2. I always pay back my debts	give back, return, pay back

Table of verbs: *tabela czasownikowa*

1	2	3	4	5	6
odpocząć	odpoczywać	🖐 odpoczywam, odpoczywają 📖 odpoczywał[a] 🖐 odpocznę, odpoczniesz 📖 odpocząłȩ, odpoczęła[a]	1. muszę odpocząć 2. najlepiej odpoczywam w górach [LOC]	1. I must rest 2. I relax best in the mountains	rest, relax
odpowie-dzieć	odpowiadać	🖐 odpowiadam, odpowiadają 📖 odpowiadał[a] 🖐 odpowiem, odpowiesz 📖 odpowiedział[a]	1. proszę odpowiedzieć nam [DAT] na pytanie [ACC] 2. nie chciał odpowiadać przed sądem [INST] za morderstwo [ACC] 3. twoja propozycja mi [DAT] odpowiada 4. nie mogę odpowiadać za wszystko [ACC]	1. please answer our question 2. he didn't want to answer for the murder before the court 3. your proposal / offer suits me 4. I cannot be responsible for everything	answer, answer for, be responsible, suit, agree with
odwiedzić	odwiedzać	🖐 odwiedzam, odwiedzasz 📖 odwiedził[a] 🖐 odwiedzę, odwiedzisz 📖 odwiedzał[a]	1. często odwiedzamy babcię [ACC] 2. odwiedź mnie [ACC], proszę	1. we often visit our grandmother 2. please come and see me	visit, call on, go
obejrzeć	oglądać	🖐 oglądam, oglądają 📖 oglądał[a] 🖐 obejrzę, obejrzysz 📖 obejrzał[a]	1. lubię oglądać telewizję [ACC] 2. wczoraj oglądałam nasze zdjęcia [ACC]	1. I like to watch television 2. yesterday I looked at our photos	watch, look at
okazać (się)	okazywać (się)	🖐 3 SG okazuje 📖 3 SG NEUT okazywało 🖐 3 SG okaże 📖 3 SG NEUT okazało	1. okazało się, że Adam mówi nieprawdę [ACC] 2. niech pan okaże paszport [ACC] 3. okazało się, że można na nim polegać	1. it turned out that Adam was lying 2. please show your passport 3. he proved to be reliable	turn out, show, present, demonstrate

Table of verbs: *tabela czasownikowa*

15

1	2	3	4	5	6
za-	opiekować się	☞ opiekuję się, opiekujesz się / ☞ opiekował się	opiekuj się młodszym bratem INST	look after your younger brother	look after, take care
opowie-dzieć	opowiadać	☞ opowiadam, opowiadają / ☞ opowiadał / ☞ opowiem, opowiesz / ☞ opowiedział	1. wieczorem należy opowiadać dzieciom DAT piękne bajki ACC / 2. opowiedz mi DAT coś ACC o sobie LOC	1. in the evening you should tell your children beautiful fairy tales / 2. tell me something about yourself	tell (a story), narrate, describe, relate
z-	organizować	☞ organizuję, organizujesz / ☞ organizował	firma organizuje wycieczkę ACC pracownikom DAT / dla pracowników GEN	the company is organizing a trip for its employees	organize, set up, establish, arrange, fix up
otworzyć	otwierać	☞ otwieram, otwierają / ☞ otwierał / ☞ otworzę, otworzysz / ☞ otworzył	1. otwórz mi DAT drzwi ACC / 2. pan Kowalski otworzył konto ACC w Szwajcarii LOC	1. open / unlock the door for me / 2. Mr Kowalski opened a bank account in Switzerland	open, unlock
paść s-	padać	☞ padam, padają / ☞ padał	1. pada (deszcz NOM) / 2. kurs NOM dolara spada / 3. spadłam kiedyś ze schodów GEN	1. it's raining / 2. the dollar is falling / 3. I fell down the stairs once	fall, rain, drop, tumble down
za-	palić (się)	☞ palę, palisz / ☞ palił	1. czy palisz papierosy ACC, czy cygara ACC? / 2. już nie palę / 3. pali się!	1. do you smoke cigarettes or cigars? / 2. I don't smoke anymore / 3. it's burning! / there is a fire!	smoke, burn

1	2	3	4	5	6
za-	pamiętać	⟱ pamiętam, pamiętają / ⟰ pamiętał[a]	1. pamiętasz jeszcze swój pierwszy pocałunek [Acc]? 2. pamiętasz mnie [Acc]? 3. pamiętaj o innych [Loc] 4. pamiętaj, że masz zapłacić za mieszkanie [Acc]	1. do you still remember your first kiss? 2. do you remember me? 3. be mindful of others 4. bear in mind that you have to pay rent	remember, bear in mind
po-	patrzyć (się) / patrzeć(się)	⟱ patrzę, patrzysz / ⟰ patrzył[a]	1. nie patrz tak na mnie [Acc] 2. na co [Acc] (się) patrzysz? 3. popatrz tu!	1. don't look at me like that 2. what are you looking at? 3. look here!	look, observe
wy-	pić	⟱ piję, pijesz / ⟰ pił[a]	piję kawę [Acc] z mlekiem [Inst], ale bez cukru [Gen]	I drink coffee with milk but without sugar	drink
1. na- 2. o- 3. od- 4. pod- 5. za- (się)	pisać (się) (pod- / pisywać) see § 4.5. i 4.8.	⟱ piszę, piszesz / ⟰ pisał[a] / ⟱ pisuję, pisujesz / ⟰ pisywał[a]	1. wczoraj napisałem do ciebie [Gen] list [Acc] 2. umie pan opisać podejrzaną osobę [Acc]? 3a. muszę odpisać na list [Acc] 3b. na egzaminie [Loc] odpisywał od kolegów [Gen] 4a. chciałbym podpisać umowę [Acc] o pracę [Acc] z firmą zagraniczną [Inst] 4b. proszę się tu podpisać 5a. lekarz zapisał / przepisał mi [Dat] nowe lekarstwo [Acc] 5b. zapisz się na semestr letni [Acc] 5c. chcę sobie [Dat] zapisać (= zanotować) twój numer [Acc] telefonu 6. jak to się pisze?	1. I wrote you a letter yesterday 2. can you describe the suspect? 3a. I have to write back to him 3b. during the exam he copied off his friends 4a. I would like to sign a work contract with a foreign firm 4b. please sign here 5a. a doctor prescribed me a new medicine 5b. enrol for the summer semester 5c. I want to write down your phone number 6. how do you spell it?	write, describe, write back, copy, sign, write down, prescribe, enrol

Table of verbs: tabela czasownikowa

1	2	3	4	5	6
za-	płacić	👆 płacę, płacisz 🔊 płacił[a]	1. znowu zapłaciłem za ciebie ᴬᶜᶜ rachunek telefoniczny ᴬᶜᶜ 2. robotnikom sezonowym ᴰᴬᵀ nie płaci się za urlop ᴬᶜᶜ	1. I paid the phone bill for you again 2. they don't pay seasonal workers for holidays	pay
za-	płakać	👆 płaczę, płaczesz 🔊 płakał[a]	1. nie płacz 2. płakała przez ciebie ᴬᶜᶜ całą noc ᴬᶜᶜ 3. umiesz tylko siąść i płakać	1. don't cry 2. she cried the whole night because of you 3. you can only sit and weep	cry, weep
po-	pływać, płynąć	👆 pływam, pływają 🔊 pływał[a] 👆 płynę, płyniesz 🔊 płynął ɸ, płynęła △	1. lubię pływać 2. płyniemy statkiem ᴵᴺˢᵀ po Dunaju ᴸᴼᶜ / do Budapesztu ᴳᴱᴺ 3. umiesz pływać żaglówką ᴵᴺˢᵀ?	1. I like to swim 2. we are going by boat down the Danube / to Budapest 3. can you sail?	swim, go (by boat), row, sail, float
podpisać	podpisać podpisywać	👆 podpisuję, podpisujesz 🔊 podpisywał[a]	możesz podpisywać te listy ᴬᶜᶜ w naszym imieniu ᴸᴼᶜ	you can sign those letters in our name	sign
podkreślić	podkreślać	👆 podkreślam, podkreślają 🔊 podkreślał[a] 🔊 podkreślę, podkreślisz 🔊 podkreślił[a]	proszę podkreślić czasowniki ᴬᶜᶜ czerwoną kredką ᴵᴺˢᵀ	please underline the verbs with a red pencil / crayon	underline
s-	podobać się	👆 podobam się, podobają się 🔊 podobał[a] się	1. Kraków bardzo mi ᴰᴬᵀ się podoba 2. ten pomysł mi ᴰᴬᵀ się podoba	1. I like Krakow a lot 2. this idea appeals to me / I like this idea	like, appeal
pokazać	pokazywać (się)	👆 pokazuję, pokazujesz 🔊 pokazywał[a] *see* okazywać	1. pokaż mi ᴰᴬᵀ rękę ᴬᶜᶜ 2. nie lubię pokazywać się publicznie	1. show me your hand 2. I do not like to be in the public eye	show, demonstrate
pomóc	pomagać	👆 pomagam, pomagają 🔊 pomagał[a] 🔊 pomogę, pomożesz 🔊 pomógł ɸ, pomogła △	1. pomóż mi ᴰᴬᵀ w budowie ᴸᴼᶜ (domu) / pomóż mi ᴰᴬᵀ budować dom 2. to lekarstwo mi ᴰᴬᵀ nie pomaga	1. help me build my house 2. this medicine is not working	help, facilitate, be of use

1	2	3	4	5	6
	potrafić *see § 4.3.1.*	⬇ potrafię, potrafisz ⬛ potrafił[a]	1. potrafię chodzić na rękach LOC 2. zrobię to ACC najlepiej jak potrafię 3. potrafisz to ACC naprawić?	1. I can walk on my hands 2. I will do the best I can 3. can you repair?	be able to, can, manage
	potrzebować	⬇ potrzebuję, potrzebujesz ⬛ potrzebował[a]	potrzebuję szybko twojej pomocy GEN	I need your help fast	need
powtórzyć	powtarzać (się)	⬇ powtarzam, powtarzają ⬛ powtarzał[a] ⬇ powtórzę, powtórzysz ⬛ powtórzył[a]	1. powtórz mi DAT to ACC jeszcze raz 2. nie powtarzaj się	1. say that one more time 2. don't repeat yourself	repeat, return, retake, replay, revise
pozwolić	pozwalać	⬇ pozwalam, pozwala ⬛ pozwalał[a] ⬇ pozwolę, pozwolisz ⬛ pozwolił[a]	1. nie pozwalam ci DAT na to ACC 2. pozwól mi DAT spać u koleżanki GEN	1. I won't allow you that 2. let me sleep at my friend's	allow, let, permit
po-	pracować	⬇ pracuję, pracujesz ⬛ pracował[a]	1. pracuję w dużej firmie LOC 2. pracuję jako koordynator NOM tego projektu 3. ona pracuje naukowo 4. silnik pracuje bardzo dobrze	1. I work in a big company. 2. I work as the coordinator of this project 3. she does research 4. the engine functions perfectly well	work, function, do research
wy-	prać	⬇ piorę, pierzesz ⬛ prał[a]	1. wełnę zawsze piorę w zimnej wodzie LOC 2. wszystko można prać chemicznie	1. I always wash wool by hand in cold water 2. everything can be dry-cleaned	wash, do laundry
wy-	prasować	⬇ prasuję, prasujesz ⬛ prasował[a]	on sam prasuje swoje koszule ACC	he irons his shirts himself	iron, press
za-	proponować	⬇ proponuję, proponujesz ⬛ proponował[a]	1. jakie warunki ACC proponuje panu DAT nowy pracodawca? 2. proponuję, żebyśmy spędzili wakacje ACC w Polsce LOC	1. what conditions does your new employer propose? 2. I propose / I suggest we spend our holiday in Poland	propose, suggest

Table of verbs: *tabela czasownikowa*

1	2	3	4	5	6
po-	prosić	🖐 proszę, prosisz 📖 prosił[a]	1. poprosić rodziców ᴬᶜᶜ o pomoc finansową ᴬᶜᶜ 2. (po)proszę o kawę ᴬᶜᶜ 3. proszę, tu jest kawa ᴺᴼᴹ 4. czy mogę prosić pana Nowaka ᴬᶜᶜ (do telefonu ᴳᴱᴺ)? (*talking by phone*)	1. he asked his parents for financial assistance 2. a coffee, please 3. here you are (here is your coffee) 4. could I speak to Mr Nowak, please?	request, ask, please (used in polite requests), here you are, there you go (used when handing something over)
1. za- 2. po- 3. w- 4. wy- 5. od- 6. *prze-* się	prowadzić (się)	🖐 prowadzę, prowadzisz 📖 prowadził[a]	1. chcę (po)prowadzić własną firmę ᴬᶜᶜ 2. zaprowadź mnie ᴬᶜᶜ do domu ᴳᴱᴺ 3. mój syn się do nas ᴳᴱᴺ wprowadził 4a. mój syn wyprowadził się z domu ᴳᴱᴺ 4b. wyprowadź psa ᴬᶜᶜ do parku ᴳᴱᴺ 5. czy mogę panią ᴬᶜᶜ odprowadzić do domu ᴳᴱᴺ? 6. jutro się przeprowadzamy	1. I want to run my own company 2. lead me home 3. my son has moved in with us 4a. my son has moved out of the house 4b. take the dog out to the park 5. can I walk you home? 6. we are moving tomorrow	run, operate, lead, show the way, move in, move out, take out, accompany, move (house)
s-	próbować	🖐 próbuję, próbujesz 📖 próbował[a]	1. spróbuj tego wina ᴳᴱᴺ 2. spróbuj wstać wcześniej 3. dlaczego nie próbujesz rozwiązać tego problemu ᴳᴱᴺ?	1. try / have a taste of that wine 2. try to get up earlier 3. why do you make no attempt to solve this problem	try, taste, attempt
przebrać	przebierać (się)	🖐 przebieram, przebierają 📖 przebierał[a] 🖐 przebiorę, przebierzesz 📖 przebrał[a]	1. muszę się przebrać 2. muszę się przebrać do obiadu ᴳᴱᴺ 3. przebierz dziecko ᴬᶜᶜ w suche rzeczy ᴬᶜᶜ 4. przebrała się za kota ᴬᶜᶜ	1. I have to change (clothes) 2. I have to change for dinner 3. put dry clothes on the child 4. she dressed up as a cat	change clothes, to dress up as, disguise, sort out, sift

Table of verbs: tabela czasownikowa

1	2	3	4	5	6
przejść	przechodzić	przechodzę, przechodzisz, przechodziłem ♂, przechodziłam ♀, przejdę, przejdziesz, przeszedłem ♂, przeszłam ♀	1. tu można przejść przez ulicę ᴬᶜᶜ 2. ona wiele przeszła 3. przeszła ci grypa ᴺᴼᴹ? 4. kiedy on przeszedł na chrześcijaństwo ᴬᶜᶜ?	1. you can cross the street here 2. she's been through a lot 3. have you recovered from the flu? 4. when did he convert to Christianity?	cross, go through, walk past, spread, convert, turn into, develop
przedstawić	przedstawiać (się)	przedstawiam, przedstawiają, przedstawiał[a], przedstawię, przedstawisz, przedstawił[a]	1. czy mogę się przedstawić? 2. przedstaw mi ᴰᴬᵀ swoją rodzinę ᴬᶜᶜ 3. przedstaw mnie ᴬᶜᶜ swojej rodzinie ᴰᴬᵀ 4. chciałbym przedstawić mój projekt ᴬᶜᶜ	1. may I introduce myself? 2. introduce your family to me 3. introduce me to your family 4. I would like to present my project	introduce, present, appear, show
przeprosić	przepraszać	przepraszam, przepraszają, przepraszał[a], przeproszę, przeprosisz, przeprosił[a]	1. on mnie ᴬᶜᶜ nigdy za to ᴬᶜᶜ nie przeprosił 2. przepraszam za spóźnienie ᴬᶜᶜ 3. przepraszam, która godzina?	1. he has never apologised to me for that 2. I am sorry for being late / I am late 3. excuse me, what is the time?	apologize, say sorry, excuse
przeszko-dzić	przeszkadzać	przeszkadzam, przeszkadzają, przeszkadzał[a], przeszkodzę, przeszkodzisz, przeszkodził[a]	1. nie przeszkadzaj mi ᴰᴬᵀ w pracy ᴸᴼᶜ 2. przepraszam, czy mogę na chwilę ᴬᶜᶜ przeszkodzić?	1. don't disturb me at work 2. excuse me, can I interrupt for a moment?	bother, disturb, interrupt, distract, hamper, hinder, intervene
przyjść	przychodzić	przychodzę, przychodzisz, przychodziłem ♂, przychodziłam ♀, przyjdę, przyjdziesz, przyszedłem ♂, przyszłam ♀	1. przyjdź do nas ᴳᴱᴺ wieczorem ᴵᴺˢᵀ 2. paczka jeszcze nie przyszła	1. come to our place / come and visit us in the evening 2. the parcel has not arrived yet	come, arrive

Table of verbs: *tabela czasownikowa*

1	2	3	4	5	6
przygoto-wać	przygoto-wywać (się)	przygotowuję, przygotowujesz / przygotowywał^a / przygotuję, przygotujesz / przygotował^a	1. przygotowałem się do wyjazdu GEN 2. przygotuj duże śniadanie ACC	1. I got myself ready for the trip 2. prepare a big breakfast	prepare, get ready
przyjechać	przyjeżdżać	przyjeżdżam, przyjeżdżają / przyjeżdżał^a / przyjadę, przyjedziesz / przyjechał^a	1. Anna przyjechała do rodziców GEN na tydzień ACC 2. czy ten pociąg przyjedzie punktualnie?	1. Anna came to her parents' for a week 2. will this train arrive on time?	come, arrive
przyjąć	przyjmować	przyjmuję, przyjmujesz / przyjmował^a / przyjmę, przyjmiesz / przyjął ◊, przyjęła ◊	1. czy przyjmuje pan moją propozycję ACC 2. lekarz przyjmuje we wtorki ACC 3. ona to ACC dobrze przyjęła	1. do you accept my offer / proposal 2. the doctor sees patients on Tuesdays 3. she took it well	accept, receive (visitors), take, assume, adopt, engage
przynieść	przynosić	przynoszę, przynosisz / przynosił^a / przyniosę, przyniesiesz / przyniósł ◊, przyniosła ◊	często przynoszę jej DAT kwiaty ACC	I often bring her flowers	bring, carry
za- / s-	pytać	pytam, pytasz / pytał^a	zapytaj / spytaj profesora ACC o termin ACC egzaminu GEN	ask the professor about the date of the exam	ask
z-	robić	robię, robisz / robił^a	1. jak robisz tę sałatkę ACC? 2. co robisz wieczorem INST? 3. muszę zrobić zadanie domowe ACC 4. nie rób mi DAT nadziei GEN 5. zrób zakupy ACC	1. how do you make this salad? 2. what are you doing this evening? 3. I have to do my homework 4. do not raise my hopes 5. do the shopping	do, make, cause

1	2	3	4	5	6
u-	rodzić (się)	🔼 rodzę, rodzisz 🔽 rodziła	1. urodziła bliźniaki ^{ACC} 2. urodził się dwunastego września tysiąc dziewięćset siedemdziesiątego dziewiątego roku ^{GEN} 3. urodził się w maju ^{LOC}	1. she gave birth to twins 2. he was born on 12TH September, 1979 3. he was born in May	give birth, be born, be in labour / labor, breed, bear, give rise
rozebrać	rozbierać (się)	🔼 rozbieram, rozbierają 🔽 rozbierał^a 🔼 rozbiorę, rozbierzesz 🔽 rozebrał^a	1. rozbierz się 2. rozbierz dziecko ^{ACC}	1. get undressed 2. undress the child	take off, undress, strip, disassemble, dismantle, disjoint, take apart
po-	rozmawiać	🔼 rozmawiam, rozmawiają 🔽 rozmawiał^a	chętnie rozmawiam z teściową ^{INST} o mężczyznach ^{LOC}	I gladly talk to my mother-in-law about men	speak, talk, converse
rozpocząć	rozpoczynać (się)	🔼 rozpoczynam, rozpoczynają 🔽 rozpoczynał^a 🔼 rozpocznę, rozpoczniesz 🔽 rozpoczął ◊, rozpoczęła ◊	1. pięć razy rozpoczynała studia ^{ACC} 2. przedstawienie rozpoczęło się wcześnie rano	1. she started university 5 times 2. the performance began early in the morning	begin, start
z-	rozumieć	🔼 rozumiem, rozumieją 🔽 rozumiał^a	1. nie rozumiem go ^{GEN} 2. rozumiem trochę po polsku ^{LOC} 3. nie rozumiem, jak to działa	1. I do not understand him 2. I understand a little Polish 3. I have no idea how it works	understand, comprehend, grasp, see, have an understanding
ruszyć	ruszać (się)	🔼 ruszam, ruszają 🔽 ruszał^a 🔼 ruszę, ruszysz 🔽 ruszył^a	1. ktoś ruszał moje rzeczy ^{ACC} 2. rusz się, zrób coś! 3. ruszaj, już jest zielone światło!	1. someone's moved / touched my things. 2. move! do something! 3. get going; the light's green	move, touch, set off, start, pull out, budge, be lose
na- po-	rysować	🔼 rysuję, rysujesz 🔽 rysował^a	1. narysuj auto ^{ACC} nowym ołówkiem ^{INST} 2. nie (po)rysuj mi auta ^{GEN}	1. draw the car with a new pencil 2. do not scratch my car	draw, sketch, scratch

Table of verbs: tabela czasownikowa

Table of verbs: *tabela czasownikowa*

1	2	3	4	5	6
rzucić 1. wy- 2. po- 3. w- 4. z-	rzucać	👆 rzucam, rzucają ▣ rzucał[a] € rzucę, rzucisz ▣ rzucił[a]	1. wyrzucitam stare listy ACC 2. on ją ACC (po)rzucił 3. wrzucali kamienie ACC do wody GEN 4. rzuć palenie ACC!	1. I threw away the old letters 2. he left / abandoned her 3. they threw stones into the water 4. give up smoking!	throw, leave, cast, fling, hurl, dash, dump, chuck, abandon, drop
(u)siąść	siadać	👆 siadam, siadają ▣ siadał[a] € usiądę, usiądziesz ▣ usiadł[a]	1. proszę siadać / usiąść 2. nie siadaj na moim miejscu LOC 3. siedź cicho	1. please sit down / be seated 2. don't sit in my seat 3. be / keep quiet	sit down, take a seat, be seated (be in prison)
po-	siedzieć (see siadać ⇕)	👆 siedzę, siedzisz ▣ siedział[a]	1. lubię tu z tobą INST siedzieć 2. ona tylko siedzi w domu LOC 3. on siedzi już dwa lata (w więzieniu LOC)	1. I like to sit here with you 2. she sits at home all the time 3. he's been in prison for two years	be sitting, remain seated, perch, roost, be in prison
skoczyć	skakać	👆 skaczę, skaczesz ▣ skakał[a] € skoczę, skoczysz ▣ skoczył[a]	1. nie skacz (po łóżku LOC)! 2. lubię skakać do wody GEN 3. skocz po piwo ACC (COLL)	1. don't jump on the bed! 2. I like to jump into the water 3. go and get some beer	jump, bounce
złożyć (się)	składać (się)	👆 składam, składają ▣ składał[a] € złożę, złożysz ▣ złożył[a]	1. złóż swoje rzeczy ACC 2. to się dobrze składa 3. złożymy Ewie DAT życzenia ACC na urodziny ACC 4. ta sztuka składa się z trzech aktów GEN 5. chłopcy złożyli się na rower ACC 6. złożytam wniosek o stypendium ACC 7. złóż scyzoryk ACC	1. fold your things 2. that works out well 3. we'll send Ewa birthday wishes / greetings 4. this play consists of three acts 5. the boys chipped in for a bike 6. I applied for a scholarship 7. fold up your penknife	fold, work out, send (wishes, application, etc.), consist of, chip in, clasp, fold up, put together

1	2	3	4	5	6
po-	słuchać	🔼 słucham, słuchają 🔽 słuchał[a]	1. słuchamy koncertu fortepianowego GEN 2. posłuchaj tego koncertu GEN 3. słucham? 4. ona nie słucha rodziców GEN	1. we're listening to a piano concert 2. listen to this concert 3. hello (when picking up the phone) Pardon? I beg your pardon? 4. she does not listen to/obey her parents	listen (to), obey
	słychać	—	1. co słychać? 2. tu słychać morze ACC	1. what's new? / what's up? 2. you can hear the sea here	be heard
u-	słyszeć	🔼 słyszę, słyszysz 🔽 słyszał[a]	1. słyszałem, że wyjeżdżasz 2. usłyszałam to ACC wczoraj od sąsiadki GEN 3. nie słyszę cię GEN	1. I heard (that) you were leaving 2. I heard that yesterday from my neighbour 3. I can't hear you	hear
po-	spać	🔼 śpię, śpisz 🔽 spał[a]	1. nie mogę spać 2. spałam z kotem INST na fotelu LOC	1. I can't sleep 2. I slept with the cat in the armchair	sleep
	spodziewać się	🔼 spodziewam się, spodziewają się 🔽 spodziewał[a] się	1. spodziewamy się dziecka GEN 2. spodziewam się nagrody GEN	1. we are expecting a baby 2. I am hoping for a prize	expect, hope for, await
spotkać	spotykać (się)	🔼 spotykam, spotykają 🔽 spotykał[a] 🔼 spotkam, spotkają 🔽 spotkał[a]	1. spotkałam listonosza ACC (Accusative: *by coincidence*) 2. spotkałam się z przyjacielem INST w restauracji (Instrumental: *on purpose*) 3. spotkajmy się w kawiarni LOC 4. czy pan spotkał się z jakimiś trudnościami INST?	1. I met the postman 2. I met with my friend in a restaurant 3. let's meet in the cafe 4. did you encounter any difficulties?	meet, encounter, stumble, across, run into
po-	sprzątać	🔼 sprzątam, sprzątają 🔽 sprzątał[a]	1. posprzątaj swój pokój ACC 2. sprzątnij ten bałagan ACC	1. tidy up your room 2. clean up that mess	tidy up, clean up

Table of verbs: *tabela czasownikowa*

1	2	3	4	5	6
sprzedać	sprzedawać	sprzedaję, sprzedajesz / sprzedawał^a / sprzedam, sprzedadzą / sprzedał^a	1. sprzedaj mi DAT swoje auto ACC / 2. to się dobrze sprzedaje	1. sell me your car / 2. it sells well	sell, vend
stanąć	stać	stoję, stoisz / stał^a / stanę, staniesz / stanął, stanęła	1. co tak stoisz? / 2. samochód stanął przed skrzyżowaniem INST / 3. stoimy w kolejce LOC / 4. mój zegarek stanął	1. what are you standing there for? / 2. the car stopped before the intersection / 3. we are standing in a line / we are queuing up / standing in a queue / 4. my watch has stopped	stand, stop
stać się	stawać się	staję się, stajesz się / stawał^a się / stanę, staniesz się / stał^a się	1. po ślubie LOC stał się inny / 2. nic się jej DAT nie stało	1. after the wedding he turned into a different person / 2. nothing has happened (to her)	become, happen
	studiować	studiuję, studiujesz / studiował^a	studiuję historię ACC na Uniwersytecie Warszawskim LOC	I study history at Warsaw University	study (be enrolled at university)
za-	szkodzić	szkodzę, szkodzisz / szkodził^a	1. (to) nic nie szkodzi / 2. szkodzi mi DAT czerwone wino ACC / 3. to tylko zaszkodzi sprawie DAT	1. it doesn't matter / never mind / 2. red wine is bad for me / 3. it will only make matters worse	harm, damage, be bad
po-	szukać	szukam, szukają / szukał^a	1. szukał wszędzie swoich kluczy GEN / 2. poszukaj tej książki GEN w Internecie LOC	1. he looked for his keys everywhere / 2. search the internet for this book	look for, search, seek, hunt for
	śmiać się	śmieję się, śmiejesz się / śmiał^a się	nie śmiej się ze mnie GEN	don't laugh at me	laugh
za-	śpiewać	śpiewam, śpiewasz / śpiewał^a	1. czy to ty śpiewałaś dziecku DAT tę piosenkę ACC? / 2. śpiewaj z nami INST	1. was it you who sang that song to the child? / 2. sing with us	sing

1	2	3	4	5	6
za-	tańczyć	🖐 tańczę, tańczysz 📖 tańczył[a]	1. tańczyła tango ᴬᶜᶜ tylko z nim ᴵᴺˢᵀ 2. on świetnie tańczy	1. she danced the tango only with him 2. he dances very well	dance, swing
za-	tęsknić	🖐 tęsknię, tęsknisz 📖 tęsknił[a]	1. tęsknię za tobą ᴵᴺˢᵀ 2. tęsknię za wakacjami ᴵᴺˢᵀ	1. I miss you 2. I long for vacation / holiday(s)	miss, long for, yearn for
s-	tracić	🖐 tracę, tracisz 📖 tracił[a]	1. straciła zaufanie ᴬᶜᶜ do matki ᴳᴱᴺ 2. straciłem na giełdzie ᴸᴼᶜ wszystkie pieniądze ᴬᶜᶜ 3. nie trać nadziei ᴳᴱᴺ 4. nie trać czasu ᴳᴱᴺ	1. she has lost faith in her mother 2. I lost all my money on the stockmarket 3. do not abandon hope 4. do not waste your time	lose, abandon, waste
po-	traktować	🖐 traktuję, traktujesz 📖 traktował[a]	1. traktowała go ᴬᶜᶜ jak psa ᴬᶜᶜ 2. potraktuj to ᴬᶜᶜ poważnie	1. she treated him like a dog 2. take this matter seriously	treat, handle, take
po-	trwać	🖐 trwam, trwają 📖 trwał[a]	1. jak długo trwa ten egzamin ᴺᴼᴹ? 2. to nie potrwa długo 3. strajk będzie trwał	1. how long does the exam last? 2. it won't last / take long 3. the strike will continue	last, continue, take, remain, stay, keep, persist, endure
	trzeba	—	trzeba to ᴬᶜᶜ zrobić	one must / should / ought to do this	one must, should, ought to
1. po- 2. za- 3. wy-	trzymać (się)	🖐 trzymam, trzymają 📖 trzymał[a]	1. (po)trzymaj dziecko ᴬᶜᶜ za rękę ᴬᶜᶜ 2. zatrzymaj auto ᴬᶜᶜ 3. wytrzymasz to ᴬᶜᶜ? 4. nie, ja tego ᴳᴱᴺ nie wytrzymam 5. zatrzymaj to ᴬᶜᶜ sobie ᴰᴬᵀ	1. hold the child by the hand 2. stop the car 3. can you endure this / stand it? 4. no, I can't endure this / stand it 5. keep it	hold, stop, tolerate, endure, stand, cling to, keep
ubrać	ubierać (się)	🖐 ubieram, ubierają 📖 ubierał[a] € ubiorę, ubierzesz 📖 ubrał[a]	1. ubierz się ciepło 2. w grudniu ᴸᴼᶜ ubieramy choinkę ᴬᶜᶜ 3. nie mam w co ᴬᶜᶜ się ubrać	1. dress warmly 2. we decorate the Christmas tree in December 3. I have nothing to wear	dress, put on clothes, decorate, adorn

1	2	3	4	5	6
uciec	uciekać	☞ uciekam, uciekają ☷ uciekał[a] ☴ ucieknę, uciekniesz ☵ uciekł[a]	1. Ewa znów ucieka z domu ᴳᴱᴺ 2. autobus mi ᴰᴬᵀ uciekł	1. Ewa has run away form home again 2. I missed the bus	run away, escape, miss
na-	uczyć	☞ uczę, uczysz ☷ uczył[a]	1. uczę geografii ᴳᴱᴺ 2. on uczy na Uniwersytecie Jagiellońskim ᴸᴼᶜ	1. I teach geography 2. he teaches at the Jagiellonian University	teach
na-	uczyć się	☞ uczę, uczysz się ☷ uczył[a] się	uczę się gramatyki ᴳᴱᴺ	I am studying grammar	study, learn
	umieć	☞ umiem, umieją ☷ umiał[a]	1. umiem pływać, ale na razie nie mogę, bo jestem przeziębiony 2. czy umiesz to ᴬᶜᶜ zrobić? 3. nie umiem kłamać	1. I know how to swim, but now I can't because I have a cold 2. do you know how to do it? 3. I cannot (tell a) lie	know how, be able, can
umrzeć	umierać	☞ umieram, umierają ☷ umierał[a] ☴ umrę, umrzesz ☵ umarł[a]	1. dawniej ludzie umierali na grypę ᴬᶜᶜ 2. umieram z głodu ᴳᴱᴺ	1. people used to die of flu 2. I am dying of hunger / I am starving to death	die, pass away, decease, starve
	uważać	☞ uważam, uważają ☷ uważał[a]	1. uważaj na siebie ᴬᶜᶜ! 2. uważam, że to ty powinnaś uważać, a nie ja 3. uważałam cię ᴬᶜᶜ za przyjaciela ᴬᶜᶜ	1. watch out for yourself 2. I think that you have to watch out and not me 3. I considered you (to be) my friend	watch out, think, consider, pay attention
wejść	wchodzić	☞ wchodzę, wchodzisz ☷ wchodził[a] ☴ wejdę, wejdziesz ☵ wszedł ◊, weszła ◮	1. wszedł do pokoju ᴳᴱᴺ bez pukania ᴳᴱᴺ 2. proszę wejść! 3. nie wchodź! 4. nie wchodź na drabinę ᴬᶜᶜ	1. he entered the room without knocking 2. come in 3. don't come in 4. do not climb up the ladder	enter, come in, climb, go up
	wiadomo	—	1. wiadomo, że on kłamie 2. czy wiadomo, kto to zrobił?	1. everyone knows he's lying 2. is it known who did it?	it is known

1	2	3	4	5	6
zobaczyć	widzieć	☞ widzę, widzisz ☞ widział[a] ☞ zobaczę, zobaczysz ☞ zobaczył[a]	1. widziałem ten film ᴬᶜᶜ już trzy razy 2. świadek niczego ᴳᴱᴺ (official) / nic ᴬᶜᶜ (colloquial) nie widział	1. I have seen this film three times already 2. the witness did not notice anything	see, notice, visualise
	wiedzieć	☞ wiem, wiedzą ☞ wiedział[a]	1. wiem, że to ᴬᶜᶜ zrobiłeś 2. wiemy dużo o tobie ᴸᴼᶜ	1. I know you did this 2. we know a lot about you	know
u-	wierzyć	☞ wierzę, wierzysz ☞ wierzył[a]	1. wierzył w Boga ᴬᶜᶜ, ale nie wierzył duchownym ᴰᴬᵀ 2. nikomu ᴰᴬᵀ nie wierzę 3. w nic ᴬᶜᶜ nie wierzę 4. wierzę, że on mnie ᴬᶜᶜ kocha	1. he believed in God, but he didn't believe the clergy 2. I don't believe anyone 3. I don't believe (in) anything 4. I believe he loves me	believe
przy-	witać (się)	☞ witam, witają ☞ witał[a]	1. witam państwa ᴬᶜᶜ serdecznie 2. przywitałeś się z ciocią ᴵᴺˢᵀ?	1. welcome, Ladies and Gentlemen 2. have you greeted your aunt?	welcome, greet
	woleć see Table 4.3.a.	☞ wolę, wolisz ☞ wolał[a]	1. wolę Ewę ᴬᶜᶜ niż Hannę ᴬᶜᶜ 2. wolę Ewę ᴬᶜᶜ od Hanny ᴳᴱᴺ 3. wolałbym tego ᴳᴱᴺ nie wiedzieć	1+2. I prefer Ewa to Hanna 3. I would rather not know about it	prefer
	wolno	—	1. tu nie wolno palić 2. tu wolno palić	1. you can't smoke in here 2. you are allowed to smoke here	can, be allowed
wrócić	wracać	☞ wracam, wracają ☞ wracał[a] ☞ wrócę, wrócisz ☞ wrócił[a]	1. wróć do domu ᴳᴱᴺ 2. wracaj do pracy ᴳᴱᴺ 3. czy on wrócił do zdrowia ᴳᴱᴺ po wypadku ᴸᴼᶜ?	1. go back / come back home 2. go back to work 3. did he recover after the accident?	go back, return, come back, get back, recover, regain
wstać	wstawać	☞ wstaję, wstajesz ☞ wstawał[a] ☞ wstanę, wstaniesz ☞ wstał[a]	1. wstań! 2. wstań z łóżka ᴳᴱᴺ! 3. nie lubię rano wstawać 4. słońce wstaje	1. get up! 2. get out of bed! 3. I do not like to get up in the morning 4. the sun is rising	get up, rise, stand up

Table of verbs: *tabela czasownikowa*

1	2	3	4	5	6
wyjść	wychodzić	👋 wychodzę, wychodzisz 🔲 wychodził[a] 🔽 wyjdę, wyjdziesz 🔽 wyszedłem 🔹, wyszłam 🔺	1. wyszła z domu GEN za późno 2. wyszła 🔺 za mąż ACC za sąsiada ACC (*masculine*: ożenić się) 3. wyjdź stąd 4. ta propozycja wyszła od nas GEN	1. she left her house too late 2. she married her neighbour (only of a woman) 3. get out of here 4. this suggestion came from us	leave, go out, come out, get married (only of a woman), get out, come from
wydać	wydawać (się)	👋 wydaję, wydajesz 🔲 wydawał[a] 🔽 wydam, wydadzą 🔽 wydał[a]	1. lubię wydawać pieniądze ACC 2. „Gazetę Wyborczą" ACC wydaje się od 1989 roku GEN 3. wydaje mi DAT się, że nasz pies jest głodny	1. I like to spend money 2. Gazeta Wyborcza has been published since 1989 3. it seems to me that our dog is hungry	spend (money), publish, issue, seem
	wyglądać	👋 wyglądam, wyglądają 🔲 wyglądał[a]	1. w tej czapce LOC wyglądasz jak idiota NOM / na idiotę ACC 2. dobrze wyglądasz	1. you look like an idiot in that cap 2. you look good	look (appear)
wyjechać	wyjeżdżać	👋 wyjeżdżam, wyjeżdżają 🔲 wyjeżdżał[a] 🔽 wyjadę, wyjedziesz 🔽 wyjechał[a]	1. wyjeżdżam z garażu GEN 2. chcę wyjechać za granicę ACC	1. I'm driving out of the garage 2. I want to go abroad / to emigrate	leave (by vehicle), drive out, emigrate
	wymagać	👋 wymagam, wymagają 🔲 wymagał[a]	1. od żołnierza GEN wymaga się posłuszeństwa GEN 2. wymagam, żeby studenci pracowali systematycznie	1. obedience is required from a soldier 2. I demand that students work systematically	demand, require, need
wynieść	wynosić	👋 wynoszę, wynosisz 🔲 wynosił[a] 🔽 wyniosę, wyniesiesz 🔽 wyniósł 🔹, wyniosła 🔺	1. wynieś śmieci ACC 2. rachunek wynosi dużo: 200 euro 3. wynoś się stąd (COLL)	1. take out the rubbish 2. the bill comes to 200 euros 3. get out of here	take out, carry out, add up to, total, come to
wyobrazić (sobie)	wyobrażać (sobie)	👋 wyobrażam, wyobrażają 🔲 wyobrażał[a] 🔽 wyobrażę, wyobrazisz 🔽 wyobraził[a]	1. wyobraź sobie, że jesteś królem INST 2. w zimie LOC / zimą INST wyobrażał sobie DAT lato ACC	1. imagine that you are a king 2. in the winter he imagined summer	imagine

1	2	3	4	5	6
wysiąść	wysiadać	wysiadam, wysiadają / wysiadał / wysiądzie, wysiądziesz / wysiadł	wysiadł z pociągu GEN za wcześnie	he got off the train too early	get off, get out
wystarczyć (=starczyć)	wystarczać (= starczać)	wystarczam, wystarczają / wystarczał / wystarczę, wystarczysz / wystarczył	1. jedna porcja NOM frytek GEN nie wystarczy na obiad ACC dla naszych dzieci GEN 2. dziękuję, wystarczy (= starczy) 3. wystarczy napisać krótki komentarz ACC	1. one portion of chips is not enough for dinner for our children 2. thank you, that's enough 3. it's enough to write a short comment	be enough, suffice
zabrać	zabierać	zabieram, zabierają / zabierał / zabiorę, zabierzesz / zabrał	1. zabrała mi DAT wszystkie pieniądze ACC 2. zabierz mnie ACC do kina GEN 3. nie zabieraj mi DAT torebki GEN	1. she took all my money from me 2. take me to the cinema 3. do not take away my bag	take away, take (along)
zabić	zabijać	zabijam, zabijają / zabijał / zabiję, zabijesz / zabił	1. w czasie LOC wojny GEN zabija się niewinnych ludzi ACC 2. nie zabijaj	1. innocent people are killed in times of war 2. thou shalt not kill	kill
zacząć	zaczynać	zaczynam, zaczynają / zaczynał / zacznę, zaczniesz / zaczął, zaczęła	1. zaczynamy dzień ACC od początku GEN 2. musisz zacząć coś ACC robić	1. we start off the day with a kiss 2. you have to start doing something!	begin, start
założyć	zakładać (się)	zakładam, zakładają / zakładał / założę, założysz / założył	1. załóż dziecku DAT buty ACC 2. chcemy założyć firmę ACC 3. zakładam, że on przyjdzie sam 4. założę się, że on przyjdzie sam	1. put the shoes on the child 2. we want to set up a company 3. I assume he'll come alone 4. I bet he'll come alone	put on, set up, assume, bet
	zależeć	zależę, zależysz / zależał	1. to zależy od ciebie GEN 2. nie zależy mi DAT na bogatym mężu LOC	1. that depends on you 2. I don't care about having a rich husband	depend, care about

Table of verbs: *tabela czasownikowa*

1	2	3	4	5	6
załatwić	załatwiać (się)	☞ załatwiam, załatwiają / ☞ załatwiał[a] / ☞ załatwię, załatwisz / ☞ załatwił[a]	1. ja ci DAT to ACC załatwię 2. dziecko musi się załatwić 3. załatw to z rodzicami INST	1. I will take care of that 2. the child has to relieve himself 3. settle this with your parents	take care of, relieve oneself, settle
zamówić	zamawiać	☞ zamawiam, zamawiają / ☞ zamawiał[a] / ☞ zamówię, zamówisz / ☞ zamówił[a]	1. proszę, zamów pokój dwuosobowy ACC 2. kolega już zamówił mi DAT kawę ACC 3. czy możesz nam DAT zamówić dwa bilety ACC na ten koncert ACC ?	1. please, order a double room 2. a friend has already, ordered me coffee 3. can you order / book two tickets for us to this concert?	order, book, reserve
zamknąć	zamykać (się)	☞ zamykam, zamykają / ☞ zamykał[a] / ☞ zamknę, zamkniesz / ☞ zamknął Ǫ, zamknęła	1. zamknij drzwi ACC 2. zamknij się w łazience LOC 3. zamknij się (COLL)	1. close the door 2. lock yourself in the bathroom 3. shut up (COLL)	close, lock, shut up, bar, bolt
zapomnieć	zapominać	☞ zapominam, zapominają / ☞ zapominał[a] / ☞ zapomnę, zapomnisz / ☞ zapomniał[a]	1. zapomnij o kłopotach LOC 2. zapomniałem klucza GEN 3. zapomniałem zadzwonić	1. forget about your troubles 2. I forgot the key 3. I forgot to phone	forget
zaprosić	zapraszać	☞ zapraszam, zapraszają / ☞ zapraszał[a] / ☞ zaproszę, zaprosisz / ☞ zaprosił[a]	zapraszam cię ACC na moje urodziny ACC	I invite you to my birthday party	invite
zebrać	zbierać (się)	☞ zbieram, zbierają / ☞ zbierał[a] / ☞ zbiorę, zbierzesz / ☞ zebrał[a]	1. zbieram znaczki ACC 2. właśnie zbieramy jagody ACC 3. zbieraj się do wyjścia GEN	1. I collect stamps 2. we are gathering berries right now 3. prepare to leave	collect, gather, pick assemble, accumulate
zdać	zdawać (wydawać) się	☞ zdaję, zdajesz / ☞ zdawał[a] / ☞ zdam, zdadzą / ☞ zdał[a]	1. jutro zdaję egzamin ACC 2. zdaje mi DAT się / wydaje mi DAT się, że pada 3. zdaj się na niego ACC	1. I am taking / sitting an exam tomorrow 2. it seems to me that it's raining 3. you can count on him	take (an exam), pass, seem

1	2	3	4	5	6
zdjąć	zdejmować	zdejmuję, zdejmujesz / zdejmował^a / zdejmę, zdejmiesz / zdjął Ø, zdjęła Δ	1. zdejmij buty ᴬᶜᶜ 2. Adam nie zdjął czapki ᴳᴱᴺ przy stole ᴸᴼᶜ	1. take off your shoes 2. Adam did not take off his cap at (the) table	take off, take down, remove
zmienić	zmieniać (się)	zmieniam, zmieniają / zmieniał^a / zmienię, zmienisz / zmienił^a	1. chciałabym zmienić pracę ᴬᶜᶜ 2. chcę zmienić nazwisko ᴬᶜᶜ 3. on się zmienił	1. I'd like to find a new job 2. I want to change my surname 3. he's changed	change
	znaczyć	znaczę, znaczysz / znaczył^a	1. co to znaczy? 2. on dużo dla mnie ᴳᴱᴺ znaczy 3. to znaczy, że nie przyjdę	1. what does this mean? 2. he means a lot to me 3. that means I'm not coming	mean, signify
po-	znać	znam, znają / znał^a	1. czy znasz Barbarę ᴬᶜᶜ? 2. poznałem ją ᴬᶜᶜ wczoraj	1. do you know Barbara? 2. I met her yesterday	know (be familiar with), meet (for the first time)
znaleźć	znajdować	znajduję, znajdujesz / znajdował^a / znajdę, znajdziesz / znalazł^a	1. znalazł dokumenty ᴬᶜᶜ w szufladzie ᴸᴼᶜ 2. tu często znajdowaliśmy grzyby ᴬᶜᶜ	1. he found the documents in the drawer 2. we often found mushrooms here	find
znaleźć się	znajdować się	znajduję się, znajdujesz się / znajdował^a się / znajdę, znajdziesz się / znalazł^a się	1. toaleta znajduje się na parterze ᴸᴼᶜ 2. znaleźliśmy się dopiero wieczorem	1. the toilet is on the ground floor 2. we found each other only in the evening	be located, find one another
zostać	zostawać	zostaję, zostajesz / zostawał^a / zostanę, zostaniesz / został^a	1. zostanę pisarzem ᴵᴺˢᵀ 2. zostanę w domu ᴸᴼᶜ 3. czy coś zostało? 4. na jej płaszczu ᴸᴼᶜ została plama	1. I'll become a writer 2. I will stay home 3. is anything left? 4. the stain remained on her coat	become, remain, stay
zostawić	zostawiać	zostawiam, zostawiają / zostawiał^a / zostawię, zostawisz / zostawił^a	1. zostaw książki ᴬᶜᶜ w domu ᴸᴼᶜ 2. zostaw go ᴬᶜᶜ w spokoju ᴸᴼᶜ 3. zostaw to sobie ᴰᴬᵀ	1. leave the books at home 2. leave him alone 3. keep it	leave, keep

16 Bibliography: *bibliografia*

Bańko, Mirosław, Dorota Komosińska i Anna Stankiewicz. 2003. *Indeks* a tergo *do Uniwersalnego słownika języka polskiego.* Warszawa: PWN.

Dąbrowska, Anna, Anna Burzyńska-Kamieniecka, Urszula Dobesz, Małgorzata Pasieka. 2005. *Z Wrocławiem w tle. Zadania testowe z języka polskiego dla cudzoziemców.* Wrocław: Wrocławskie Wydawnictwo Oświatowe ATUT.

De Knop, Sabine, Teun De Rycker. 2008. *Cognitive Approaches to Pedagogical Grammar.* Berlin – New York: Mouton de Gruyter.

Fisiak, Jacek, Maria Lipińska-Grzegorek, Tadeusz Zabrocki, 1978. *An Introductory English – Polish Contrastive Grammar.* Warszawa: PWN.

Flynn, Suzanne, Wayne O'Neil (red.). 1998. *Linguistic theory in second language acquisition.* Dortrecht: Reidel Press.

Gass, Susan M., Larry Selinker. 2008. *Second language acquisition.* Warszawa: Exliblis.

Kaipio, Clara. 1977. *201 Polish Verbs fully conjugated in all the tenses.* New York: Barron's Educational Series.

Kurzowa, Zofia, Halina Zgółkowa. 1993. *Słownik minimum języka polskiego.* Poznań: Kantor Wydawniczy SAWW.

Lipińska, Ewa. 1999. *Nie ma róży bez kolców.* Kraków: Universitas.

Madelska, Liliana. 2004. *Słownik wariantywności fonetycznej współczesnej polszczyzny.* Kraków: Collegium Columbinum.

Madelska, Liliana. 2007. *Polnisch entdecken.* Kraków: Prolog.

Madelska, Liliana. 2008a. *Odkrywamy język polski.* Kraków: Prolog.

Madelska, Liliana. 2008b. *Praxis-Grammatik Polnisch. Das große Lern- und Übungsbuch.* Poznań: PONS LektorKlett.

Madelska, Liliana (in print). *Posłuchaj, jak mówię.* Wien: artJam Studios.

Mędak, Stanisław. 2003. *Słownik odmiany rzeczowników polskich.* Kraków: Universitas.

Mędak, Stanisław. 2004. *Liczebnik też się liczy!* Kraków: Universitas.

Mędak, Stanisław. 2005a. *Praktyczny słownik łączliwości składniowej czasowników polskich.* Kraków: Universitas.

Mędak, Stanisław. 2005b. *Słownik form komunikacyjnych czasowników polskich.* Kraków: Universitas.

Miodunka, Władysław. 2006 (Video). *Uczmy się polskiego. Kurs podstawowy.* Warszawa: Polska Fundacja Upowszechniania Nauki.

Miodunka, Władysław. 2006 (Video). *Uczmy się polskiego. Kurs zaawansowany.* Warszawa: Polska Fundacja Upowszechniania Nauki.

Miodunka, Władysław. 2007 (DVD). *Uczmy się polskiego. Kurs podstawowy.* Warszawa: Polska Fundacja Upowszechniania Nauki.

Miodunka, Władysław. 2007 (DVD). *Uczmy się polskiego. Kurs zaawansowany.* Warszawa: Polska Fundacja Upowszechniania Nauki.

Mizerski, Witold (red.). 2000. *Język polski. Encyklopedia w tabelach.* Warszawa: Adamantan.

Pasieka, Małgorzata. 2001. *Język polski dla cudzoziemców. Ćwiczenia dla początkujących.* Wrocław: Wydawnictwo Uniwersytetu Wrocławskiego.

Pyzik, Józef. 2006. *Przygoda z gramatyką. Fleksja i słowotwórstwo imion. Ćwiczenia funkcjonalno- -gramatyczne dla cudzoziemców (B2, C1).* Kraków: Universitas.

Serafin Barbara, Achtelik Aleksandra. 2005. *Miło mi panią poznać. Język polski w sytuacjach komunikacyjnych.* Katowice: Wydawnictwo Uniwersytetu Śląskiego.

Seretny, Anna, Lipińska Ewa, Waldemar Martyniuk. 2004. *Opisywanie, rozwijanie i testowanie znajomości języka polskiego jako obcego.* Kraków: Universitas.

Styczek, Irena. 1982. *Badanie i kształtowanie słuchu fonematycznego.* Warszawa: WSiP.

Zgółkowa, Halina. 1983. *Słownictwo współczesnej polszczyzny mówionej.* Poznań: Wydawnictwo Naukowe UAM.

The book Discovering Polish. A Learner's Grammar was written within the framework of the "Hurra!!!" Socrates Lingua 2 Project (103360-CP-2002-1-PL-LINGUA-L2)
SOCRATES TRANSLATIONAL CO-OPERATION PROJECT LINGUA 2 – DEVELOPMENT OF TOOLS AND MATERIALS HURRA!!! A COMPREHENSIVE SET OF POLISH TEACHING AND LEARNING MATERIALS 103360-CP-2002-1-PL-LINGUA-L2

This project has been carried out with the support of the European Community in the framework of the Socrates programme.
The content of this project does not necessarily reflect the position of the European Community, nor does it involve any responsibility on the part of the European Community.

Hurra!!! Series Editor-in-chief: Agata Stępnik-Siara
Reviewer: Adaptation of the German language version reviewed by:
Prof. Katarzyna Dziubalska-Kołaczyk, PhD, Prof. Stefan Michael Newerkla, PhD
Collaborating and testing institutes: Vienna University, Slavic Institute (www.univie.at/slawistik);
The Brasshouse Center Birmingham (www.birmingham.gov.uk/brasshouse);
Kolleg für Polnische Sprache und Kultur Berlin (www.kolleg.pl)

Graphic Design: Studio Quadro (www.quadro.com.pl)
Typeset: Pracownia Słowa
Jacket Design: Quadro (www.quadro.com.pl)
Illustrations: Bogna Sroka, Bartosz Mucha

Linguistic editing and proofreading: Ron Mukerji, Guy R. Torr, Joanna Śmiecińska, Małgorzata Grabania-Mukerji, Barbara Owsiak, Joel Paisley, Anna Socha-Michalik
Substantive editing: Justyna Krztoń

Printed by Know-How

PROLOG Publishing
ul. Bronowicka 37, 30-084 Kraków
tel./faks +48 (12) 638 45 50, tel. +48 (12) 638 45 25
e-mail: books@prolog.edu.pl
online shop: www.prologpublishing.com